CW01498941

CRYPTO
CONFIDENTIAL

CRYPTO
CONFIDENTIAL

AN INSIDER'S ACCOUNT FROM
THE FRONTLINES OF FRAUD

JAKE DONOGHUE

For Abigail

First published 2024

FLINT is an imprint of The History Press
97 St George's Place, Cheltenham,
Gloucestershire, GL50 3QB
www.flintbooks.co.uk

British Library Cataloguing in Publication Data.
A catalogue record for this book is available from the British Library.

ISBN 978 1 80399 618 9

Typesetting and origination by The History Press
Printed and bound in Great Britain by TJ Books Limited, Padstow, Cornwall.

Trees for LYfe

Praise for *Crypto Confidential*

Crypto Confidential is the final word on the cryptocurrency industry. Its lively and dramatic account of greed, corruption, and scandal will captivate you from start to finish. I have been speaking out about Bitcoin and cryptocurrency for nearly ten years, and this book is a visceral illustration of why. It shines an uncompromising light on the dangers and pitfalls of the 21st century's most malevolent fad, and I would recommend it as essential reading for anyone considering dabbling in digital assets.

Frank W. Abagnale, subject of *Catch Me If You Can*

Before investing in crypto, read this tale of 'Grifters' Groundhog Day', in which investors, even the grifters themselves, fall for age-old scams, again and again. I can't vouch for the accuracy of every performance in this circus of fraud, but they're all more plausible than the rosy outcomes dangled by crypto-evangelists and swallowed by gullible investors.

Paul Romer, 2018 winner of the Nobel Prize for Economics and co-author of *Looting: The Economic Underworld of Bankruptcy for Profit*

A brilliant and fascinating description of crypto, the 21st-century high-tech version of age-old bubbles. It makes painfully clear that, on the buying side, there is no limit to human credulity, and in the faith in magic returns. And, on the selling side, no limit to hubris, deception and scamming. Read the book, and cry. Message to investors: do not touch the stuff. Message to regulators: kill the beast before it affects all of us.

Olivier Blanchard, former chief economist of the IMF, and Robert M. Solow, Professor Emeritus of Economics at MIT

Everything you feared was true about crypto and much worse are laid bare in this gripping and infuriating insider account of his time at the forefront of the industry. Funny, illuminating and beautifully written.
Liam Vaughan, author of *Flash Crash: A Trading Savant, a Global Manhunt and the Most Mysterious Market Crash in History*

A fascinating insider's perspective into what life was like in the fast lane of the crypto shilling mania of 2021 and a must-read for all those still being actively wooed by crypto and blockchain lobbyists, from politicians and regulators to central bankers. Don't be surprised to learn it was even worse than you ever suspected.
Izabella Kaminska, former editor of *FT Alphaville*, senior finance editor POLITICO Europe and founder and editor of *The Blind Spot*

I didn't expect a book about cryptocurrency to be racy, funny and gobsmacking all at once ... Deliciously gossipy as the book is, you'll need a strong stomach to digest some of its revelations ... At a time when so many face relentless financial pressure, it's a reminder that others have so much loose cash that they'll throw it at an environmentally ruinous industry, where, even after the jailing of Sam Bankman-Fried, fraudsters are still mistaken for IT whizz-kids who want to save the world. In the lawless world of crypto, Charles Ponzi would recognise what's going on right now; so would Bernie Madoff.
Andy Verity, BBC financial investigations correspondent and author of *Rigged: The Incredible True Story of the Whistleblowers Jailed after Exposing the Rotten Heart of the Financial System*

Just when you were thinking it might be safe to dip a toe into the crypto waters, along comes Jake Donoghue's brilliant and propulsive *Crypto Confidential*, a cautionary tale if there ever was one about the dangers still lurking in that roiling sea.
William D. Cohan, bestselling author of *House of Cards* and co-founder of Puck

A fascinating and gripping insider's account of the nefarious world of crypto. Donoghue takes the reader behind the scenes of the crypto industry, guiding the reader through its Byzantine complexity, and exposing the immorality and corruption at its heart.

Grace Blakeley, author of *Vulture Capitalism: Corporate Crimes, Backdoor Bailouts, and the Death of Freedom*

Jake Donoghue's *Crypto Confidential* is a roll-call of infamy, providing an unparalleled insight into the nefarious bunch of chancers, charlatans, con men and fraudsters who control, or controlled, the global crypto space.

Ian Fraser, author of *Shredded: Inside RBS The Bank that Broke Britain*

Pacey and authoritative, this is the sort of thing we need the most at present – an honest book about a thoroughly dishonest industry

Dan Davies, author of *Lying for Money: How Legendary Frauds Reveal the Workings of Our World*

Crypto Confidential is a unique insider's view of a legal and regulatory nightmare, and an illustration of why crypto scams remain endemic and pervasive ... It raises important questions about the future of crypto influencers, yield farming, staking, auctions, and other practices that would be closely regulated if they involved securities instead of crypto assets ... If you weren't in the crypto industry from 2020–22, this book will take you there.

Frank Partnoy, the Adrian A. Kragen Professor of Law at UC Berkeley, International Research Fellow at Oxford University, and author of *The Match King: Ivar Kreuger, the Financial Genius Behind a Century of Wall Street Scandals*

This book provides a bird's-eye insider view of the crypto industry's highs and lows. Other books have recounted the lows, but it is Donoghue's vivid description of the industry's heyday that serves as the most searing indictment of crypto's hollow cynicism. This account makes clear that the crypto industry was never about building anything; instead, it was always about making a quick buck for the lucky (or just plain dirty) few. Readers are left with the sobering impression that – even when there was no outright fraud or money laundering – it's hard to point to a good apple in the crypto industry.

Hilary J. Allen, Professor of Law at the American University Washington College of Law and author of *Driverless Finance: Fintech's Impact on Financial Stability*

From his insider's seat at the table, Jake Donoghue takes us behind the scenes of the shadowy world of crypto grifters and reveals how so many worthless tokens were promoted with the aid of a legion of anonymous influencers and corrupt crypto media outlets. *Crypto Confidential* reads like the modern version of the movies Boiler Room and The Big Short. This book is a must-read for anybody who has ever invested, or is thinking of investing, in the cryptocurrency market.

Joe Saluzzi, co-author of *Broken Markets: How High Frequency Trading and Predatory Practices on Wall Street Are Destroying Investor Confidence and Your Portfolio*

An eye-opening insider's look into the crypto industry, which sheds a stark and uncompromising light on its nefarious incentive structures and lays bare the dark side of digital assets.

Stephen Diehl, author of *Popping the Crypto Bubble*

Crypto Confidential finally blows the whistle on one of the most fraudulent industries in history. Like Mackay's *Extraordinary Popular Delusions*, Donoghue's insider take will be the go-to history lesson for understanding the mania in digital-asset markets for generations.

Peter Howson, author of *Let Them Eat Crypto: The Blockchain Scam That's Ruining the World*

As a crypto insider, Jake writes from a unique vantage point, offering a rare peek behind the curtain of one of the world's most opaque and misunderstood industries. He offers his insights with humour and intelligence, and almost every page comes with a revelation or an explanation to clear some of the muddiest waters in finance.

George Harrison, co-author of *Inside Allenwood: The Story of a British Banker Inside a US Prison*

Contents

Author's Note

This book is based on my experiences working in the world of crypto. I've tried to capture, as best as possible, just what it was like working at the epicentre of an industry that is often, and most accurately, described in superlatives: the fastest-growing asset class in history; the greatest redistribution of wealth ever seen; the worst financial crimes ever committed, etc.

One problem I kept encountering when attempting this was something I had experienced many times working in the industry: the pace at which crypto moves, and the speed with which the whole landscape can change. This story is primarily concerned with the 2020–22 crypto boom: a period that saw the value of all the cryptocurrencies on the market top $3 trillion – more than the GDP of France at the time. However, even now, fresh developments are taking place almost daily in consequence of the events that transpired during that three-year period.

If you've glanced at the finance pages of any newspaper at any point over the past year and a half, you'll know that the crypto industry has been in a precarious position for a long time. When I started writing this book, bitcoin was trading below $20,000. Less than a year before that, it was worth over $65,000. A long line of high-profile frauds and company implosions had eviscerated its value. And yet, at the time I'm writing this now in 2024, it's back above $40,000. And it's not just bitcoin that is subject to volatile, unpredictable and often unexplained changes in circumstance.

Just as I finished a section detailing the fall of a crypto bro's once-great company, my phone would ping with a news alert saying the character in question had been arrested that morning. Just as I put the final touches on an anecdote about a player whose escapades resulted in his reputational ruin and exile from the industry, I would see on his social media that he'd managed to pull off a redemption arc.

The approach I settled on to deal with this issue was to treat this book as something of a history project. I have tried, in so far as it's possible, to focus solely on the three-year period in question, and the events that led up to it. I've endeavoured to avoid getting lured into the Sisyphean task of providing a fully exhaustive, conclusive account of the fates that befell a whole cast of characters. In most cases, not only is this impractical, but impossible: many of them are still at large, and will continue to leave both stories and victims in their wake as long as they remain so.

Instead, this book is intended to serve as a snapshot, not just of the time period across which it's set, but of my insights into the crypto industry. It's an insider's view, into the lives and livelihoods of some of the inner circle to which I used to belong. It's a record of the sheer extravagance, excess and absurdity which seemed to take place on a daily basis. And what it illustrates is how the people behind one of the most captivating, disruptive and incomprehensible industries the world has ever seen act when the cameras are off, and their guards are down.

In telling this story, I have changed some names, dates and locations where necessary, to protect the privacy and identity of individuals. Some events (and some players) have been simplified, or even amalgamated, and some dialogue and details have been recounted from memory or constructed for the sake of the narrative. However, at all times I have endeavoured to remain true to the essence of the markets as I worked in them.

To sum up: this is all based on a true story. Or, at least, parts of that true story. Everything that happens in this book is based on what actually happened in real life. Even if, at times, I wish it hadn't ...

PART ONE

Prologue

The Swindler's Symposium

I forced my way through the frenzied crowd, holding my phone like a man overboard with a lifeline. For the past 2 hours it had been pinging almost constantly with horrifying updates and even more alarming projections. It was a bloodbath; I had never seen this much red.

With a million sharply declining charts searing into my vision, I picked a precarious path through swathes of inebriated partygoers. The atmosphere may have been one of celebration, but I was a one-man island of terror. I had to find Archie; I knew he would be hidden somewhere in this heaving mass of bodies. I had to speak to him to make sense of what was going on. To ask how we were going to pull through this.

The year was 2022. Bitcoin was crashing, and everything was totally and irrevocably fucked.

In light of the market meltdown, I had arrived late to my own party. Midnight had come and gone before I found the entrance to the bar. We were in Canary Wharf, after all: a maze of endless, hollow boulevards. Here was the dark heart of British finance – a gleaming playground for capital and an apt setting for such an event.

Stealing out of the cold November night, I was ushered into the foyer of tonight's low-ceilinged, clammy venue by Claire, our none-too-impressed events coordinator. She shouted over the blaring music, gesticulating wildly and speaking a novel and hybrid language – a fusion of English, French and general exasperation.

With much effort, I managed to catch the gist of her discontent: London's crypto bros had arrived in force, and now they were letting down their hair as only the sickeningly rich can.

I told her she could dispense with door duties and join the party, and we both strode into the main room – I in search of my co-founder, she in search of the open bar. I eventually spotted Archie, holding court in a quieter corner of the bar, surrounded by an audience of young men with glazed eyes and vacant expressions. Whatever he was saying, it would have to wait.

I hurried over to him, stammering an apology to the pack of hangers-on I pushed out the way.

'Archie,' I said, my voice a heady blend of relief and distress. 'Archie, mate, you need to see this.'

I held out my phone, a price chart filling the display. I studied Archie's expression as he looked at the chart, his face aglow in malevolent red light. Archie raised his eyes to meet mine, then reached out and snatched the phone from my hand. He swiped at the screen and started typing, watching for a reply from whoever he had just messaged.

'Fucking hell,' he eventually said.

'Right,' I said. 'It's bad, isn't it?'

'It's awful,' he said. Then, with a grin, he added, 'I just messaged the manager, and he's saying we've still got eight grand on the bar tab. What the fuck have these people been doing all night?'

With a laugh, Archie thrust my phone at my chest. Then he seized me and the nearest of the bystanders and marched us both to the bar, gesturing for another round of whatever overpriced concoction he had been quaffing all evening.

'Right,' Archie said, turning to me as the barman busied himself with an array of bottles. 'What was that shit you were showing me on your phone?'

I blinked and looked into Archie's drunken eyes. Music was pounding and strobes flashed from above, lending a dreamlike glow to the scene.

'Are you fucking mental? Have you seen what's happening to the markets? This is the lowest bitcoin has traded for over two years, and everything else is getting rekt with it.'

'Rekt' is a morsel of crypto slang that is used to describe a collapse in the price of an asset – or, in this case, the entire market. A deliberate misspelling of 'wrecked', the term originated in the gaming community before being appropriated by crypto commentators. It's a light-hearted term but is often used to describe even the most cataclysmic events.

But Archie wasn't fazed. He simply laughed and said, 'You could do with getting a bit more rekt yourself. You're bringing the vibe down.'

Archie's admonishment did nothing to calm the anxiety that had been overpowering me for the last few hours. Surveying the bar once more, I found yet more cause for concern in the sheer *lack* of concern around me. These were some of the most prominent, influential people in the entire industry, and not one of them seemed bothered by what was happening to the market. Their house was on fire and, rather than rushing for the door, grabbing the family photo albums on the way, they didn't even appear to have noticed.

In one corner, the CEO of a crypto company worth just under half a billion dollars (and less still by the second) was attempting to 'long arm' a pint of beer. He held the pint at full arm's length and raised it into the air. Some beer gushed into his open mouth, but most of it spilled over his face and down his shirt. Onlookers cheered, and the sodden CEO set down his glass, wiping flecks of foam from his chin.

In another corner, a group of try-hard traders, sporting slicked-back hair and shirts two sizes too small, laughed as they poured Cristal champagne over their plate-sized Patek Philippes. I rolled my eyes, having always considered this one of the more obnoxious practices of crypto millionaires.

Surely, I thought, everyone in the room couldn't be so rich or stupid that they didn't know or care about what was happening? Surely these erstwhile successful people wouldn't fiddle all night while their empire burned?

I left Archie at the bar and plunged back into the crowd. This time, I was just looking for anyone who appeared sober or sensible. I needed a frame of reference, to vindicate my instinct that everyone else's reaction was wrong.

I remembered hearing whispers of strange people who came to events like these to actually talk about business: to debate the goings-on of the industry, exchange contact details and build a web of useful connections. I realised in my desperation that this was exactly the type of person I needed now. Unconscionably, and in a sign that things really had gone to shit, I began to seek out that creature I had always shunned. The semi-mythical being I had pushed from my mind so many times. The Networker.

Soon enough, I spotted someone who seemed to fit the bill. With a bottle of mineral water in one hand and a deck of business cards in the other, this guy looked the right type to provide a sound take on the market turmoil.

'Tim!' revealed the name tag stuck to his lapel. And, indeed, Tim needed no prompting; as soon as I drifted into earshot, he launched into a lecture on the state of the gaming industry. He described, in an effortless monologue, how he was going to use blockchain technology to 'disrupt legacy business practices', 'return gaming to the gamers' and accomplish a number of other meaningless clichés.

'That's great,' I said, when I understood he had finished. 'And tell me, Tim, what do you make of what's happening in the markets?'

'What do you mean?'

'The crash! Do you think this might be it for the industry? And how bad do you think the contagion is going to be?'

Tim said nothing. He merely stared with an expression as still and flavourless as his mineral water.

'I haven't heard anything about a market crash,' he eventually said. 'Or, uh ... contagion?' His expression changed, so that he was now looking at me like you might regard a person shouting at themselves on the Tube.

Luckily, though, I didn't need an excuse to extricate myself from Tim. Just before I could make something up about checking in with our events team, the music died all throughout the bar. An alien silence enveloped the dancefloor, followed shortly by the sharp sound of silverware striking glass. It was time for the speech.

I nodded goodbye to Tim and squeezed my way through the tangle of limbs. I was heading for the other side of the room, where I knew Archie had planned to deliver his address. After much exertion, I saw him clambering onto an empty crate of Bollinger – an improvised soapbox that seemed particularly fitting, given the night's mood. Holding a microphone in his left hand and a half-smoked cigarette in his right, Archie was clearly in a bad way. But it helped that everyone else seemed to be in a bad way too. And it also helped that one of Archie's greatest talents was being able to chat an astonishingly articulate amount of shit, no matter the state he was in.

Archie raised the microphone to his lips. He took a second to compose himself, and said, 'Thank you all for coming!'

The crowd cheered. Glasses were raised, and drinks were sloshed.

'Thankfully,' continued Archie, 'only one person got their phone out tonight to try to show me a price chart. And what I saw on the screen scared me, I won't lie.'

I took a breath. Here it comes, I thought.

'Yeah, I was very concerned that there wasn't a single green dildo in sight. Plenty of big red ones though!'

The crowd burst into laughter, and I shook my head. For some context, in the world of trading, the movement of asset prices on charts is depicted with a series of 'candlesticks'. These charts look a bit like your typical bar graph, except each solid bar has a 'wick' at the top and/or bottom. The purpose of the wick is to show the high and low extremes the asset has traded at each day. When the price moves up, the candlestick turns green, and red when it trades down. Crypto bros, having the mental maturity of prepubescent kids, refer to these bars as either 'red dildos' or 'green dildos', even though it would take a herculean stretch of the imagination for them to look even vaguely phallic.

'Jokes aside,' said Archie, his voice taking on a more sober edge as he found his rhythm, 'I want to congratulate each and every person in this room tonight. We're making generational change. I've been in crypto for a decade, and I've seen a lot of people come and go. It's the people who keep their heads down and build who get through the tough times. Make no mistake, crypto is going to bounce back bigger and better than ever before. Thank you, and thank you all for coming!'

Archie raised his microphone triumphantly into the air, accepting the applause of the crowd, before clambering down from the soapbox. As soon as I saw him handing the mic to the next speaker,

I made my way towards the exit. I had stuck around for Archie's speech out of a sense of duty to my co-founder, but there was no chance I was going to participate in this extracurricular circle-jerk for a second longer than I had to.

I slipped from the bar and returned to the bracing November air. With red candlesticks burning behind my eyes, I ordered a cab, relishing the prospect of bringing this night to its long-overdue close.

In itself, the general farce and idiocy on display that night in Canary Wharf was nothing out of the ordinary. On the surface, it was a typical Wednesday night affair in the London crypto scene. But what dragged the egregious evening down to the level of downright degeneracy was the timing of it all. The party took place on the same night that FTX collapsed.

Prior to its fall, FTX was one of the most prominent cryptocurrency exchanges in the industry. Exchanges are essentially trading platforms that allow users to make bets on whether the prices of crypto assets will rise or fall. Or, at least, that's what they used to be.

Over the years, some exchanges – including FTX – have made astronomical sums of money. And, in some cases, the meteoric rise of these crypto exchanges has brought out the latent megalomania of their founders. And then, somewhere along the road, some of these founders convinced themselves that their companies were actually more like banks than exchanges. FTX was one such crypto exchange that started acting like a quasi-bank (when they were not simply buying banks outright to skirt local licensing laws, that is).

In recent years, a familiar playbook has emerged. As the C-suite gets high off its own fumes, the mega-exchanges start to create and issue currencies like they're going out of fashion. At the same time, they roll out every financial service under the sun – from capital lending to the provision of credit cards and savings accounts – and even start trading the market like hedge funds. With so many fingers in so many pies, the exchanges afford themselves ample opportunity to commit financial misdeeds. Combine this with a non-existent regulatory framework (much of crypto remains, even to this day, wholly unregulated) and we arrive at what a financial journalist struggling for originality might well term a perfect storm of corruption.

And, indeed, the crimes and corruptions of FTX were truly immense, in both scale and quantity. The charge sheet against Sam Bankman-Fried (the disgraced former CEO of the company) was so encyclopaedic that it would've made Bernie Madoff wince. It ranged from fraud, money laundering and embezzlement to more ambitious and specialist crimes like making illicit political donations. His crimes were so extensive that prosecutors even had to drop some of the charges, as otherwise it simply would've taken too many years to process all the evidence. And on 2 November 2023 he was found guilty of all the counts brought against him. At the time of writing he's awaiting sentencing and is facing over a century in prison.

It's no exaggeration, then, to say that the case of FTX is one of the grossest and gravest cases of fraud in the twenty-first century, if not the entire history of finance. Not only was a $36 billion company wiped out overnight, but billions of dollars of customer funds, which were being stored on the exchange, were lost. And that's not to mention the knock-on effects that reverberated through the space; investor confidence descended into a death spiral, causing the value of other assets, like bitcoin, to plunge. Some estimate that as much as $200 billion in value was wiped off the market over the course of just a few days.

And yet, for those who came to our event on the night of the grand crypto collapse, it was as if none of this was happening. These were supposed to be the most engaged and invested participants in the crypto industry – the inner circle of the ultimate insider's game. While this indifference may seem shocking to those on the outside, it can be easily explained: for many of them, the events that came to light that evening were par for the course. Just another day in the office. Just another fraud that got found out.

These were people who had built their careers and made their living from fraud. It was a core component of their business model. In the pursuit of ever more obscene wealth, they had become desensitised to malpractice and acclimatised to corruption, to the point where they regarded it as a banality – an expediency, even an inevitability.

Crypto founders and industry insiders have been getting away with all this for far too long. It's time their sordid story was brought to light – the full story, with all the gory details. One that is so ludicrous, so fraught with absurdity, about a con so large in scale and so cleverly masked and so convincingly abjured, that it simply has to be told.

But, in order to tell that story, I first need to tell my own. It's the story of a player on the inside who became so blinded by greed that he didn't even realise he had lost his way until it was almost too late.

1

Slowly, then Suddenly

'So, Miles, how's everything with you? You've been quiet this evening. Everything okay with that digital coin thing you're working on?'

Miles glanced up from the phone he had been glued to all through dinner. His cheeks were flushed, either from awkwardness or from the heat, or both. It was a particularly warm night in August 2020. Back in those days, I was working as a PR consultant. A spinner for a large transatlantic agency, massaging the public perception of hedge funds and asset managers. The kind of firms that make billions on oil investments, and then bring people like me in to drum up press coverage for their CEO's keynote speech at a climate conference.

That night, I was at a dinner party hosted by my old university friend Eliza, to celebrate her new job. We were all quite surprised that Miles had joined us. He was another friend of ours from university, but we hadn't seen him much in the years since we graduated. And, in fact, we didn't see him much when we were at uni either; he was a maths undergrad, who shunned nightclubs and student bars in preference to staying in on the weekends and studying the financial markets. He thought his flair for numbers gave him an edge, which he could use to make his fortune.

'Yeah, no, I'm all good, thanks,' came Miles's reply. 'Things are ticking along well with the crypto. Me and my cousin have just brought a head of branding on board, to design our white paper and stuff.'

Miles had been an early bitcoin evangelist. Along with an older cousin of his, he began buying it when we were students in 2016.

Despite his usually reserved disposition, he was never shy when it came to talking about money. He would seize every opportunity that came his way to tell us just how much bitcoin he was holding. When the price was hovering around the $800 mark, he and his cousin had tens of thousands of pounds' worth of it.

We all thought he was crazy. We thought the bitcoin thing was just a fad, and that he should cash out while he was ahead. That is, until bitcoin crossed the $10,000 threshold later that year. Miles was quick to inform us he had made over 1,000 per cent profit, and his bitcoin position was now worth more than a quarter of a million. At this point, he became something of a campus celebrity. The contemptuous amusement previously felt towards his bitcoin fanaticism quickly morphed into envy. And I felt the envy more than most. Miles had been exhorting me to get involved in his operation from the start, but I hadn't taken his advice.

From then until the time of the dinner party, it had always been a bitter source of regret, and the cause of many sleepless nights spent imagining what I could have done with the small fortune I'd turned down.

As soon as he made the comment about his crypto project going well, I sat bolt upright in my seat. And I wasn't alone in wanting to hear more; the conversations in his vicinity ground to a halt, heads turned his way, and he suddenly found himself with half a dozen pairs of eyes staring at him.

'Oh, right,' came the response from the girl sitting opposite him. Miles looked uncomfortable, and a bit apprehensive. He could sense the impending cross-examination. 'I didn't know you were into crypto. I thought bitcoin crashed and died a few years ago?'

'It crashed, but it didn't die. It nearly topped $19,000 at the end of 2017, but then dropped back down to around 3,000 within a year or so. Things were pretty slow for a while after that, but we're back above ten K now.'

Miles had barely finished speaking when the next question came from someone two seats down: 'And what do you mean you've just hired a head of branding? How can you be hiring anyone? I thought you were just investing?'

'We were investing back at uni, but we're launching our own crypto project now. We've been fundraising and need to bring more people on board.'

'And what the fuck is a white paper?'

'Umm, well it's kind of like a document, which just explains what a crypto project does, and what benefits the token has. The bitcoin white paper set the precedent for this and was a document of great elegan—'

'Right. Got it. Cool.' After the initial wave of curiosity, the crowd seemed to quickly lose interest. Their previous conversations were resumed, and Miles went back to scrolling through his phone. My interest, on the other hand, had intensified. I was surprised to learn that Miles was still into crypto, and not just investing, but running what sounded like a proper company. I resolved to find out more.

I stood up and extricated Miles from the frivolous chatter taking place around the table, steering us to a quieter corner of the flat. He didn't need much encouragement to tell me more about his project and the broader state of the crypto industry. While he floundered somewhat in social situations, he relished talking shop.

He started to explain that the crypto markets were undergoing a substantial uptick. He said that the $12,000 mark was in sight for bitcoin and reckoned it would only be a matter of time before a new all-time high was set. And it wasn't just bitcoin that was flourishing: there was a slew of new projects entering the market. Every week, dozens of tokens were being launched. Their prices were skyrocketing, as speculators who hadn't bought bitcoin early enough were now snapping up other tokens to get some skin in the game.

This was a renaissance period for crypto, after the 2018 slump. Commentators were calling it the 'DeFi Summer', with 'DeFi' being an abbreviation of decentralised finance. And Miles was getting in on the action. He was setting about founding his own DeFi project, called Portent Protocol.

He explained that Portent Protocol would be composed of two elements: a platform and a token. This is the typical project set up in the industry. All the money in crypto lies in launching tokens onto the market, so there's often little incentive to launch a platform without an accompanying token. And, conversely, there's an abundance of incentive to launch a token without the inconvenience of having to build a platform.

Portent Protocol, I learned, would essentially be a gambling platform, enabling users to bet on the future price of bitcoin. Unlike other trading or betting platforms, however, Portent wouldn't make users pay if they made a bad bet. Users would simply state how much money they wanted to gamble, input their price prediction, and wait the given amount of time to see the outcome. If their bet was right, they would win a payout. And, if it was wrong, then they would get their initial stake back, fully intact and undiminished. Miles thought he had invented risk-free gambling and discovered a source of free money for all.

Of course it sounded too good to be true. However, Miles quickly reassured me that his project was the exception to the otherwise immutable saying around propositions of this nature. He told me that, after launch, a large amount of tokens would be set aside to pay out the betting rewards. This, combined with a small usage fee that users would pay to place their bets, would more than cover the amount needed to pay winning gamblers. It wasn't until much later that I discovered this to be a totally implausible business model. One that would ultimately bring about the downfall of the project. However, for now, it sufficed to dismiss any doubts I had.

Miles then went on to inform me that the platform – and its fanciful logistics – weren't his priority at the time. The token was. And the token had to be launched, he asserted, before the platform could be launched or even built. He cited a number of compelling reasons for this, chief among them being that people would not be able to use the platform without the token. It was only through buying and holding the Portent token – called TENT – that users could access this economic fairy tale of a gambling site.

I didn't question Miles any further on this point. I didn't cast any doubts on the necessity of launching a token. Nor did I put forward any counter arguments (for example, that his platform would work just as well if a token wasn't used to access it, with bettors just gambling their funds directly). I simply marvelled at the entrepreneurship of it all, impressed to think of a 25-year-old peer as a 'founder' of anything, let alone something as esoteric and explosive as a cryptocurrency.

After I lathered the praise on thick, Miles carried on justifying his project and the practices of the industry in general. He started to talk at length about why crypto tokens are launched, explaining that tokens typically serve two functions: 'access' and 'governance'. The former of these he had already covered with the spurious argument around needing tokens to use platforms, thereby lending the tokens a facade of utility and drumming up demand for people to buy them. The question of 'governance' is slightly more nuanced. But while it may appear more convincing on the surface, at heart this concept is just as fundamentally flawed.

Essentially, 'governance' means decision making. Token holders, in many projects, are given the right to vote on decisions affecting the project in question. As a user, your voting power is often proportionate to the number of tokens you hold. These voting rights cover all manner of sins and allow for a wide range of management decisions to be outsourced to the community of investors. From budget allocation to developer priorities and even things like where the companies should be headquartered, major questions in the running of any given crypto project are often outsourced to the user base. Whatever answers are thrown up, that's governance.

Needless to say, this method of decision making is fraught with problems. To put it plainly, the system is just too easy to exploit. Anyone of a morally reprehensible inclination can take advantage of a shoddy governance structure. And nowhere was this displayed more brazenly than in the case of the Uniswap grants fiasco.

Uniswap is the largest decentralised exchange in the crypto industry. Decentralised exchanges (or 'DEXs') operate in much the same way as normal exchanges, in that they enable users to swap one crypto token for another. However, the difference is DEXs have no central intermediary to the transaction, and no one can ever be stopped from using the platform. It runs by itself, following a set of pre-written algorithms that dictate how it operates.

Uniswap was launched in 2018 and, because this is the crypto industry, the launch didn't just consist of the DEX itself. Naturally, Uniswap launched a token too. Like all cryptocurrencies, Uniswap's

UNI coin enjoyed huge price appreciation when the markets started taking off in the DeFi summer. Thanks to this, and the often hefty fees that Uniswap charges users for the pleasure of swapping tokens without an intermediary, the company was soon sitting on a vast treasury. At its peak, Uniswap's coffers topped $2 billion.

At a loose end as to what to do with all this cash, the team formed a grants fund to reward good actors within the crypto ecosystem and encourage the positive progression of its principles. Interested participants from the wider world of decentralised finance were invited to enter their own governance proposals, recommending worthy causes or organisations that deserved to be funded. Around this time, as the first submissions started rolling in, a new profile appeared on Twitter. Here was an account calling itself the 'DeFi Education Fund'. Nobody had ever heard of this group before but, as the bio explained: 'We do policy and advocacy work to help DeFi flourish.'

The DeFi Education Fund profile was created in June 2021. Within a month or so, this so-called 'Education Fund' had entered a governance proposal suggesting that they be allocated $20 million from the Uniswap treasury. The proposal said they wanted the money to help facilitate their grand ambitions of brightening the future and broadening the horizons of decentralised finance, onboarding a billion users into DeFi, saving the world, etc.

For the wider community, this was quite disconcerting, given the Education Fund's opaque origins and less-than-clear mission statement. However, the Education Fund quickly reassured the community by highlighting a pledge they had made within their proposal. These funds, they affirmed, would be allocated gradually over a period of four to five years, with all spending decisions explained and justified in full on their social media channels. The crypto community, the wider DeFi ecosystem and fellow UNI token holders had nothing to fear: these guys had promised, as a condition of receiving the grant itself, that they were in it for the long term.

These entreaties had the desired effect: UNI token holders used their governance rights to vote the proposal through. The Education Fund received $20 million in UNI tokens. And, two days later, they sold $10 million worth of them.

From then until now, next to nothing has been done with the proceeds. Their social media profile is still active and posts regularly, but the Education Fund has given no indication that it has engaged in any educational initiatives whatsoever. For all we know, these self-professed proponents of decentralised pedagogy have sailed off into the sunset, and their Twitter account is being run by an intern whom they occasionally check in on between barbecues and bouts of maniacal movie-villain laughter.*

However, when Miles was giving his project the hard sell at that fateful dinner party, none of this was known to me. It only became apparent later, as I waded deeper through the quagmire of crypto. Miles, for his part, may have known that such practices existed within the industry. But, if he did, he made no effort to disclose them to me that night. Instead, he decided to succinctly sum up the prevailing state of the industry with the eloquent exclamation: 'There's absolute shit out there sitting at a $40 million market cap. There's a fucking fortune to be made.'

And, with this, Miles had me. I was wrapped around his little finger. He could've played me like a fiddle, and all I would've said was a simple and sincere, 'Thank you for the opportunity.' We spoke into the small hours of the morning, and I took my leave long after the sun had risen, the light ushering in a new dawn for my career. I knew that, one way or another, I had to get involved with the operation Miles was running.

If there really was a fucking fortune to be made, I wanted in.

---

* In April 2024, Hayden Adams, the founder of Uniswap, got drawn into defending the Education Fund against criticism being levied against it on Twitter, and highlighted some of the initiatives the group had been busy with over the years. These amounted to three amicus briefs (essentially just informative documents filed to a court on behalf of a party involved in a lawsuit), a letter commenting on an SEC proposal, and, bizarrely, a lawsuit the Fund filed against the SEC in conjunction with a small Texan leather-goods startup. All of that in a mere three years and with a paltry $20 million at their disposal. Nice work if you can get it …

2

Vulture Capital

My eyes were bleary from overuse, and my mind was fuzzy. Squinting against the bright light of my laptop, I groped across my desk in search of a mug. I needed coffee if I was going to get this finished tonight. I took a fortifying glug and turned back to the task at hand. My laptop's tiny fan whirred; the screen was a stark and vicious white, a cursor blinking on the page.

For several weeks, ever since that fateful dinner party, I had been working into the early hours, putting together the document that was to be my golden ticket into Miles's money factory. It was a PR strategy for the launch of his token, presenting a variety of desirable narratives we could spin up to attract institutional investors and the public. Miles had never asked for it, and he didn't know I was busting a gut to get it done. My hope was that I would demonstrate my marketing nous and prove how determined I was to get involved with his project.

A few days after I sent Miles the strategy document, he invited me to meet his cousin, Archie, on a Zoom call. It seemed my efforts had been vindicated, those many nights of coffee-fuelled sacrifice paying off at last. I knew this was the final hurdle, one last screening with the co-founders before my official invite to join the project.

I logged on early to the call. Alone in the virtual waiting room with only my webcam feed for company, I watched myself counting the seconds as they ticked by on the clock in the taskbar. My dreams of generational wealth were closer than ever, but I knew there was still time for things to go wrong. Winning over Miles was one thing, but something told me Archie would be a tougher nut to crack.

After what seemed like a lifetime, Miles joined the call, followed shortly by his cousin. For our first meeting, Archie was sporting a black T-shirt and baseball cap. Staring into his webcam with inscrutable eyes, he puffed assiduously on a vape, stopping only to sip from the hip flask that stood on the corner of his desk. We dispensed with pleasantries in record time, and Archie got down to business.

'Podcasts,' he said, with a scrutinising intensity in his tone. 'I didn't see anything about podcasts in the doc you sent over. Did you look into podcasts at all?'

'Yeah,' I said. I had a copy of the document open on my computer, and now I started scrolling, slipping down the pages in search of the relevant section. 'They're right there, on page ... seventeen.'

'Yeah, nice. Of course. Just remind me which ones you wrote down again?'

Unsure if I was being had – or being tested in an obscure way, like I heard they sometimes did with interviewees at cutting-edge tech firms – I rattled off a few names from the top of the list. I couldn't quite keep the hesitation from my voice. Just as I was about to finish, Archie muted himself. He picked up his phone and started talking into it. I could see his lips moving, but I couldn't hear the words. A moment later, he turned his camera off, and his portion of the screen was plunged into total blackness.

'Those suggestions are brilliant,' said Miles, playing the diplomat as best he could. 'Cheers for that, mate.' There was silence for a moment, and then Miles felt compelled to fill it. 'Sorry, shouldn't be a minute. It's a pretty hectic day for Archie.'

'No worries.'

After an awkward 5 or 6 minutes, in which Miles mostly monologued about the project, Archie returned and unmuted himself. The phone was gone; the vape was back.

'When did you say you can start?' he asked. 'There's some stuff that we need to sort out this afternoon. Are you free to help?'

I looked at Archie's portion of the screen and watched him take another puff. There was no trace of a smile on his face – or, if there was, it was hidden behind a cloud of vapour. I sensed I was at an inflection point, one of the moments on which a whole life can hinge. I took a breath and smiled at Archie.

'I can start right now,' I said. 'No problem. Let me know what you need, and I'll get it sorted.'

'Brilliant, cheers. Need to run, so Miles will send over the vesting docs now and explain what you need to do.' And, with that, Archie was gone.

I got the email from Miles around an hour after the call ended. It consisted of a single attachment and some instructions. Miles and Archie were gearing up for the big launch of the Portent Protocol project, which was still a few months away. As part of their pre-launch marketing, they wanted to publish a series of blogs and articles about the project, drumming up interest and raising awareness of what they were trying to achieve. One of the first morsels of content would explain the vesting schedule of the TENT token to prospective investors. They wanted me to write it for them, based on the information in the attachment.

I knew this would be an easy enough job, a fairly straightforward task to mark my ascension to the inner circle. I was delighted to have made it past Archie and, in my head, I was already spending the fortune I was sure to make. Of course, there was still plenty of work to do before I could sail off into the sunset, starting with the vesting document. But, before I could write it, I had to get myself up to speed on what, exactly, it was ...

Back in those days, crypto launches tended to follow a standard playbook, and Portent Protocol was to be no different. In almost all cases, founders had to start by going after venture capital.

Before a new token hits the market, a select cohort of venture capitalists is usually given the opportunity to buy a load of them at a discounted rate. This guarantees they can get there first, before Joe Public has a chance to buy or sell. It's not like there's one flat rate for all VCs though. Instead, VCs will be grouped into rounds, with the best and most desirable VCs in the first round. Here the token will be offered at its lowest price, creating more of an incentive to invest. The price will then increase with subsequent rounds, with the less desirable VCs having to fork out more than the first-round contingent, but still getting a potentially vast discount on the eventual public sale price.

The process of selling tokens to VCs is known as a private sale, so called because it precedes the public sale round, in which the token is made available to ordinary investors. A project can have as many token sale rounds as its founders want, but the norm is to have at least four: seed, private, strategic, public. The seed round is for the crème de la crème of the venture capital world, investors who back the project early and put their money where their mouth is. The strategic round is for influencers, marketers, or others whose backing would be a strategic benefit to the project. Sometimes, you'll come across a launch with an additional round, like pre-seed, slotted in somewhere, and sometimes the rounds will have different names. But you get the gist.

Token sales weren't always conducted like this, however. In fact, they have come a long way from the 2017–18 boom. In many ways, this was the golden age of crypto, also known as the 'ICO era'. ICO stands for initial coin offering – a play on the concept of an initial public offering (IPO), which happens when a company floats on the stock market. The handful of crypto projects that floated back in the ICO era made an absolute killing, inspiring subsequent waves of ICOs and sparking a tide of interest from retail investors.

In the heady days of the ICO era, the industry was nowhere near as developed as it is now. There were fewer projects and tokens being launched, and the ICO process was a lot less sophisticated. The founders of any given project would simply let prospective investors know their token valuation, post a link to a bitcoin wallet address, and encourage buyers to send as much bitcoin as they wanted. Investors would then receive their share of the tokens. Throughout this process, all investor communications were conducted through Telegram, a highly encrypted messaging platform that promotes user anonymity and that has always been a cornerstone of the industry. Even now, most of the industry is still run on this one messaging app.

Even though this crude ICO process inspires about as much confidence as an email from a Nigerian prince, the projects that launched back then raised unbelievable sums of money. Notable among these was the fundraise conducted by EOS, a 'layer 1 blockchain network' (that is to say, a base blockchain network through which payments can be made, like bitcoin or Ethereum). EOS raised just over $4.2 billion through a year-long ICO, which tops every other crypto token sale in history. For perspective, the EOS fundraise was larger even than the three biggest venture fundraising rounds for equities in 2018 – Uber, Epic Games and Juul – combined.

Despite this astronomical figure, the sale followed a typically unsophisticated procedure. Would-be investors were directed to a website, where they were provided with a wallet address. Buyers then sent their funds to the wallet and waited to receive a corresponding stack of EOS tokens.

It should come as no surprise to hear that this far-from-foolproof process was soon exploited by scammers. The fraud was about as primitive as the actual ICOs that were taking place: the only difference was that, after investors sent funds to the scammers (thinking they were buying into a legitimate ICO), they didn't receive any tokens in return. After countless cases of ICO fraud, and untold fortunes of stolen funds, investors began to tire of being so predictably conned. Eventually, they stopped investing in ICOs altogether, and the market went flat. Crypto founders needed to come up with a way to restore investor confidence and to keep the money printer whirring. And, from this necessity, ICOs gave way to IDOs.

IDOs, or initial DEX offerings, essentially have the same objective and perform the same function as ICOs. An IDO just has a few extra steps, ostensibly to promote equity and security. One of the key additions in the IDO process is the introduction of those private VC rounds before the public token sale. This serves many purposes: not only does it allow projects to secure early funding, thereby mitigating the inherent uncertainty around how well a token will sell when it's offered to the masses, but it also imbues the project with a sense of legitimacy.

Retail investors treat VC backing as proof that a project and its founders are credible. The thinking goes that vast investment institutions, prior to committing any capital to a project, will conduct thorough research and due diligence, thus relieving retail investors of the need to go digging through the project's paperwork and accounts. In essence, retail investors tend to think that VC backing means the hard work has already been done for them, so they can invest confidently, knowing that they're buying a reputable product that has serious backing. It's due diligence by proxy. What could go wrong?

The problem with this system is that VCs, by their nature, are incredibly mercenary. If a VC has backed a project, they will naturally expect a return on their investment. VCs have also come to learn that much of the cryptocurrency ecosystem is propped up by flimsy and fickle hype on the part of founders and investors. Hype circles are generally self-sustaining ... until they aren't. Consumer confidence can crash in the space of seconds, and a token that might have seemed watertight this morning can hit $0 by lunchtime. Savvy VCs know this, and their response is to make sure they always cash out long before the wheels have a chance to come off. As such, they have gathered a well-earned reputation for being 'dumpers' – a loaded industry term for individuals or institutions that habitually sell their tokens the second they get their hands on them.

To counteract this, founders began imposing 'vesting schedules' onto the VCs taking part in their launches. This just means that a portion of the tokens, although already paid for, will only be handed down to the VCs after a given amount of time. Until then, the VCs can't do anything with them, which prevents VCs from dumping all their tokens onto retail investors on launch day (and crashing the price in the process).

For example, a project may subject VCs to a ten-month vesting schedule with equal instalments, meaning that every month, for ten months, the VC receives 10 per cent of their tokens. Or there might be a 'cliff', meaning that, for a given number of months, no tokens will be available, with vesting to commence after this period. Typically, the longer the vesting schedule, the more it looks like the project is making efforts to reduce VC sell pressure. This then results in greater investor confidence.

All of this was relevant to my first task as a member of the Portent Protocol team. I pieced together the particulars of our own vesting schedule and wrote it up for the Portent blog, as Archie had instructed. I felt, as I was hammering away at my keyboard, that every word took me closer to unimaginable wealth. And every second did indeed take us closer to the launch – potentially the biggest moment of my life. Across London, somewhere in the middle of a cloud of sweet-scented vapour, Archie was a knot of ever-increasing tension, and I knew Miles was spending every waking minute working through the various angles. All we had to do was get it right, and then we would be rich.

I sent over the vesting doc, and both Archie and Miles approved it. I was rewarded with a title: chief communications officer, no less. And, as only the fourth team member to come on board – after Miles, Archie and a guy called Paul, our head of brand – I was also named a co-founder. Now I was really looking forward to getting immersed in the industry, working directly with sophisticated investors, entrepreneurs and innovators. Never mind the snoozefest that was traditional PR: I felt that this was my real purpose. After all, I was joining the frontline of a revolution, forging a wholly new financial system underpinned by fairness and transparency. And if I happened to make an absolute killing while I was at it, well, that was just a perk of the job.

'Mate, it's fucking febrile out here!' As Miles laughed down the phone, I caught a twinge of mania in his voice.

'Listen,' he continued, and I duly pressed my phone closer to my ear. 'I just got off a call with CS Equity. You know them? They're one of the biggest crypto VCs in China. They said they have a hundred grand to send us, and they want our contribution address right now.'

'Bloody hell.' I blew out a mouthful of air. This was more investment than we could accommodate, based on the structure of our investment rounds. 'So we got through their due diligence?'

'What due dil? No questions asked, mate – they want in. They want to send the money right now, but there's only fifty grand left in the private round. Can you quickly edit the doc you sent over?'

'Sure thing, mate.' Miles hung up, and I was left staring at my phone.

It was around 7.30 a.m., and I was exhausted. I had just left Monument station and was marching to Pret for my third coffee before heading into the office. It was February 2021, and I was still working full time in PR. Initially, I had tried to keep crypto separate and do my work for Portent after hours. But, as the launch approached, I had let the side hustle take priority over my day job. Portent had already grown into an all-consuming colossus; the launch was practically all any of us could think about. And now, with so much VC money pouring in, the stakes were higher than ever and rising all the time. Already, I was working around 100 hours per week, and we hadn't even reached the launch date yet. It was scheduled for early March and, while still relatively new to the crypto game, I had picked up enough by now to know this was likely to change. Fair to say, I was feeling the strain.

As soon as I arrived at the office, I made the latest changes and sent the document to Miles. We were now on version eight of what should have been a straightforward blog post about VC fundraising. Every time we thought we were prepared to move on with the IDO process, another irresistible offer would come in, and we would have to change everything to accommodate the latest VC who wanted to throw money at us. Word was going round about our project, and VCs were clambering over each other for allocations (or 'allos', as they're more commonly called). They couldn't hand over their cash fast enough, and I knew it wasn't because they believed in us as founders or loved our project or shared our vision. It was because of our starting market cap. Our laughably low, total joke of a market cap.

When a company floats, and its shares are offered to the public for the first time, an investment bank is hired to determine the value of the company before it is listed. This is a highly complex, stringently regulated part of the IPO process, accompanied by intense public and professional scrutiny. Scores of independent accountants, lawyers and regulators take a close look at not only the floating company but also at the investment bank providing its valuation. Everyone's on the lookout for wrongdoing, and everyone involved is keeping an eye on everyone else. This results in a lengthy process designed to protect retail investors and ensure they end up paying a fair price for the stock when it becomes tradable. But that's equities. Needless to say, crypto valuations are not done the same way.

When a crypto token is launched, the initial price is decided upon by the team that created it. This, in turn, allows the team to control the initial market capitalisation (also known as 'market caps' or just 'mcaps') of their project. Market caps show the total value of a token or, in the case of stocks, of a company. You calculate the market cap by taking the number of tokens in circulation and multiplying that by the price per token.

Because there are no investment banks or other professional observers tasked with keeping the process fair and transparent, crypto founders are free to set the initial market capitalisation of their tokens at a deliberately low level. They do this knowing full well that the price will only skyrocket on launch day. A low valuation helps to generate hype among retail investors and VCs alike, since early investors are all but guaranteed huge returns. It also makes it more likely that the founders in question will make a fortune from dumping their stash of tokens when the price is right.

At Portent Protocol, we set our listing price fantastically low, even by industry standards, to entice as much pre-launch investment as possible. And, so far, our plan was working. We already had over half a million dollars in the bank, and more was arriving by the day – not bad for an as-yet unlaunched token with next to no real-world application.

And we weren't finished there, either. In fact, we were just getting started.

3

Auditory Blindness

We had not long rewritten our investment plan when the topic of an audit first cropped up. I was on a call with Miles, continuing to neglect the duties of my actual, salaried job to talk through the next step in the launch process: the strategic investment round. I was concerned about how much it would cost to hire a batch of influencers to pump the token. But these concerns, I was about to discover, paled in comparison to what Archie and Miles were busying themselves with.

'Don't worry too much about the influencers,' said Miles, towards the end of our call. 'Archie's on hand to help with that. He's got some ideas which should bring the costs down. He's actually here now, I'll pass the phone over. I need to drop to speak to the auditors.'

For weeks, I had been busy working all the marketing angles, leaving the guts of the launch preparations to Miles and Archie. They were driving the audit process, which in our case was being carried out by a major player in the space: a firm called Tutus Security. Although we weren't doing anything wrong, I feared a sober, external observer might not be too impressed by our small, on-the-hoof operation. I thought the deliberately low valuation might also ring alarm bells.

'What are you speaking to the auditors about?' I asked, but Miles had already gone.

'Mate, where are the fucking influencers?' That was Archie's voice, cutting me off. He sounded distant, as if he hadn't had time to put the phone to his ear and was instead shouting across the room.

'I'm working on it,' I said. 'Just quickly, do you know what Miles is speaking to the auditors about?'

'Yeah, they want an allo, the dirty dogs.' Archie sounded closer as he tutted down the phone. 'We really need to start closing off these rounds. We're oversubscribed already.'

'What? As in our auditors want to invest in the project?'

'As in they want to do their audit in exchange for an allo. They want to buy our tokens so badly that they'll audit us for free just to get their foot in the door. Bloody brilliant. Saves us an absolute fortune.'

I was stunned. I knew you could find some unsavoury practices within the crypto space – after all, this was the Wild West of the modern internet – but what I had just heard was something else entirely.

I had been engaging with influencers for a while. They wanted money in return for hyping up our token to their followers, with zero transparency, which seemed distasteful enough. But I figured that was just how influencers were, and I wasn't going to lose any sleep over it. Auditors, though, paying to invest in a project they're supposed to be scrutinising? This was a magnitude of malpractice that I hadn't encountered before.

In recent years, it has become common practice for crypto projects to be audited before they go to market. These audits were supposed to be one of the few parts of the launch process that required at least a degree of external oversight. And the auditors who carry them out were supposed to be the good guys: reputable, impartial service providers who analyse and evaluate the code that underpins a project – the technology governing the platform and the token. The code presents a key vulnerability for any given project, and for hackers it's pure bait.

Anyone who has glimpsed a financial newspaper in the past couple of years will doubtless be familiar with the regularity with which high-profile, high-value crypto projects are undone by cybercriminals. Take, for example, the Ronin Bridge hack, orchestrated by a shadowy collective known as the Lazarus Group: a state-sponsored hacking organisation that operates on behalf of the North Korean government. The Lazarus Group is known to have orchestrated a raft of cyber attacks dating all the way back to 2009, with victims including Sony Pictures, countless South Korean citizens, and numerous banks and businesses all around the world. Since 2017, the group has focussed on stealing crypto assets, with the laundered proceeds going straight into the hermit kingdom's national coffers.

The Ronin Bridge hack was their largest ever heist, and also the largest in the history of digital assets. The Lazarus Group was able to make off with over $650 million, plundered from Ronin, a platform that powers the largest blockchain game in the industry, Axie Infinity.

The hackers were able to gain back-door access to Ronin's 'bridge', which is a protocol that allows a token to be swapped between networks. For example, if you're holding money on Ethereum, you can use a bridge to swap the same amount of money over to Solana, another blockchain network. Bridges are common targets for hackers, as they typically hold large amounts of money and have multiple points of entry. The Lazarus Group found one of these points of entry, and then drained the funds being stored on the bridge.

However, they didn't stop there; the hack went undetected for about a week and, in that time, the group decided to reinvest some of their ill-gotten proceeds. They placed short positions on the Axie Infinity native token. In non-finance speak, this just means they made a bet against the performance of the token linked to Axie Infinity. They anticipated that, once the news got out about the hack, the value of the project and its token would collapse. Not content with making off with the best part of a billion dollars, they wanted to commit even more crimes to profit further still.

However, they were thwarted in this endeavour. And it was the sheer incompetence of the Axie and Ronin teams that was their undoing. Because it took the developers so long to notice the hack, the token price not only remained buoyant but actually continued appreciating. The Lazarus Group's shorts eventually got liquidated, which is to say that they lost so much money from the market moving against them that the platforms they were trading on automatically closed their positions. However, even in spite of the failed bet, the North Koreans were still able to make off from the heist with a fortune, which no doubt the rogue state found useful for funding its illicit weapons and surveillance programmes.

It's exactly these kinds of situations that auditors are supposed to protect against. The whole reason they exist is to meticulously check the code that governs platforms and tokens to make sure there are no technical faults, bugs or weaknesses that can allow hackers to steal funds. It's beyond dodgy, then, to think of an auditor investing in a project they're supposed to scrutinise, as it softens the incentive for them to do a thorough and honest job. But for an auditor to entirely forgo payment in favour of a token allocation is something else entirely; it completely undermines their role as an independent evaluator of a project's merits and pitfalls.

If you have a vested interest in the success of a project, or in the price of its token, then why bother checking the code too thoroughly? And if you do come across something that rings alarm bells, why make a fuss and risk crashing the price? Instead, you're incentivised to gloss over any shortcomings, turn a blind eye to bugs, and write a favourable report about the project's tech and security. After all, you benefit directly from greater investor confidence. It's a conflict of interest on a scale that simply would not be countenanced in any other industry.

Imagine, for instance, if one of the 'Big Four' accounting firms took payment for their services in the stock of the companies whose accounts they were contracted to audit. Such a scandal would incur not just astronomical sanctions from regulatory authorities but also criminal prosecutions under the severe investor and consumer protection laws that protect traditional industries. However, in the world of crypto no one has ever been charged for this egregious conflict of interest. Indeed, nobody responsible has ever faced any consequences whatsoever. And yet, as shocking and deplorable as all this was, I was soon to discover that it got even worse.

Tutus was supposed to be one of the biggest, best-known and most reputable auditors in the space. They positioned their audits as the gold standard of security within the crypto industry. Around the time we were due to announce our own audit, however, disaster struck several prominent projects Tutus had rubber-stamped. Notable among these was the hack of Challenger Group, a project run by a highly flamboyant and vocal founder named Chad Granger. With his fake teeth and perma-tanned skin, and bolstered by enough botox to rejuvenate half of Beverly Hills, Granger had taken pains in recent years to position himself as the surgically enhanced face of the crypto industry. His slick, if strange, appearance, bubbly online presence, and silver-tongued media appearances endeared him to many, and he inspired enough confidence to elicit a staggering cascade of capital inflows for his latest project: a toolkit of decentralised financial products, covering everything from the lending and borrowing of capital to insurance provision.

In no time at all after its launch, Challenger Network boasted a $100 million market cap. Or it did, until it got exploited. Shortly after Tutus partnered with Challenger Network and announced they had completed their audit, hackers succeeded in carrying out an 'infinite mint' attack against the project. Essentially, they managed to access the code that allows the project to create new tokens. They then minted billions of these and sold them on the platforms where the PAID token was trading. In the process, they drained the project's liquidity, netted themselves millions, and sent the project's $100 million market cap to zero.

Needless to say, distraught users quickly turned to Tutus. Thousands of investors started asking how Challenger Network could have been so obviously compromised when it had just received a glowing report from one of the industry's best auditors. And then, perhaps inevitably, some of crypto's more astute observers noticed that this fitted a wider pattern. Challenger Network wasn't the first project to be hacked or compromised soon after a Tutus audit, and this raised alarm bells for the crypto community. Some even started wondering if it wasn't Tutus themselves who were behind these hacks. It would, after all, make sense: Tutus had an inside-out view of where the weaknesses were in the code base. Of course, this could never be proved, but the mere insinuation (which spread like wildfire at the time) was enough to cast serious doubts over the reputation of the auditor.

For us, this presented a big problem. On the one hand, there were still large sections of the crypto community who wouldn't invest in a project unless it had been audited, believing an auditor's rubber stamp added a layer of protection and certainty. On the other hand, Tutus's reputation was going through a rough patch, to say the least, and a lot of investors were pointing fingers in the wake of the high-profile hacks. We wanted to release an audit, but Tutus wasn't exactly the flavour of the month. We felt that, no matter what, we were going to end up alienating some of our future investors.

We decided to roll the dice and go ahead with the audit. We made a finger-in-the-air judgement that the number of people who wouldn't invest without an audit would be greater than the number of people who were so sceptical about our auditors that they wouldn't invest with one. Plus, our community was still relatively small, consisting of only several hundred people across our social channels at the time. This meant that, if the sentiment went south, we could always just memory-hole the audit, the details of which we were planning to pub-lish on our blog. But what ultimately tipped the balance was a cold, hard financial consideration. The audit wouldn't cost us anything; we were giving the auditor an allocation, after all, so in essence *they* were paying *us* for the provision of their services. And we certainly were not the types to turn down free money, under any circumstances.

In the end, our worries turned out to be entirely unfounded. We uploaded the audit report (no problems detected, of course) and, not only did they not take any exception whatsoever to our choice of auditors, some even took the time to congratulate us on taking our security so seriously. This came as quite a surprise to us all. We knew there were at least a few people in our community who had invested in Challenger Network. After scanning the Telegram groups of the disaster-stricken project, we discovered that, not only had some of our backers invested in it, but they had also been very vocal in their condemnation of Tutus's role. Now those same people were delight-ing in Tutus's appraisal of our own project.

'They're deluded,' was the analysis of Paul, our head of brand. 'They only care about these things after the fact. All of them cling on to the hope that they're going to make generational wealth off these projects, so they just don't pay attention when they see something that could jeopardise that. It's selective blindness on an industrial scale. They're all full of hope until something goes wrong, at which point the pitchforks and torches come out.'

Paul's sentiments ring true enough today. At the time, however, I was overworked and impatient to get to launch day, so I accepted the involvement of Tutus as a win and moved on. I still had plenty of work to be getting on with, and my number-one priority at the time was finding some influencers who would agree to pump our project.

I was excruciatingly aware that the launch was getting closer all the time. Each day meant more pressure and less room for manoeuvre. And yet each day brought me closer to the fortune I, like our selectively blind investors, was hell-bent on chasing. Our public profile still wasn't close to where it needed to be, however, so I was devoting a lot of my mental processing power to what I was starting to think of as the influencer problem.

I was quickly learning that working in crypto involved a lot of jumping between tasks, across multiple business lines, and putting out fires. It was sporadic, chaotic and disorganised. And, despite operating in a near-constant state of panic, I was loving every second of it. There was so much energy, so much urgency. My years spent working in traditional PR seemed like a geriatric ward in comparison. This was life in the fast lane, and I felt like I was on the frontline of a revolution. Safe to say, I was getting hooked.

4

Influence for Hire

'After CS Equity, we really need to stop giving ad hoc private allocations,' Miles said. He was speaking over the phone, but I could still hear his mind whirring away; he was always thinking about the next step. At last, our VC funding was all wrapped up – for real, this time – and attention was now turning to the influencers, or the lack thereof. 'We've got to move on and get our asses in gear for the strategic round. They're the guys who will get the price up. This shit isn't going to pump itself.'

Based on the unbelievable demand from VCs, we were convinced that the TENT token was a golden egg. And what we needed next was a means of hatching the most eye-watering profit. This was why Miles was so focused on the strategic investment round – the tranche in which tokens are offered to influencers who might buy into a project and then pump it all over social media. As soon as the token looked like it was nearing its peak, we co-founders would sell our own TENT reserves and cash out, having made a fortune. That was the plan, anyway. But first, our golden egg needed an incubator.

In a finance context, an incubator is essentially a VC who plays a much more active role in a project's development. While all VCs are, in theory, supposed to add value to the companies they invest in, the reality is that most are as apathetic and aloof as they come. They invest, they make money, they fuck off. That's the cliché, anyway.

Incubators, on the other hand, are supposed to offer much more guidance and support to the projects they invest in. Theirs is a very broad remit; a decent incubator might, for example, connect a project to more VCs, point founders to service providers who can work with them, or even help with marketing by making introductions to prominent influencers.

'I'm about to land us a great incubator,' Miles continued. 'They're planning to intro us to all of their influencers, which should be more than enough to fill the strat round.'

Influencer marketing is a big deal in crypto, but it can be ruinously expensive to pay one of these bellwethers to promote your token. It's much cheaper to give influencers a chance to buy presale tokens in a strategic investment round, which then creates an incentive for them to promote the project to their followers. It's quite an ingenious (and highly nefarious) system: ingenious because, by buying tokens, the influencers are actually paying the projects they're working for, and nefarious because influencers seldom, if ever, tell their loyal followers that they have a vested interest in the project they're promoting.

'Yeah, the quicker we start getting some influencers in the better,' I said. 'I DM'd that Ghost DeFi guy yesterday, and he wants 5 ETH per tweet. Fuck spending almost ten thousand dollars on a tweet from a guy with less than twenty thousand followers.'

Most conversations with influencers take place via direct message (or 'DM') on social media platforms like Twitter, which is hardly the ideal place to conduct business deals worth tens or even hundreds of thousands of dollars. It doesn't help that most crypto influencers, even the most prominent ones, are completely anonymous. They mostly have cartoon avatars as their profile pictures and go about calling themselves something like 'Ghost DeFi'. Often, an influencer will also attach a crypto-related suffix to their pseudonymous name – something like 'XBT', which was an early trading symbol for bitcoin. The prefix 'ox' is also commonly used, especially for newer influencers who market Ethereum-based projects. (Wallet addresses on the Ethereum network all start with the characters ox.)

Miles passed me over to Archie, who seemed to be in a bad mood, as was increasingly common these days. I put it down to the stress of the launch, which was creeping up on us, threatening to overtake our plans. Still, it rankled when Archie asked, in typically brash fashion, if one conversation was the sum of my progress on the influencer front.

'Well,' I said, 'we've also got that call with CryptoCroc later. Plus, I've had some very encouraging—'

'Look, mate, forget all that shit. Leopard Labs are going to put us in touch with their network. That'll be thirty to forty influencers all pumping us, round the clock. You like that, don't you?' Archie paused, as if actually expecting a response.

'Yeah, nice,' I said. 'Who are Leopard Labs again?'

'That's the incubator me and Miles have been speaking to. They're already in for a hundred grand in the private round, by the way, so you need to change that article again. It should be the last time.'

'Right,' I said. We were into double digits now with that article, something like the eleventh draft. 'What about other influencers?'

'Listen, Leopard Labs are going to pump us. Let's get the Croc on board, but the Leopards will sort the rest. Come to my flat, and we'll take the Croc call together.'

'Okay. But how much allo do we have to offer the influencers?'

'All the changes to the private round fucked us a bit, so we need to tighten the strat round. The influencers will need to share about a hundred grand or so of allo. Let's see if the Croc will take three grand, and whatever you do, don't tell him Leopard have a hundred in private. He knows them, and we don't want to cause any bitterness.'

At that moment, I was struck by the bizarreness of the situation that I had somehow got myself into. We were raising hundreds of thousands of dollars (which still seemed like an awful lot to me, back then, before the real money started rolling in) from individuals and organisations called Leopard and Croc. I was starting to wonder if all this was some kind of joke. Who on Earth could take this mangy menagerie seriously?

Well, there was the CryptoCroc, for one.

'Three K?' he fumed. Archie and I were on one end of the call; Croc was on the other. And it seemed we had inadvertently poked him. 'Three K? You've got to be kidding. The last project I invested in, I wrote a check for a quarter of a million. I literally would not bend down to pick up $3,000 if I dropped it on the floor.'

Croc had a thick Eastern European accent but, beyond this, we knew absolutely nothing about him. His camera was off, and his portion of the screen was filled with an image of a cartoon crocodile.

He wouldn't tell us his real name or even what country he was in. I would go on to find out that this was the norm when dealing with crypto influencers.

'Three thousand is all we can offer,' I said. 'We're a low-cap gem, so we're not raising very much, but the price is going to absolutely skyrocket on launch.'

Croc snorted. 'I heard you're working with Leopard Labs?'

'Bloody hell,' said Archie. He cast a sideways glance at me. 'How'd you hear about that?'

'I've worked with them a lot,' said Croc. 'I'm one of their main influencers. Look, normally I wouldn't bother with this, but everything they've touched recently has turned to gold. I'll take the three grand if that's all you can offer, but don't expect much if I'm making such a small investment.'

'Perfect,' I said. 'We'll get a SAFT over to you straight away.'

A SAFT is a simple agreement for future tokens. It's basically a contract between projects and whoever invests in the token before it launches – influencers, VCs, service providers and the like – which confirms the buyer's rights and supposedly protects against either one of the parties pulling out of the deal. But I later found out that, because most crypto firms are structured to be little more than shell companies, and because they're all registered in countries with judicial systems about as robust as a wet paper bag, these SAFTs usually aren't worth the paper they're written on. Still, SAFTs were standard industry practice and, if nothing else, there was an outside chance they might help with disputes – like if an influencer were to chance it and claim they didn't get the allocation they were promised (a situation that is certainly not unheard of). Generally, everyone in the industry goes through the motions with SAFTs, just as an insurance policy. Except, that is, for people who don't want their identities known.

'I don't fuck with SAFTs,' said Croc. He was indignant, as if the very notion of a SAFT was absurd – offensive, almost. 'If I need to sign something to get these tokens, I'm out.'

'Well, what do you want us to do then?' I asked. 'Our hands are tied. Our lawyers say we need SAFTs from everyone we give tokens to.'

'Are you getting influencers through the Leopard network?'

'Yeah, they said they'd help us get people on board.'

'Okay, don't worry then. I'll get my allo through them.' And with that, Croc hung up.

I looked over at Archie. 'What was he on about?' I asked. 'How can he get his allo through an incubator? Surely all the influencers they give us will also just have to sign SAFTs later down the line?'

Archie stared back at me for a while. His brow creased. He had also never procured influencers for a project; all this was as new to him as it was to me.

'Fuck it,' he said at last. 'It'll be fine.'

As it turned out, Archie was right. Leopard Labs had a system in place for dealing with their more privacy-conscious influencers. The incubator simply asked for a single SAFT, made out to them, for the full strategic round allocation. They would then divide up their allocation and dish it out to the influencers, without making any of them sign individual SAFTs. It was an efficient solution, although somewhat problematic for us.

As we later discovered, quite a few incubators and influencer management firms employed this method, and not always with the utmost honesty. It's a system that lays the groundwork for exploitation. If an incubator is given $100,000 to distribute among their influencers, the incubator might just pocket $50,000 of this and either give their influencers a smaller allocation or procure fewer of them. This poses quite significant risks for projects, as a single entity holding a large number of tokens necessarily has a lot of power. A sell-off of too many tokens in one go could potentially spook other investors and crash the price. But in the case of Portent Protocol we weren't really in a position to argue with Leopard Labs's proposed solution. We needed influencers more than we needed assurances about the stability of our as-yet unlaunched token. And, without Leopard Labs to assist with our marketing drive, our token would never even become valuable enough to crash.

So, we agreed to the demands of our incubator and, in no time at all, they sent back a signed SAFT. Before you could say 'unlawful promotion of securities', we had forty influencers on our roster. Leopard Labs set up a Telegram group with all of them in it, where we could send them important tweets that we wanted them to 'amplify'. (In this case, 'amplify' is an industry euphemism for 'promote without a disclosure'.)

Our legion of social media opinion formers started tweeting for us round the clock. The low market cap of our token provided them with plenty of additional motivation to make sure this thing took off on launch; in those days, 10,000 per cent price increases were not uncommon for new tokens, meaning that even Croc's measly $3,000 allocation could quickly grow into a $300,000 holding. Soon we had some of the most prominent crypto personalities, a couple of them with over a million followers, writing comprehensive threads about how unmissable this opportunity was. Our social media following grew from the low hundreds to the tens of thousands.

Needless to say, none of the influencers' tweets were ever marked as ads or sponsored content. None of them ever mentioned that they had personally invested in our project at presale prices and therefore stood to gain more than any of their followers if the token took off. On some level, the influencers must have known that what they were doing was wrong – or at least dubious – as they often deleted their tweets about TENT a few days after posting them.

When we raised questions with Leopard Labs about why our influencers were doing this, we were told it was standard practice. Our paid cheerleaders didn't want a digital footprint showing which tokens they had promoted in case any of the projects were hacked, turned out to be scams or simply didn't perform well. They were deleting the evidence as they went along so that they didn't risk ruining their credibility further down the line. At the time, however, I swallowed my distaste and got on with it. All that mattered was our ever-rising follower count.

'This is bloody brilliant,' Miles said one evening over after-work beers. He clapped me on the shoulder. 'We're absolutely pumping, lad! We're up to fifteen K followers on Twitter.'

Archie glared over the head of his pint. The ever-present vape was resting in his other hand. 'It's not enough,' he said. 'Where's the fucking PR?' As chief comms officer, I knew this question was directed at me.

'Well, we haven't really had any newsworthy stories to write about,' I said. 'All we've really posted on our blog is the audit and then a few inconsequential bits of content about our mission and vision. If you're expecting articles in the press, then don't. No journalist is going to write about that stuff.'

'Mate, the journalists will write what we tell them to write.'

'What?'

'The journos are in on it too,' said Archie. 'Everyone wants an allo; just dangle one in front of their faces. Tell them we want to test out the results first, so we'll commission a couple of articles for cash and then discuss an allo if it all goes well.'

I looked from Archie to Miles and back again. I couldn't believe what I was hearing. Surely, I thought, Archie must be taking the piss? I understood that corruption was par for the course among influencers; after all, these were individuals with cartoon profile pictures who made a living promoting volatile financial investments on social media without disclosures or caveats. But surely journalists couldn't be so brazen? Surely the rules were different for traditional media outlets, where content was written and edited by named and accountable professionals?

Of course, all my PR experience before now had come in the asset management sector, which is highly regulated. The first two weeks at my agency were spent reading the financial promotion rules and nothing else; there was even an internal exam they made us sit at the end of it. Because if the wrong thing is said about a hedge fund – or even if the right thing is said in the wrong way – the regulators will come down on you like a ton of bricks. At the firm, a fuck-up of that magnitude meant you'd be sacked on the spot.

Archie must have noticed my disturbed expression. He took another puff and, when the cloud of fruit-flavoured vapour disappeared, I saw he was smiling.

'Look, mate,' he said, 'it's the fucking Wild West out here. There's none of that posh PR stuff in crypto. There are no rules. It's all unregulated. So just go out there and buy some media coverage.'

That night, more out of curiosity than anything else, I began sending out Twitter DMs to as many crypto journalists as I could find. It was a crude method of outreach, and one that I wouldn't have dreamt of in traditional PR. But I reckoned if it worked for influencers it might work for reporters as well. Plus, I figured any journalist open to taking bribes likely wouldn't mind transacting via social media. It would surely beat an approach via their work email, which their employers would be able to monitor.

I'll admit, though: I didn't have high hopes of getting any bites. I imagined a reporter might, at best, respond to tell me that they wouldn't think of taking money in return for favourable coverage. At worst, I feared being reported to some kind of legal authority. But my fears, I quickly learned, were completely unfounded.

Within minutes of sending out my initial batch of messages, I had my first reply. It was from a leading reporter at *The Blockchain Gazette*: a medium-sized crypto news outlet, with over 50,000 unique monthly visitors. The reporter told me that he was interested in our project and thought it had a great value proposition. He would publish an article about it, he said, for $250, and then, if we were happy, he'd be delighted to discuss an allocation. He even offered to throw in a complimentary tweet from his outlet's official account promoting the article – a means of sweetening the deal and increasing his chances of an allo, I presumed.

I was stunned, even as the sound of cash registers started ringing in my ears. How low were the moral standards in this industry that journalists, supposedly the conveyors of truth and objectivity, could be so easily bought and sold? All it took was a 5-minute chat over Twitter.

This was cowboy stuff compared to what I was used to in traditional PR, but it suited my purposes perfectly. I asked the reporter when he would like to interview Miles, as the project's CEO, for his article.

'Unnecessary,' he replied. 'Just send me the article you want published, and I'll post it to our site.'

I stared at his response in a state of disbelieving scorn. Not only was this joker taking bribes for commissions over Twitter DMs, but he wouldn't even write the story himself! Did that mean he would republish any old puff piece with zero editorial oversight?

I wanted to test the waters, to see how far we could go, so I sent him the most self-indulgent piece of content I had to hand: a blog post I had written about the mission, vision and values of Portent Protocol. This article was so packed with self-aggrandising platitudes and meaningless banalities that it was almost too syrupy for our own blog. It was nowhere near newsworthy, and no serious third-party outlet had any business publishing such reheated nonsense. But I went ahead and sent over the copy anyway. I crossed my fingers and waited for a reply.

The reporter asked me if I would like him to publish it immediately or schedule it for later.

So it was that the next morning, at exactly 11 a.m., I found myself reading an article about the mission, vision and values of Portent Protocol on the homepage of a well-known crypto media outlet. The only edit the 'reporter' had made was to change the point of view to the third person so it sounded like he had written it all himself. Shortly after the article was posted, he sent me his crypto wallet address for payment. Not the bank details of the news site or even a company crypto address. His own personal wallet. I wondered if his editor or the site's owners knew he was taking article commissions and keeping the cash to himself. Then it dawned on me that his bosses were almost certainly doing the exact same thing.

'Excellent work, mate,' was Archie's response to all this. 'I told you, you just needed to grease the wheels a bit.' He laughed down the phone. 'Now just churn out five or six of those a day, and we'll be in business. Also, for the big journos, try to get them over for some pints. They'll bloody love that. And if you become friends with them, they might give a discount or do it for free. No one can say no to a free pint.'

'Sure, mate,' I said. I was strangely disheartened by the whole episode. 'I'll send more messages today.'

'Good man. Hang on, Miles wants a word.'

'All right.'

'Yes, mate,' came the voice of our CEO, our fearless leader. 'Loved the article. Great stuff.'

'Cheers.'

'Look, this is just a heads up, but we've got a bit of a situation unfolding on the legal front. Long story short, I might have to go out to the Cayman Islands for a while.'

'Right, okay.' My heart rate picked up an extra beat or two. 'How come?'

'It's a bit complicated. I'll explain later. But I need some help from you.'

'What is it?'

'We need to go back through all of our articles, and make sure that nothing – absolutely nothing – references gambling in any way.'

'It doesn't.'

'Referencing gambling doesn't just mean using the word "gambling". I mean we need to go back and check that every time we've spoken about users betting on the platform, we don't say "bet", or "winnings", or anything like that. And all that shit about it being "risk-free", that needs to go as well.'

'Right, got it. So, what do we say instead?'

'Mate, you're the PR guy. Think of some similes and use those.'

'Synonyms, you mean?'

'Exactly! Good man, I'll leave you to it. Let me know as soon as it's done.'

'Yeah, no problem.' I paused. 'What's all this for?'

But Miles had already hung up, and it wasn't until later that I discovered the cause of his nervous urgency.

Portent Protocol, like the overwhelming majority of crypto companies, was legally registered in an offshore domicile. This is very easy to do; in most cases, the company doesn't even need to do any real business in the place where it is registered. Nor do any of the team need to be based there. In fact, a whole economy exists of third-party individuals who will legally register themselves as a director just so the company in question meets the requirements for being headquartered in a particular offshore location.

An onshore domicile would be somewhere like the UK, the EU, or the US, where the regulatory frameworks governing companies are typically more robust. Compare these to offshore domiciles – somewhere like the Cayman Islands, Panama, or any other exotic location commonly mentioned in news reports about financial scandals. (They don't all need to be remote tropical islands, though; Jersey is technically an offshore domicile.)

If you're registered in an offshore domicile, you'll end up paying less tax and complying with fewer regulations. For Portent Protocol, the domicile of choice was the Cayman Islands. Here you could find irresistibly low taxes, a very straightforward set-up process and a regulatory framework that was more lax, to say the least. But, even so, there were a few hoops through which we needed to jump.

In the Cayman Islands, while the laws governing crypto were lax, the laws governing gambling were highly stringent – unsurprising, given that gambling has been around for millennia. The handful of crypto laws, by contrast, have mostly been rushed through in the past few years to capitalise on a gold rush of cash-rich founders looking for a friendly domicile in which they can set up shop.

To avoid falling into a regulatory web of gambling laws, we needed to obtain what's known as a 'legal opinion' – an official, legally binding document issued by a licensed law firm stating that, in the opinion of the experts working at the firm, our company was not dealing in gambling products. These legal opinions are essentially very serious and important pieces of paperwork; they determine how regulatory authorities classify and govern the companies in their jurisdiction, and they're issued by large, reputable law firms, many of which have been operating for decades and employ some of the leading individuals in the industry. It is common practice for offshore-domiciled crypto firms to obtain a legal opinion outlining the scope of their business. In fact, most crypto firms could not survive without one.

It came as a shocking surprise, then, to learn just how readily and cheaply you could buy a favourable legal opinion.

At the start of the crypto boom, offshore law firms – just like all the other service providers who have gotten into bed with the crypto bros in recent years – realised there was a fortune to be made by delving into the world of digital assets. So, they set up dedicated blockchain divisions and put their services out for hire. Crypto companies in need of legal opinions can approach one of the major firms in whichever domicile they choose and obtain a quote for an opinion. This opinion will state that the crypto firm is not a gambling company, or a security, or any other type of product that carries strenuous regulatory burdens.

But crypto bros are shrewd business operators, and no self-respecting founder would just take the first offer on the table. Like true wheeler-dealers, they shop around for bargains. After a CEO has received a quote for an opinion, they'll then go to a competing firm and present the initial figure to see if the rival is willing to undercut their competitor. Which they often do. It's a race to the bottom, and the end result is that crypto firms can secure their must-have legal opinions at bargain-basement prices. To date, the cheapest I've ever heard a legal opinion being sold for is $5,000. An inconceivably low price, given the level of protection they give projects, and how essential they are to the most fundamental operations of a crypto outfit.

I was shocked when I learned about this practice – perhaps more shocked than I had been about any other dodgy dealings I had come across. The power of these legal opinions really cannot be overstated; if a crypto project receives an opinion stating, for example, that their token isn't a security, then they have de facto immunity from any regulatory action that might be taken against them under securities law. If a regulator decides to investigate them – following, say, a class action lawsuit from cheated investors – the project's legal opinion greatly narrows the tools the regulator has at their disposal to prosecute them and obtain justice for the investors. The project can simply point the regulator in the direction of the law firm that issued it. They're the ones who said the token isn't a security, so they're the ones who bear the liability.

You might think that this would make law firms reluctant to dish out opinions for cash, but you'd be sorely mistaken. While the regulators can, in theory, prosecute the law firms for issuing dodgy opinions, the lawyers are protected by the best insurance money can buy. They all have policies that cover against regulatory sanctions and penalties. This means that if they're fined for negligence or bad judgement, it's always the insurers who pay out. For the lawyers, it's all water off a duck's back and they carry on cashing in, auctioning off their opinions and their integrity to the lowest bidders.

I remember being mortified when I learned that even law firms were wrapped up in the web of crypto corruption. It was only then that it started to dawn on me just how long the arms of the crypto bros truly were. How vast their venal network was. And just how many people, how many institutions, would abandon their moral principles as soon as they caught a whiff of crypto dollars. And yet, as shocking as this all was, it would pale in comparison to the revelations still to come.

I was torn about what to do. As much as I wanted to voice my concerns with Archie and tell him I wasn't comfortable with what was going on, I couldn't. He wouldn't listen; he would take it as a sign of weakness, or as a lack of commitment to the project, and likely boot me out. I thought about going to the press, but that seemed just as futile as speaking to Archie: many outlets were already acutely aware of what was happening in the industry and were up to their necks in it themselves. Of all the things I considered, though, doing a U-turn and going back to PR wasn't one of them. I was already in my notice period, having resigned from my job when I saw the big VC tickets coming in for Portent.

Of course, I knew I could just get another gig somewhere else. But, if I'm honest, even with how shocked I was about what was going on in crypto, the thought of going back into an ordinary day job just wasn't an option. If I went back into PR, it would feel like a monumental waste of all the time and effort I had put in over the past months. I had come this far, so I could go a little further. And if I went all the way, and things went according to plan, I'd never have to worry about work ever again.

So I put my head down, held my nose, and got on with my job. Miles had clearly been worried that our own publicity material might inadvertently make us look like a gambling firm, so I set about making things right. I combed through the Portent Protocol content, making sure any allusion to gambling or gambling-related language was amended. Then I sent everything over to Miles and awaited my next task.

The launch was nearly here, which meant it was almost time to start pumping the artificially low token price as high as we could get it. But first, before we could float the token and make our fortune, there was one more hurdle in our way.

5

Hysteria and Hype Cycles

Thanks to the efforts of the influencers and the journalists on our payroll, the buzz around our token was approaching fever pitch. We were inundated with messages from chancers looking to secure an allocation; we had scores of influencers in our DMs offering to promote us if we let them buy tokens at massively discounted presale prices. To prove their worth, some of them even started giving us freebies, making videos about us or inviting us onto their podcasts in the hope that this would get them a foot in the door. It never did. We had long reached our hard cap funding target, and we had already been forced to extend our private sale rounds to fit newcomers in. We were now completely closed, and there was not a penny more we could offer in allocations. No amount of grovelling and no sum of cold, hard cash could change that.

By now, we had most of our legal, operational and promotional ducks in a row. But there was still one more service provider we had to secure. This next one was arguably the most important of all, and certainly the most illicit – the market maker.

Market makers are liquidity providers. Take an asset that's tradeable on an exchange, like our TENT token would be when it launched. Market makers will hold large reserves of this asset and offer buyers a price at which it can be purchased. And for holders looking to sell their tokens, the market maker will always be there to buy them. When they work how they're supposed to do, market makers guarantee efficiency by ensuring there will always be a market to sell or buy the assets they deal in.

But this is crypto we're talking about. And in crypto, market makers (like all the other actors in the industry) don't always work the way they're supposed to. In addition to fulfilling their core service of providing liquidity to markets, many have taken advantage of the industry's non-existent regulatory framework to provide a whole host of other services besides. Most are of questionable legality and some of them are outright criminal.

'Without a market maker, how the hell are we supposed to dump our tokens?' Archie said to me one day, when I asked him to shed some light on the shadowy subject.

'If we sell on the open market,' Archie continued, 'people will see on the blockchain that the tokens have come from one of our project wallets. We don't want people to think we're dumping on our investors. So we'll send the tokens to the market maker, and they'll do the dumping for us.'

'What if we just send the tokens to an exchange account?' I asked. 'People won't be able to see what we're doing with them, and we can just sell them like that. That way, we won't have to pay the market maker's fee.'

Contrary to what many outsiders would expect, centralised exchanges provide far more privacy than when you transact on a public blockchain. When you trade tokens on a centralised exchange, other users can't see the transactions. They see the funds going into the exchange and then nothing else, meaning you can sell your holdings without anyone noticing. In industry terms, this is known as transacting 'off-chain' – as in, not on the public blockchain. If you use a decentralised exchange, on the other hand, keen-eyed observers will be able to follow all your transactions. They'll see how many tokens you've swapped, which tokens you've swapped them for and when each and every transaction has been made. This is known as transacting 'on-chain'.

'Yeah, sure,' said Archie. 'We could do that. But who the hell wants to be sitting at a screen for hours every day selling shitcoins? Plus, we're not traders. The market makers are, so they'll know how to minimise fees and make sure the exchange isn't taking all our profits.'

'Well, we could just sell them all in one go, couldn't we? So there's just one fee. It will only take about 2 seconds.'

'Yeah right, and crash our own token while we're at it. Put in too big of a sell order, and you'll fuck the price. The market maker knows how to sell them off in batches, so it doesn't tank the whole market and cause panic and a huge sell-off.'

'Right,' I said. 'I see.'

'It isn't just that,' Miles interjected. 'Market makers are pretty much essential for revenue generation. They don't just sell; they buy as well.'

'Yeah, I know,' I said. My experience with traditional finance had taught me that much. 'They buy from other users. They provide liquidity for both sides of the order book.'

A smirk started creeping up the side of Miles's face. 'No, mate. They don't just buy from other users. They buy from themselves.'

'What? So the market makers *take* liquidity as well?'

'Exactly.'

'Why the hell would they do that?'

As it turned out, there are many reasons why they would do that, which Miles was all too willing to explain to me. In crypto, the market makers start off by being given a pool of volatile tokens and then roughly the same amount of stablecoins or US dollars (with a stablecoin simply being a non-volatile cryptocurrency, with each token exactly equal to $1). And with these two pools of cash, their manipulation of the markets can get under way.

They go about this in a number of ways, all intended to bag as much profit as possible for the projects who employ them and, in turn, for themselves. One of their favourites is a staple in the world of financial malpractice: market manipulation. When market makers see the price of an asset is rising organically – as prices do in ordinary markets – they'll use the US dollars they have on hand to start buying up the token across exchanges, augmenting the rally and causing the price to rise even further. Traders watching the prices will take notice of the rally, but they won't necessarily know what's behind it. Either way, they're likely to want to load up on tokens in the hope of making some profit themselves. Once enough capital starts pouring into an asset, market makers will then start liquidating not only the tokens they've bought up but also the stock of tokens they were given by the project. Through the artificial price action they engineered, they're able to sell at much higher prices, vastly amplifying profit margins.

In addition to using their cash reserves to manipulate asset prices, market makers are also able to manipulate trading volumes in a practice known as 'wash trading'. This is when a market maker buys and sells tokens to and from themselves. This isn't intended to influence the price, but it does inflate the volume figures: stats that show how many times any given token has been traded on any given day. These volume figures are very important, allowing traders to get a sense of how healthy a market is. If a token has a low daily trading volume, then no one is going to want to trade that market. The low figure might indicate that the project is dead or dying, that there is very little demand for the token, or that traders' orders aren't being filled due to a lack of liquidity on the other side of the trade. Essentially, wash trading paints a false picture of a project and its token, making investors think the market for an asset is thriving and far more attractive than it actually is. It amounts to a manipulation of public perception, and it's spectacularly illegal in regulated markets.

With all this in mind, it's easy to see why founders put so much stock in market makers. When markets can be manipulated to such an extent, there's a fortune to be made. In the case of Portent Protocol, our market maker came highly recommended: Krasus Capital, one of the best players in the space at the time. They offered a suite of essential services, which included managing our liquidity across both centralised and decentralised exchanges, liquidating our team tokens for us and washing our trade volume to make our token seem even more appealing. It all added up to profit, for us and for them – just not for the poor retail traders who would find themselves playing a rigged game against an all-powerful house.

But it didn't stop there: I soon learned that Krasus Capital also provided an optional, additional service – one reserved for only their most trusted clients. This was a highly unconventional, uncommon and unconscionable practice, even for a crypto market maker.

Archie explained everything one day during an internal catch-up call with the Portent Protocol inner circle. By this point our project numbered around twelve people, but there were five of us at the core: me, Archie, Miles, Paul and Spencer, who had recently been hired as our chief technical officer.

We were just wrapping up what had been an otherwise routine video call when Archie said, almost as an afterthought, 'By the way, guys, if anyone ever needs any laundry done, the market maker says they can help with that.'

'Archie, mate ...' Miles looked and sounded deeply uncomfortable.

'It's fine! It's only us here, and nobody's recording.'

'What do you mean "laundry?"' I asked.

'They said that if any of us ever has any cash that needs to look like it's come from somewhere else, they can connect us with exchanges that will make OTC deals for tokens.'

OTC stands for over the counter. It's a trade that takes place between two parties – say, a crypto founder and an exchange – but that happens off a trading platform. For example, if I have a load of tokens and an exchange wants to buy them from me, we'd be able to make a direct trade without routing it through their usual trading system. I would simply send them the tokens, and they would send the money. There's nothing inherently illegal or illicit about OTC deals – they can even aid efficiency by allowing large trades without platform fees or burdensome admin. But, of course, they can easily be manipulated and misused.

'How does that work then?' I asked. I didn't envisage I would ever need, or want, to use the market maker's laundry service, but I was curious to understand the logistics of it.

'First the market maker connects you with a dodgy exchange,' said Archie. 'Maybe in China or Venezuela or something. You send them your money, and the exchange will send you some shitcoins. You then send the tokens over to the market maker, and they liquidate them for you. They'll then send back the money, into whatever bank account you want, and it just looks like you've made money trading, or the market maker has made money for you. They keep 10 per cent of the funds, and the exchange keeps 10 per cent, so you get 80 per cent back.'

'But what if someone wants to know where the money actually came from in the first place?' I asked. 'You can't exactly receive a load of money into your account, and say you made it trading, without showing a deposit into a trading account for the funds you traded with in the first place.'

'Mate, you're dealing with an exchange. They just set you up with an account and make up your deposit history. All these records are just numbers on a screen, and they control the screen.'

'Blimey. So you just send them money, the exchange forges a trading history for your account, sends you back a load of tokens, and the market maker liquidates them for you?'

'Yep,' said Archie. He smiled at his webcam. 'Pretty clean, isn't it? Also, if it's physical cash you need laundered, the market maker can send someone round to pick it up. Talk about a premium service.'

At this point, Miles interjected. 'Why the hell would any of us need physical cash laundered, Archie?' He sounded exasperated and a little embarrassed.

Archie merely shrugged. 'You never know, son. You never know. I'm just passing on what they told me on my last call with them. Make of it what you will.'

Archie was clearly showing off, but nonetheless it was quite astounding that our market maker had offered him this additional service – not least because Archie had only spoken to them a few times. I thought, at first, that perhaps they could just tell Archie was the kind of person who might appreciate it.

It wasn't until later that I obtained a copy of our market maker's pitch deck for prospective clients. It contained a list of all their most popular services, including those that involved manipulating the markets. I realised then just how brazen this firm was; most others tended to treat their more clandestine services with some degree of discretion, and certainly didn't include the details in a highly leakable document. But this outfit was clearly more risk tolerant than others, which could explain why they were so quick to advertise their money laundering services. They did, however, still have the good sense to leave this particular service out of their deck.

Money laundering aside, the acquisition of a market maker was a big step forward for us. It marked the end of our preparatory period. Launch was now just around the corner and, with our excitement reaching its zenith, we started to cast our eyes to the competition.

We wanted to assess how other token launches were performing, so we could get an indication of retail investor sentiment. From this, we hoped to be able to estimate just how much money we would make. We were also looking at the marketing tactics that other projects had successfully employed during their launch campaigns – particularly those that we could repurpose for our own.

Luckily for us, there was an abundance of case studies to work off. It was early 2021, the height of the bull run, and exuberance in the crypto markets was reaching unprecedented levels. The world was mired in Covid lockdowns, and the US government, in lockstep with most other developed nations, had unleashed record-breaking quantitative easing measures to combat the pandemic's economic turmoil. In the US, these measures were accompanied by a series of enormous stimulus packages. With hundreds of millions of people around the world stuck in their bedrooms, many of them with a government-issued cheque burning a hole in their pocket, the conditions were perfect for speculating on magic internet money. Every day, a new token launched onto the market, achieving exponential increases in its price as soon as it hit the exchanges.

We decided to pay particular attention to projects that had received investment from the same VCs or used the same staple of influencers as us. We thought we would likely share an investor base with these ventures, so their performance would give us the best indication of what kind of capital inflows we could expect.

The first project to catch our eye was called Polkapledge. Like Portent Protocol, this was a kind of betting platform; Polkapledge allowed users to make predictions on a wide variety of future events or asset prices. The key difference was that they promised a broader scope of markets, as they allowed for betting on sports, political events and the like. Our users, by contrast, could only speculate on the price of bitcoin.

The name 'Polkapledge' is worth highlighting briefly. Back then, a lot of projects were attaching 'Polk' or 'Polka' prefixes to their project name. This was a highly disingenuous practice employed by founders in an attempt to cash in on the hype surrounding Polkadot: a layer 1 blockchain, which topped a $35 billion market cap in March 2021. This was pretty astounding, considering their DOT token did absolutely nothing. The network had not launched yet, meaning no one could make any transactions or build other applications on it and, as such, the token didn't even have a semblance of utility. Buying the token was an act of pure speculation: blind faith in a project that might never come through.

Seeing this monumental (if unmerited) market cap, other projects in the space wanted to cling to the coattails of Polkadot's success. So they used deceitful prefixes to hint at an association. Some, including Polkapledge, even had the effrontery to add the tagline 'Powered by Polkadot' to their social media platforms and marketing materials. A particularly misleading stunt, considering that their PLEDGE token would in fact be launched on the Ethereum network – a Polkadot rival.

This was a blatantly duplicitous marketing strategy. Of course, that didn't stop us trying to do exactly the same thing as PLEDGE. For a while, 'Powered by Polkadot' adorned all our marketing collateral. Many of our followers took notice, congratulating us for positioning ourselves within such a thriving ecosystem. The praise was short lived, though. We eventually had to remove the tagline after a series of questions from a few of our more scrupulous observers. They kept asking in our Telegram group how, exactly, we were going to be 'powered' by a network that currently existed only in the imagination.

As for Polkapledge, the betting platform had more going for them than just a sneaky prefix. They were also being pushed hard by some of the biggest influencers in the space: top-tier promoters whom they had secured thanks to the connections of their incubator, Selene Capital. Today, many of these influencers have been entirely discredited for having made innumerable undisclosed promotions of tokens they were personally invested in – all of which they then dumped onto their followers as soon as they were able to, earning millions in the process. At the time, though, these influencers were at the height of their popularity and prominence, and having them on board served as an unequivocal signal that the Polkapledge launch was going to be a huge success. And it did not disappoint.

The token launched, and the price rocketed. It all seemed to happen at once, and it wasn't until the dust had settled that anyone was able to make sense of just how well PLEDGE had performed. In the aftermath of the launch, the managing director of Selene Capital could not contain his elation, taking to Twitter to boast about PLEDGE's success.

'Sitting at $2.64, which equals 88X for IDO participants, peaking at 300X,' he wrote in a now deleted tweet. This astronomical asset price appreciation meant that if an investor had bought $10,000 worth of PLEDGE at its listing price their investment would have peaked at $3 million. However, what the overzealous managing director had neglected to mention was that virtually no one had been able to buy at the initial listing price.

Back then, when new tokens launched, they tended to appreciate in price almost instantaneously. The pump would begin long before ordinary investors even had the chance to buy a single token, because of interference from 'bots'.

Computer-savvy investors, of which there are many in crypto, managed to create automated programs capable of buying and selling tokens many times faster than a human. When a new coin listed, these bots would scoop up as many as possible, kickstarting the price rally. Ordinary human investors would then join the gold rush, boosting the price even further. Once the price was sufficiently inflated, the bots would sell their tokens, netting huge profits for the programmers who created them. Beyond making the computer nerds who owned them unfathomably rich, these bots also made every crypto launch they were used in incredibly turbulent.

They could pump a token's price by 10,000 per cent in a fraction of a second, and then just as quickly drop it right back to near where it started, leaving ordinary investors holding the bag. And yet, the allure of turning $1,000 into $100,000 in the space of minutes can prove simply irresistible. It's a whole economy driven by FOMO – the fear of missing out. Huge numbers of retail investors still play this rigged game, and, inevitably, many of them get horrifically burnt in the process. And, just as inevitably, many of them sign up to do it all over again as soon as the next hottest project comes along.

In the case of PLEDGE, the price stabilised after the initial bot-induced pump and VC-induced dump, and the buy pressure from retail investors kept the price hovering around 8,000 per cent above its initial listing price for a short while after launch. Needless to say, as more VC tokens got unlocked, and the market got flooded by insiders taking profit, the PLEDGE price started swiftly declining. At the time we had our eyes on them, though, most of their tokens were still locked, and PLEDGE was still riding high. Speculating on how long that was going to last wasn't our concern; we were busy comparing shopping lists, in anticipation of TENT replicating their 8,000 per cent pump. Our excitement was tempered slightly, however, when we realised that not every project we were keeping an eye on had quite the same happy ending.

A few days after the Polkapledge launch, a contact of ours pointed us in the direction of another project, telling us it would be worth our time to investigate it further. They were called Horderz, and they were one of the first projects to try to cash in on the NFT phenomenon.

'NFT' stands for non-fungible token, which is a one-off entry on the blockchain ledger. It's a bit like a regular crypto except that each token in a set is unique and can't be replicated. Whereas there's no difference between one bitcoin and another, each NFT can be thought of as a kind of bespoke, personal token that is completely distinguishable from every other NFT in existence. They were all the rage at one point, with the industry's flagship NFT collection Bored Ape Yacht Club (or BAYC for short) fetching six figures for a single digital image of an eccentric ape sporting various outfits.

Horderz was launching a collection of digital trading cards, each represented by an individual NFT. This was set to take place over six months before BAYC stormed onto the scene, quite some time prior to the peak of the NFT mania that swept the industry. While Horderz couldn't quite capture the full hype of the NFT fad, there was still plenty of interest in this burgeoning technology, which they could leverage. This was all with a view to drive interest in their more traditional, fungible crypto token – which, back then, before NFTs really took off, was where all the money was to be made.

Horderz had already floated their token by the time we took notice, and its launch bore all the hallmarks of success. Just a few weeks prior to our own launch, Horderz's token had a market cap of over $100 million. This figure was made even more impressive by the incendiary allegations of insider trading that plagued their launch day.

The Horderz team added liquidity for their token to the Uniswap DEX around half an hour before they released their contract address. This, in itself, wouldn't have been a problem, had it not been for the fact that they also distributed tokens to their VCs and early backers as soon as the liquidity got added. What this meant was that, for the first half an hour the token was listed, the tens of thousands of ordinary people in their Telegram group couldn't buy or sell the token. Without the contract address, they simply didn't know where to find it on Uniswap. The VCs, on the other hand, did know, which gave them a half-hour grace period in which they could dump their tokens and bank their profits before retail could start trading.

While retail traders struggled to find the contact address, and even as the VCs were busy jumping the gun, the bots arrived. The programmers who created them didn't need to wait for the contract address to be shared; they were technologically savvy enough to get the address straight from the blockchain. Because of this, for a full half an hour before ordinary investors could buy and sell, bots were able to pump the price up, and the VCs were able to dump their tokens and make huge profits. When the public was eventually able to access the token, the price was already massively inflated. Despite the epidemic of VC dumping, the bots had bought enough tokens to inflate the price many times over.

And yet, the Horderz team had managed to drum up enough retail demand to ensure that large numbers of people still bought the token, even after it had taken off. These retail investors not only propped up the price, but made it rally even further. By this point, the bots began dumping their tokens, believing the market had peaked. The retail buy orders, however, were still flying in so quickly that they counteracted the bots. When the mêlée had settled, and the VCs and bot owners had banked their profits, the token was still up by over 300 per cent on the first day of its listing. The token kept appreciating over the coming weeks, eventually peaking at an approximate 1,600 per cent gain against the initial listing price.

When we learned of this, we approached Horderz for a potential partnership. We hoped to capitalise on their hype and cash in on the NFT fad ourselves. The proposition we made to them was vague – some notion about creating a series of NFTs somehow related to Portent Protocol – but the specifics didn't matter. Back then, when projects were launching, they would form as many 'strategic partnerships' as possible. Barely any of these ever came to fruition, and the ones that did seldom produced anything tangible. But that wasn't the point. It was the announcement itself that projects were so desperately seeking. These partnership announcements were all about optics: they were marketing ploys, which allowed projects to leverage each other's profiles, access each other's community and ultimately grow their own brands.

Horderz said they were too busy following up on their launch to form new partnerships, so they turned us down. This was a tenuous reason given that all that was required from them was an article posted on their blog, which we offered to write for them, and a few social media posts. Perhaps they just didn't like the cut of our jib. Whatever the real reason, their refusal turned out to be a blessing in disguise.

Several months after turning us down, Horderz were hacked. Their token had been on the decline for some time; the retail investors holding it after their launch soon realised that all the VCs had exited the project, at which point the uselessness of the token and the wider project finally dawned on them. Then, in July 2021, every investor's worst nightmare came true. Horderz released an announcement saying their contract had been exploited, and hackers had stolen all their remaining funds. The token went to zero, millions were lost, and the reputation of the Horderz project and team went the same way. In crypto, a hack normally spells the end for a project team, regardless of the details. Investor confidence seldom recovers from a hack, as no one wants to gamble on a project that has seen its token price hit rock bottom. And in the case of Horderz the reputational damage was just beginning.

A bunch of blockchain savants claimed they could trace the source of the hack, and they followed this trail all the way back to none other than Horderz's founder. Reports soon emerged that he had fled to Bora Bora and was living a lavish beachfront life at the expense of thousands of his investors. Such was the furore in the Horderz community that one social media influencer offered a $10,000 reward to anyone who could provide concrete information on the where-abouts of the founder. (This was likely just a PR stunt, however, as the influencer had been one of Horderz's loudest cheerleaders; he was probably trying to salvage his reputation by putting some dis-tance between himself and the doomed project.) In another twist to this sordid tale, the founder was confronted by another prominent social media influencer, who coincidentally happened to be on holi-day in Bora Bora and recognised the founder lounging on the same beach as him.

Disappointingly, nothing materialised from this encounter beyond a video that went viral for a short time. For all we know, the founder could still be in Bora Bora, sipping strawberry daiquiris and living out his days in luxury.

At the time when we were prepping for our launch, however, all this was still in the future. Back then, Horderz were still enjoying a vastly inflated token price and all the kudos that went with it. We therefore looked to them as a prototype and vowed to do everything we could to emulate the success that they, like so many others, had achieved.

We realised that if there was one real danger, one obstacle to our success, it was the bot problem. Many projects encountered this issue and, while most had been able to overcome the negative con-sequences wrought by these mechanical menaces, crypto investors were becoming increasingly irate, recognising at last that the odds were stacked against them. If a launch was accused of being too heavily 'botted', for example, ordinary investors would refuse to buy the token at the inflated price. We knew we had to do something to keep the bots away if we wanted to protect the TENT token and guarantee our fortune.

We didn't know it then, but the plans we put in place to try to avoid disaster would themselves become the very cause of our pro-ject's demise.

6

Taxing Conversations

With less than two weeks to go until launch, our anxiety around the bot issue was becoming palpable. It seemed like every token that had launched recently had been marred with bot problems, and investor sentiment was suffering, to the point where even a whiff of bot interference spelt the immediate and irrevocable end of a project. If a token launched and pumped in price faster than a human could put in a buy order, no one else would touch it, and all presale investors would dump their tokens as soon as they got their hands on them. And not just that, but the team in question would find themselves with hundreds, sometimes thousands, of furious crypto community members venting their frustration with them across every social media platform imaginable.

It was with these concerns weighing down on us that we sat, distracted and in a state of near burnout, on a 9.30 p.m. check-in call with one of our lead VCs, Zapater Ventures. Founded by hot-blooded Portuguese businessman Eduardo Zapater and his nephew Francisco, it was a small operation, with only a handful of portfolio companies. While they had done well on their investments so far, they were still awaiting the project that would make their fortune and cement their reputation as a leading industry player. They hoped that we would be that project, so they were investing a lot of their time, energy and resources in setting us up for success. And, of course, they wanted to make sure that the $100,000 cheque they wrote us paid dividends.

'Guys, what's going on?' asked Eduardo, with noticeable concern in his voice. 'You guys look like shit. I know it's late and you're tired, but this is the final push. We need energy more than ever now.'

'Difficult to feel energetic when we're almost certainly going to get fucked by the bots,' Archie replied.

'Ha! Is that what you're worried about?' Francisco said, an ear-to-ear grin lighting up his heavy-set face. Archie, Miles and I sat up in our seats in unison. 'For a second, I thought it was something serious. We can get this sorted, no problem. Have you heard of Sidera Solutions?'

'Vaguely,' Miles said. 'Why?'

'I'll take that as a no then,' Eduardo was chipper, and clearly excited to have the answer to our problem. 'They're an infrastructure provider. They basically build apps and programs for other crypto projects to use. And, luckily for you guys, they've just released their latest product: an anti-bot solution.'

'Oh, shit.' Archie picked up his laptop, and was holding it in front of him as he paced around the room. 'How does it work? Does it stop the bots?'

'Guys, it's brilliant. They've already tried it out on a few projects, and their launches were phenomenal. Any bots which tried to interfere got absolutely rekt. They've got people queuing up to use their product.'

'How does it work?' Miles asked.

'How the fuck am I supposed to know? I didn't build it. But it works. And, luckily for you, I know the founder of the project. Took him on a pretty wild night last time he was in Lisbon, so I should be able to get you guys to the front of the queue.'

Miles, Archie and I were almost giddy with relief. It was like we had just got the all-clear on a cancer scare.

'This is great, thanks so much Eduardo! Let's get a meeting booked in with them first thing tomorrow.'

'Ignore Miles,' Archie said. 'Can they do tonight?'

'Yeah, tonight would be better,' Francisco nodded. 'Let's get on top of this as soon as we can. I'll speak to them now, and get it set up.'

Around half an hour later he messaged us to say that he had managed to arrange a call with the Sidera team at 1 a.m. UK time.

While this wouldn't help our exhaustion, we were all happy to forgo the much-needed sleep if it meant getting the bot situation under control, thereby guaranteeing the success of our launch. In a bid to keep my mind busy and my eyes open while I waited for the meeting to start, I decided to look into Sidera in a bit more detail. From what I could see, they were a mid-sized project, with a market cap of around $60 million. Just like Eduardo said, they'd built a variety of applications that provide infrastructure solutions to other projects. Beyond a blog post simply announcing the latest addition to their suite, there was nothing online whatsoever about how their anti-bot mechanism actually worked. But, as I was about to find out, it was troubling to say the least.

1 a.m. eventually rolled around, and we were greeted on the call by one of the founders of Sidera, Geoff Kean. A strikingly suitable surname, given how chirpy he was at the late hour.

'Absolutely stoked you guys want to use our anti-bot tech!' Geoff proclaimed, with a bit too much enthusiasm, and even a slight tinge of surprise, which I thought odd given that he supposedly had a pipline bursting with leads.

'Same here, Geoff. It would be great to hear a bit more about how your tech works.'

'What we've done is built a program which automatically detects when non-human entities attempt to input trading signals.'

'Sounds very cool,' Miles said, 'and how does it do that exactly?'

'Ah well, without wanting to go into all the gory details, it basically watches for "front-running". Say you've got a bunch of people all trying to buy a token at the same time, the Ethereum network gets congested, so they essentially go into a queue, like in a traffic jam. The network determines their position in the queue and processes their transactions depending on how much "gas" they pay. Gas is just the usage fee, which you pay to make transactions on the network.'

'We know what gas is, Geoff,' Archie said irritably. 'This isn't our first rodeo, you know.'

'Right, of course. Well, as you'll know then, smart users know how to manually adjust their gas fees, so they get put at the front of the queue, and can buy the token first. Even smarter users will look at the blockchain, see how much gas each person in the queue is paying, and then set their fee just a bit higher than the person at the front, so that they know they can buy first. The problem is, you then get a load of people jostling for position, with newcomers all setting their gas fees higher than the person who was previously front of line. And then the bots get involved. They set their gas fees many times higher than the person at the front of the queue and, if anyone tries to go even higher than that, then they readjust instantaneously. No human can input faster than a bot, meaning that the bot is always at the front of the queue. So when the network eventually processes the transactions, it's the bots who get the tokens first.'

'Yeah, right, got it,' said Archie. 'All makes sense, but how do you actually stop them?'

'Ah well, that's where things get interesting. What our tech does is it identifies these non-human transactions – which are actually quite easy to spot, given how unnaturally fast they are – and we then just blacklist the address. After that, the wallet which has been making the transaction can't buy, sell, or transfer any more tokens.'

At this point, I interjected: 'Wait, what do you mean you blacklist the wallets? How is that even possible ... how can you control a wallet which someone else owns?'

'So, it's not that they can't move *any* tokens around. They just can't move yours. Our tech essentially builds a backdoor into the codebase of your token, which allows the program to completely freeze the token if any red flags are raised. Bot activity raises that red flag, so when it's detected in a wallet, the tokens held there basically shut down and can't be interacted with at all.'

'And what about a false flag?' Miles asked.

'Good question. Hardly ever happens, but it's not a problem when it does. We can unfreeze tokens whenever we want, and manually remove any wallets from the blacklist.'

'Hang on,' I cut in, 'does that mean you can add and remove from the blacklist whenever you want, even if the wallet doesn't belong to a bot? So you can basically freeze any TENT tokens you want, whenever you want?'

Geoff looked a bit uneasy for a moment, before straining to shoot a reassuring smile into his camera. 'In theory, yes. But don't worry, we would never do that. Plus, if you want, after the launch we can just permanently disable the anti-bot program. We can remove it from your token's codebase entirely.'

Geoff's efforts to alleviate my concern fell on deaf ears. It wasn't that I was worried about Sidera going rogue and taking control of our token. Or ruining our project by freezing all our investors' tokens on a whim. It was the principle behind this that I found so disquieting. For months, ever since we had gone public with the project, we were positioning ourselves as decentralised. Just like every other crypto project operating under the banner of 'DeFi', our entire narrative centred on removing intermediaries from the financial system. I had written countless in-depth articles explaining how intermediaries exert excessive control over the finance sector and how crypto restores power to the individual by operating on a permissionless, decentralised basis. What Geoff had just told us completely undermined all that. It isn't decentralised finance if a single group of people sitting on a Zoom call can freeze the assets of potentially thousands of people at the push of a button.

Archie, on the other hand, did not share these concerns.

'Yeah brilliant, Geoff. If it fucks the bots, sign me up.'

'Perfect. I'll get a contract over to you first thing, and then our tech team can get to work installing the program into your code. We normally charge twenty-five grand for this, but if it helps I'd be happy to discuss taking payment in allo.'

'Say no more Geoff, we'll whip up a SAFT asap.'

We were riding high from the conversation with Geoff, dreaming of what we would be spending our fortunes on after launch. The bot issue, which had been the cause of so much anxiety for us, finally had a solution. There was now nothing to prevent our launch from being anything short of a triumph. Just as we started window shopping for châteaux in the south of France, we were summoned into an ominous meeting with Eduardo Zapater. He added us into a Telegram group, saying we needed to have an urgent call to discuss the liquidation of VC tokens after launch, which at this point was less than 72 hours away.

An hour after the group was made, Miles, Archie and I sat in the living room of Archie's swanky east London pad, facing Eduardo on a Zoom call. We were all visibly tense, our irregular breathing being the only noise to come out of any of us as we waited for Eduardo to start speaking.

'Guys, great job on securing Sidera. That should dispel a lot of worries, and really help with the hype. Looks like it's going to be a stellar launch, a real moonshot.'

'Cheers Eduardo,' replied Archie.

'Which is why I wanted to have this call with you guys today. I want to make sure that we're all set up for success after the token launches. We need to establish a liquidation plan, for cashing out our coins.'

This was a touchy subject. VCs, as we've seen, are well known for being prolific dumpers, and their selling can tank a token price – and a project – before it's barely got off the ground. Eduardo could see the concern in our faces, and quickly made efforts to alleviate this.

'Guys don't worry, I'm not talking about me and Francisco. Like I've said so many times, we're in it for the long run. I meant the other dumpers who have written cheques for you. We need a plan for how they can get rid of their tokens safely.'

'What do you mean safely?' asked Archie. 'They'll just sell them on the open market, like they always do.'

'Yes, that's what we need to avoid. If people see all the VCs dumping, that won't be good for general morale. People are sick of being dumped on by VCs.'

'So what do you suggest then?'

'I'm going to set up a Telegram group with all your investors and tell them to only sell on 1Inch. And I'll tell them to set limit orders, so they're only selling when the price is rising. Selling into a green candle is much better than creating a red candle.'

1Inch is what's known as a 'DEX aggregator', which compares the prices at which tokens are trading across various decentralised exchanges and allows users to buy and sell at the optimal rates. It's quite a useful tool; even to this day, crypto is still very much in its infancy, meaning there is a lot of inefficiency in the markets. It's not uncommon for the same token to trade at drastically different prices across various exchanges. This provides ample opportunity for savvy traders to engage in 'arbitrage': a risk-free investment, which typically leverages and exploits discrepancies in prices. A trader can buy a token on one exchange, where the price might be low, and then sell it on a different exchange, where it might be trading for higher. Platforms like 1Inch facilitate this.

Archie knew all this at the time, and was interested in Eduardo's idea.

'Yeah nice, 1Inch could be a good shout, Eduardo. But what do you mean by limit order?'

'Ah, it's just a trading term. Say your token is trading at $10, you set a "limit order" to sell at $12, meaning that when the price reaches that level, the platform will automatically sell your token for you. It makes it more likely that your trade will go through when the price is rising.'

'Got it. 1Inch it is then. We'll leave you to get the other VCs in line.' Archie was on the verge of hanging up when Miles interjected.

'Hang on. All sounds good with 1Inch, but do you think we should also remind the investors about the tax function? In case they've forgotten, or never read the white paper. Probably don't want to give them a nasty shock on launch day!'

Eduardo looked confused for a moment. 'What? What do you mean because of the tax function?' he asked, his eyes narrowing and his voice picking up speed. 'That's just when people enter their bets on the platform. We shouldn't even have to think about that until the platform is built.'

'Yes, it applies when people use the platform, but it also gets applied when people sell or transfer their tokens.'

In the blink of an eye, Eduardo's expression changed from alarmed to furious. 'Are you fucking serious? Guys, no one is going to buy a token which taxes them when they sell it. And when they transfer it! How much is the tax?'

'It's only 3 per cent,' Miles said pleadingly, looking at me and Archie for backup.

'Have you lost your head? So you're telling me if I send Francisco 10,000 tokens, he's only going to receive 9,700?'

'Umm ... yep.'

Eduardo put his head into his hands. 'Why have you done that? Remove the tax function, today, and don't tell anyone that it was ever there.'

'And we can't remove it,' Miles said. 'We'd have to rewrite the code for the whole token. We're working on an admin setting which will let us adjust the amount of tax, but that's still a few weeks away.'

'Delay the launch then.'

'Oh, come on,' Archie said, sounding quite frustrated with this whole exchange. 'Don't be so dramatic, Eduardo. What's the big deal here, it's not like we'd be the first token to have a sales tax.'

'Well *I've* never bought a token like that. Guys, if I'm going to get taxed 3 per cent when I sell my tokens, I want my investment back. I didn't sign up for this.'

'Yes you did, Eduardo,' said Archie. 'We've never made a secret of the tax function. It's been in our white paper from the start.'

'No one reads the white papers!'

'Look, Eduardo,' Miles said, trying to be diplomatic and diffuse the situation. 'You've been great to us, and we want to help you out. We can't blanket remove the tax function, but what we can do is put your individual wallet address on the whitelist, so that it won't apply to you specifically. How does that sound?'

That seemed to do the trick, as Eduardo sat up in his seat and looked visibly relieved. 'Yes, I think that should work. Yes.'

'Okay, perfect,' Miles said. 'Happy days then.'

'Well, not quite. We still need to think of the other VCs, and all the other people who are going to be buying the token. They're not going to like this.' Eduardo rubbed his neck pensively, and said, 'Tell me, what are you going to use the tax revenue for before the platform launches?'

'Well, we can do anything we like with it. We can give tokens to influencers for marketing, or can give them out as random rewards for investors. We can do whatever.'

'Hmm, interesting. Okay, this could be okay after all. When you send the comms out about the tax function, make sure to say that some of the revenue will be paid back to the community, and for marketing to pump the price even more. They'll love that – should take some of the sting out of the announcement.'

'Yeah, nice, will do for sure.'

'And, most importantly, make sure my wallet is exempt from the fucking 3 per cent.'

'Absolutely, I'll speak to the dev team right now, Eduardo.'

And, with that, Eduardo left the call. We let out a unanimous sigh of relief and, without saying a word to one another, got up and made our way to the kitchen. I opened the fridge and reached for the beers, but Archie held my arm back. He opened a cupboard and brought down a bottle of whiskey.

'We need it, after that,' he said, a conspiratorial smile forming across his face. 'Now let's just hope the community responds better than Eduardo did.'

We clinked our glasses together and downed our drinks in one, steeling ourselves for what we were all sure was going to be nothing short of a shitstorm.

7

Round Trip to the Moon

The next morning – just over 48 hours from our launch – I sat uploading an article to our blog, complete with accompanying social media posts, giving people all the information they needed to buy our token when it launched. Included in the article was a note reminding them of the tax function (which I dubbed a 'community development fee'). I linked to the white paper, which explained the fee in more detail. I hit send and hoped for the best.

A few minutes later, the first message came in reply to my post: 'What's this about a 3 per cent fee? Why is the team only telling us about this now? And what the fuck is community development? This sounds like a rug.'

A rug pull, from the idiom 'pulling the rug out', is a common and often unsophisticated crypto scam wherein fraudulent developers lure investors into what appears to be a lucrative new project, then disappear with the funds after a presale, or remove the liquidity from decentralised exchanges after launch, leaving the investors with a worthless asset.

As frustrating as the accusation of being a rug pull was, I was prepared for it. I quickly screenshotted the tax section of our white paper, told them that this had always been part of our revenue model, cited several other prominent projects whose tokens had a recall function built in, and emphasised that, prior to platform launch, the overwhelming majority of tokens would be reallocated to the community through rewards and incentive programmes.

I left the specific amount deliberately vague, and hoped I wouldn't be called out for it. And, just to be on the safe side, I also had a large number of 'shillers' on standby.

'Shillers' are mercenaries, typically based in Eastern Europe or the Philippines, hired to make as much noise as possible about projects across social media. They spend all their working hours sitting at their keyboards, sending out thousands of promotional messages. They can also be used to blitz Twitter with a project's chosen hashtags, to try to get it trending.

When this message came in, I gave them the green light to start their work and flood the group with paid-for positivity. In the blink of an eye we had scores of messages coming in, congratulating us on our transparency and expressing untold excitement about the generous community rewards programmes we were promising.

This seemed to do the trick and, following the activation of our hired guns, we noticed some organic positivity coming in, speculating with enthusiasm about what we had planned for the rewards and incentives. However, we didn't consider ourselves out of the woods yet, so we immediately followed this up with our last, and arguably most significant, marketing ploy: our launchpad announcement and whitelist competition.

Launchpads are platforms through which the initial stages of a token sale can take place. Prior to listing on an exchange or trading platform, many projects will decide to offer a number of their tokens to investors through a launchpad. Tokens are sent straight to the launchpad platform, or to the team that runs it, and then users are offered the chance to buy them at a predetermined, guaranteed price through a variety of mechanisms. Ostensibly, launchpads serve two functions: they provide security by offering safe access to presale tokens, and they promote equality by democratising access to otherwise inaccessible token presales. However, the reality rarely lives up to those self-declared justifications, and their real purpose is far more simple and self-interested: they generate hype for projects and revenue for the platforms.

A good launchpad will have a pre-established user base, sometimes numbering in the tens or even hundreds of thousands of investors. It can often cost the platforms millions to acquire these users, especially if they have to go through a process of KYC – or 'know your customer' – to be able to participate in the token sales, for legal or practical reasons. KYC is a huge point of contention for crypto investors, as it involves submitting identification documents to prove who you are, where you live, etc. Members of the crypto community hate this; some because they genuinely believe in the right to online privacy, and some because they are involved in illegal activities and don't want to be traced. To surmount this aversion, platforms spend fortunes on influencer marketing, ad campaigns and celebrity endorsements to convince prospective users that the platform won't misappropriate their data, and that the KYC is a necessary evil worth enduring to access their deal flow. But the substantial investments platforms make to acquire their users are well worth it; back in the height of the bull run, running a successful launchpad was one of the most lucrative rackets to be in on.

Their business models consisted of two primary revenue streams – their native tokens and the allocations they got from projects they launched. The first of these involves users purchasing launchpad tokens, after making it through the KYC process, in order to secure allocations in the projects being launched. The more tokens a user holds, the more allocation they'd be able to access. Sometimes a tiered lottery system would be used: users were arranged into tiers according to how many tokens they held, and a random ballot would be held to determine who was awarded an allocation. The higher tiers had more allocation, fewer participants and, therefore, a greater likelihood of winning.

The demand for the presale allocations on offer drove demand for the launchpad token, and pumped its price. Launchpads, like all other crypto projects that enjoyed buoyant and vastly inflated market caps, could then liquidate their own token holdings and generate capital for themselves.

The second revenue stream involved the teams running the launchpads receiving kickbacks from the projects launching on their platforms. The best launchpads, with the most users and the strongest track record for delivering sellout launches, were inundated with demand from projects to sell their tokens through their platform. The launchpad teams could then leverage this for their own benefit.

For example, if a project had $250,000 worth of presale tokens to sell, they might give the launchpad team $50,000 of this to secure their place on the platform. Sometimes this would be added into the terms of use of the platform, and would feature in the contract issued to projects conducting a token sale. However, more often than not, it was far less formal and merely involved a Telegram group between the respective teams negotiating how large a bung the project could offer the launchpad.

However, we didn't have to go through the standard negotiation route with our launchpad, as it was owned and operated by our incubator VC Leopard Labs. This was a particularly egregious conflict of interest, equivalent to a venture capital firm owning a trading platform and only allowing the stock of other companies within their portfolio to be traded there. Or, alternatively, if a VC owned a stock exchange and only allowed their own investments to undergo an IPO on the exchange. Needless to say, this wouldn't be tolerated in traditional finance and would be a serious breach of securities laws.

However, in the Wild West of crypto, no such laws exist. Which meant we were able to launch onto the Leopard Launch platform without a hitch.

Everything was in place, and now all we needed to do was launch the token. The market conditions could not have been better. Bitcoin was rallying and making new all-time highs, with its price topping $55,000. Sentiment was booming, and we were as prepared as it was possible to be. We thought nothing stood in our way, so we dived headfirst into the launch.

And, as we were about to find out, into a whole world of problems.

'Fucking hell, what was that?!' It was 1.50 p.m., and for the past 20 minutes I'd had posts on standby, announcing our token contract address. The plan was to post it at 2 p.m. across all our channels, and then sit back and watch the feeding frenzy get under way. It came as a shock, therefore, to see that, 10 minutes before I posted anything at all, the price of our token jumped up 1,000 per cent.

'Why the fuck did we just pump 10X? What's going on?' I followed up on my original question as no one had responded. There were ten of us in the living room of Miles's flat, all glued to screens. Every inch of the dining table was taken up by monitors, laptops and other bits of work equipment. This spilled out onto the sofas, and a few people – I assumed they were our developers, but I couldn't be sure as I had never met them before – were squatting on the floor, tapping away in a variety of awkward positions.

'It was a bot,' said Spencer, the CTO. 'The bot owner must have got the token address straight from the blockchain.'

'I didn't even know we had added liquidity to Uniswap yet,' said Paul, visibly confused and overwhelmed by the hive of activity buzzing around him. Being our head of branding, he was more at home on beanbags, sipping a beer and drawing some sketches. The tumult in the flat that day took him far out of his comfort zone.

'Yes, it was added at 1.37 UCT,' said someone who I thought was a dev. He spoke carefully, and unnaturally enunciated every letter of the time zone acronym in his thick Eastern European accent.

'This isn't good,' came a trembling voice from somewhere in the room. 'We haven't even launched yet, and some bot's already nabbed 150 Eth worth of TENT tokens. That's more than $300,000 worth. We need to get an emergency message out about this.' I had no idea who was speaking, and didn't want to just shout into the maelstrom of the room, so I opted for saying nothing.

Miles's unmistakable voice then let out a jubilant cry: 'Ha ha! Not a problem, the Sidera lads have got him.'

'What do you mean?'

'The anti-bot system, I'm on a call with their team: they snagged the bot!' Miles had one headphone in his left ear, and was shifting his attention back and forth between listening into the call and typing frantically at a laptop.

'So what happens now?'

'Hang on, I'll ask.'

He stormed out the room and returned about half a minute later punching the air.

'All the Eth it spent buying our token is just going to go into our liquidity pool. It means the 10X pump can't go back down.'

Cries erupted throughout the cramped, boisterous space. The mood and tempo in the flat were approaching ecstasy. We hadn't even officially launched yet, and we were already 1,000 per cent up in price.

'Nice,' came Archie's curt summation. He had been chain-smoking cigarettes since 7.30 that morning, filling the already unpleasant space with a thick, choking haze. 'Let's get some comms prepped straight away.' He looked in my direction, but I had no idea whether he saw me or not. 'Needs to go out just after the contract address, telling everyone we stopped a bot ruining the launch. They'll love that.'

'Already writing it up,' I exclaimed, hoping I had been heard.

'Okay, let's go with the contract address,' Miles said, bounding over to where I was perched on the edge of a sofa. 'Now. Let's get it out now.' It was 2.01 p.m. I hit send.

The moment the contract address landed in our Telegram group, the orders started flying in. The chart that we had hooked up to the large TV mounted on the wall started to flood with green. We had the candles set to the shortest possible time frame, meaning we could see every minuscule movement in price. The token was initially set to be listed at $0.30. Thanks to the bot, by the time I posted the announcement we were at $3. By the time two new candles had formed on the screen, indicating 2 minutes had elapsed, our token was trading at $9. Our fully diluted market cap was $90 million.

I stared at the screen in disbelief. The kind of disbelief known only to lottery winners, and to gamblers who bet their house on a hand of blackjack and get dealt a twenty-one from the off. I couldn't comprehend what was happening. $90 million. Out of complete thin air. For a moment, everyone else in the room faded into a blur, and I sat mesmerised by the peaks of the green waves surging on the screen. And then, suddenly, I was brought back into the room by a loud bang and something hitting me hard in the back. I jumped out of my seat, and, with a sharp pain throbbing between my shoulder blades, I looked round to see one of the graphic designers holding a magnum bottle of champagne, foam spraying out the end of it.

'No one's put in a single sell order yet!'

'We're on the fucking moon lads.'

'Fuck the moon, we're on Mars!'

A heated debate got under way as to what celestial body best described our token's price appreciation. I kept my eyes firmly on the screen. Launch had taken place 10 minutes ago, and our price rise showed no signs of stopping. We were at $20 and climbing. Our market cap was now $200 million.

And, despite the noise and the frenzy raging all around, I couldn't help but pick up on something shouted by some indiscernible voice just now: 'No one has put a single sell order in.' This struck me as very strange. The launchpad participants should have their tokens by now. And the VCs and influencers and other partners and service providers should have portions of theirs. They were all over 7,000 per cent up on their investment. If they had put even $1,000 into our coin, they would be sitting on over $70,000 now. Why weren't they selling? It made no sense to me.

I went over to Miles. 'Let's unmute the Telegram group,' I said. 'It should only be muted for 5 or 10 minutes after launch, and we're past that now.'

It was standard practice to mute Telegram groups around the actual moments of a token launch, so that the team could send important messages to buyers without them being lost in the noise. Also, it stopped the team getting distracted by reading hundreds of messages a minute, some of them invariably negative, and allowed for more focus on critical tasks at hand.

'Yeah, sure, whatever mate.' Miles barely seemed to register what I said. Spencer was lying on a sofa with his head dangling over the arm, as Miles stood over him and poured champagne directly into his mouth.

I pulled out my phone, went into our Telegram group settings, and hit the unmute button. And, as soon as I did, all hell broke loose. Hundreds of messages all came through instantaneously. My phone started getting hot in my hand, and its battery started noticeably depleting as it struggled to cope with the sheer volume of messages pouring in. None of them were good. I was struggling to keep up with the conversation, as I could only glance at a message for a fraction of a second before it was pushed up the group by an onslaught of new ones. I had to mute the group again, just to take stock.

My suspicions were correct. The absence of sell orders was not due to exclusive bullish sentiment. Initially, on realising no one was selling, I thought people were so confident that the price was going to continue pumping, they wanted to hold onto their tokens and not take any profits just yet. This wasn't the case. There were no sells because, for some unknown reason, no one was *able* to sell.

'Archie!' I called out, pushing aside our head of brand and one of the unknown developers. They were holding empty shot glasses and wincing as they sucked lime wedges. 'Archie! Have you seen the Telegram group?'

Archie was staring at his phone and didn't look up. 'Archie, it's fucking bad. No one can sell!'

He looked at me, the terror in his eyes plain as day, and simply said: 'Shit.'

He snatched Spencer up from the sofa, seized Miles by the arm, and thrust them both out the room, down the hall, and into Miles' bedroom. I followed them in and closed the door. Archie barked instructions at them, his words scarcely coherent, but the sentiment of them crystal clear: find out what's wrong and fix it.

Spencer hooked his laptop up to a monitor Miles had on the small desk in his room and began hitting his keyboard. Several large chat boxes were up on the two screens. Each had black backgrounds and were filled with green text. It looked like something out of *The Matrix*. Spencer sat scrolling and typing for a while, looking confused and quite distressed. He was running his fingers through his knotted, shoulder-length hair and fidgeting with his hoodie strings in between bouts of typing. Archie paced the room, while Miles scrolled through his phone, catching up on the furore that had unfolded in the now muted Telegram group during the 30 seconds people were able to send messages into it.

After what felt like a lifetime, Spencer looked at Archie, his distress now morphed into abject fear. 'Umm, so I think I've found what the issue is,' he said sheepishly. 'The Sidera anti-bot. It's blacklisted our tax wallet.'

'What the fuck does that mean? Speak English!'

'I can't be sure of the cause, but I think when people started trying to sell their tokens, the Sidera bot saw the tokens flowing into the tax wallet, realised that it was being done automatically and faster than any human can send tokens, and then classified it as a bot and blacklisted the address. So no TENT tokens can be sent to the tax address. Meaning that no sell orders can be processed.'

'Just remove the tax. Fuck the 3 per cent, this is going to kill the whole project.'

'We can't remove the tax. We'll have to disable the anti-bot.'

Miles darted out of the room and returned with his laptop and headphones. The call with Sidera, which he had previously been half-listening to through one headphone, was still going on. He went to put his headphones in, but Archie snatched them and inserted them into his own ears.

Archie didn't immediately tell the Sidera team to disable their software, opting instead to launch into a barrage of insults. After issuing one of the most imaginative arrays of expletives I've ever heard, he was eventually reined in by Miles, who seized the laptop from him and muted the call, begging Archie to calm down. Archie stormed out of the room. Miles disconnected the Bluetooth headphones from his laptop, which were still lodged in Archie's ears, and began to speak to the Sidera team over the laptop's speakers.

'Guys, sorry about that. It's all a bit hectic here at the moment. We need your anti-bot disabled, right now please.'

'What the hell's going on, and what's wrong with Archie? He got a screw loose or something? Our software just saved your launch – it prevented a massive bot order of 150 Eth. And a few smaller ones as well, about 20 or 30 Eth each. We've stopped just about half a million dollars of tokens being dumped onto legitimate investors.'

'Yep, great, that's all brilliant. But it's blacklisted our tax address as well. No one can sell the token.'

'What tax address?'

Miles explained the tax function to them, and the situation that their software had caused.

'Well, how 'bout that. That would trigger the anti-bot, yes.' Geoff from Sidera sounded calm, and curiously fascinated, in the same way a scientist might be interested in an unexpected result produced by an experiment. 'If you'd told us about this tax address, we could've recalibrated the software. Send us the wallet details, and we'll remove it from the blacklist.'

Spencer again resumed his typing, as he rushed to pull up the info Geoff needed. After a brief moment he exclaimed: 'All right, done! It's in the Telegram group we have with you.'

'Brilliant, thanks a lot. Hold the line please, while we sort this out.' Geoff seemed to have shifted his tone, from that of an intrigued scientist to a bored customer service rep.

There was then an agonising silence as Geoff and his team got to work. While we waited, and to take my mind off this calamitous turn of events, I pulled out our price chart on my phone. TENT was trading at just over $36. Our market cap was now $360 million. We were 12,000 per cent up from our initial listing price. Our token had been on the market for about half an hour. Despite the tense mood in the room, I couldn't resist showing my screen to Miles. I expected him not to register it, or even to knock it out of my hand, such was his concentration on the task at hand. But I was wrong. He put his laptop down on his bed, put his arms around me, and began jumping up and down.

'YESSSS. Come on lad! 100X, easy!'

I was suddenly aware of how volatile and unpredictable the atmosphere in this flat was. People could go from total panic to eruptive rage, to abject distress, to absolute elation, all in the space of a few moments. I didn't have time to dwell on this, though, as I was – quite literally – pulled into Miles's elation. We both knew that the price was artificially inflated due to the inability of people to sell, and I was sure Miles was also wondering the same thing I had been from the moment I found out about the anti-bot glitch: what would the price fall to, once selling could start?

We were about to find out. As we were still celebrating our artificial token price, a voice came from the laptop's speaker.

'Okay, tax address is being removed from the blacklist in about 30 seconds guys.'

I left the room to retrieve Archie. With about 10 seconds left to go until selling was allowed, Miles, Archie, Spencer and I stood huddled in Miles's bedroom, braced for our token price to plummet. I had the bot announcement ready to go, to try to dampen the sell pressure, and restore a bit of confidence among the hordes of irate investors.

'Okay here goes. Three, two ...' But Geoff needn't have bothered with the countdown; the address must have been removed from the blacklist prematurely as, before he had started counting, the price was already dropping. We were standing in silence, our eyes glued to the monitor. There was no noise coming from the other room either. In a state of increasing horror we watched as our $36 token price dipped down to $34, then to $30, then kept dipping.

'Okay, unmute the group,' Archie said after a moment, shattering the tension hanging thick in the air. 'Let's get that message about the bot posted, too.'

As soon as people were able to comment in our group, the vitriol started pouring in. Messages ranged from the confused, to the accusatory, to the downright vile and insulting. Crypto can turn very nasty very quickly, and we had thousands of people now directing their anonymity-veiled rage towards us.

Surprisingly, though, it wasn't all bad. The people who were able to get the very first sell orders in made a fortune and were understandably over the moon. One investor informed the group that, through TENT, he had turned the last $500 he had to his name into over $60,000. I tried to capitalise on messages like these as much as possible, telling our shillers to post congratulatory replies, and even to make up some of their own success stories and share them in the group.

It also seemed most of the launchpad participants were able to sell early, so they too were sprinkling some positivity into the mix. However, it very much seemed like tipping a bucket of water over a forest fire. The general sentiment in the group was overwhelmingly negative. The bot announcement did distract for a moment or two, with anger turning into amusement as people revelled in the knowledge that a single bot owner had lost $300,000. However, the sharply declining price ensured that this didn't last long, and the conversation quickly returned to upbraiding us over the botched listing.

'What the fuck are all these people complaining about?' Paul asked, bursting into Miles's bedroom. 'We're at $25, so still around 80X up on listing price. We've got a quarter of a billion dollar market cap. These guys should be fucking applauding us!'

'They think it's going to just keep dropping,' I answered flatly. 'They also saw the $36 peak, and they know that we won't ever reach that price again, probably. So, compared to that, whatever we trade at from now is going to be a disappointment.'

'Yeah, and they probably realise that the price only attained that level through a technical fault,' Spencer added, without taking his eyes from his malevolent-looking green and black text boxes. 'It did look quite artificial, what with the lack of sells.'

'All right, damage control,' Miles said, leaping up from his bed, 'I'm going to message the VCs, and find out which ones of them sold. I'll try to persuade them not to sell any more, at least for the time being. They're the ones who can make the biggest impact on price. Then we need to do the same with influencers,' he cast a look in my direction, before continuing: 'We need them not only to hold onto their own tokens, but to tell their followers they should do the same. But, before all that, there's one thing I need to do.'

'What's that?' I asked.

'I need to sell some tokens.'

I looked at Miles to ascertain whether he was joking or not. He ushered Spencer out of the desk chair, removed his laptop from the monitor and started hooking up his own equipment. When he was all set, I saw that the Portent Protocol treasury wallet was open on his screen.

'Wait, what are you doing?' I asked. 'Surely, we don't want to mess the price up any more than it already is? And surely people will see on the blockchain if we just start selling from the treasury wallet?'

'Mate, this is likely the highest the token will ever trade at. In our treasury wallet now, we have about £6 million worth of tokens. I want to liquidate at least some at this price. Don't worry, I'm only going to sell five grand's worth. Got to keep the lights on some-how. And some buy orders are coming in, which should soak up the damage. I'll only sell into green candles, when the price is rallying slightly, so I don't create any new red ones.'

I pulled out my phone and looked at the chart. Sure enough, things did look like they were levelling out. We were at just over $22. It seemed people considered this price attractive, as some quite hefty purchases were being made.

'And also,' Miles added, 'don't worry about people seeing the sells from the treasury wallet. We've done about 20 million in volume in 45 minutes, from about 5,000 individual transactions. Our treasury wallet isn't public, so someone would have to manually go through all the trading logs to find we've sold. And who the hell is going to do that?'

Before I could think up an objection to Miles's arguments, music started playing from the living room. Archie looked up from his phone, which he had been staring at in silence for the past 10 minutes, and made his way next door with Spencer in tow. I stayed and got on with shooting out some messages to the influencers. After I had sent four or five, I looked back up at Miles's screen. He had Uniswap open, and was getting ready to put his sell order in. In the box on the trading platform into which the quantity of tokens to be sold is entered, Miles had inputted $5,000 worth of TENT tokens. He cast a sideways glance in my direction. His cursor stood motionless, and I felt his eyes on me. I looked at him and saw there was a conspiratorial smile on his face. Without taking his eyes off me, he added another zero to the figure.

'What are you doing?' There was a note of alarm in my voice. Miles turned back to his screen and moved his cursor to the red rectangle containing the word 'SELL' in big white capital letters. After a moment's hesitation, his mouse let out a sharp, plastic click.

'What the fuck?! You just sold off fifty grand of tokens. You said you were only doing five. What are you doing?'

'Oh shit, did I?' The smile was still there on his face. 'My bad. Must have fat-fingered it. Oh well.' Miles shrugged and made for the door. I pulled out my phone again, unlocked it, and was greeted with a short, squat red candle interrupting the procession of green ones to its left. We were down to $18. Swinging open his bedroom door, Miles turned to me as if he had just remembered something. 'Oh yeah,' he said, 'one thing – don't tell Archie.'

He opened the door to the living room. A heady bassline pounded into the corridor, mixed with the sounds of cheers and laughter. Miles bounded in, punching the air as he entered. I was left alone, aghast, in his room. I opened Telegram and went into the Portent Protocol community chat. The first message I saw was from an investor who had bought our token at its peak of $36. He said he saw that it was only going up and up. And now, about 10 minutes later, he only had half of his money left. It was for an engagement ring for his girlfriend. He couldn't afford the one she wanted, and he thought by investing in TENT he'd be able to not disappoint her.

I sat down on Miles's bed and put my head in my hands. We were never going to recover from this.

PART TWO

8

A Picks and Shovels Play

The day after launch, with the dust somewhat settled and the turbulence levelled off, we took stock. Our token was hovering around $16, which represented a more than 5,000 per cent increase on the listing price. Many of our VCs had paid even less than this, though, and the seed investors – who bought at the cheapest price of $0.17 – were sitting on around an 9,300 per cent price increase. Our fully diluted market capitalisation was $160 million.

While this sounded like a lot, it was in fact a false picture of our token's health. The key was very much in the words 'fully diluted,' meaning that if all the tokens in existence were trading, this is what the market cap would be. However, due to vesting periods and lock-ups, not all the tokens were on the market. If all those not currently in circulation were disregarded, our market cap was actually closer to around $30 million.

Our trading volume in the first 24 hours of launch was over $40 million, which was quite substantial for a new token. We had around 2,500 token holders (with this figure being easily ascertainable from the blockchain). This was a good amount of holders; anything over 1,000 after a token's first day on the market was typically seen as decent.

All in all, the figures seemed to indicate that our launch had been a success. And yet it certainly didn't feel that way. It was all downhill from here, and we knew it. Because, despite the high price, we were anathema to many of our community members. Many bought when we were at our artificially induced peak of $36. And, surprisingly, it wasn't just the people who were out of pocket who were pissed. The people who managed to get in earlier, and were in profit, were also taking us to task. Paul had a theory as to why.

'It's because they saw the token at $36, and then saw it drop from there. For these guys, just making money isn't enough. They want to keep making more and more money. If they buy a token at $5, and then it goes up to $10 and they make $1,000 profit, they'll be happy. But then if it drops down to $7.5, and they're left with $500 profit, they're furious. Because, from their point of view, they haven't made $500. They've *lost* $500. They think they're entitled to the all-time high price. And, worse than that, they want tokens to keep going up in price indefinitely. And when they don't, they'll make sure there's hell to pay.'

Paul's somewhat cynical view of the psychology of crypto traders aside, there was one mitigating factor in all this: the negative sentiment towards us seemed to be entirely confined to retail. Once the influencers and service providers were able to dump their tokens, they went quiet. And not just *to* us, but *about* us as well.

'Why haven't the influencers tweeted anything about our launch?' Archie asked on a Zoom call the day after listing. The call was scheduled for 7 p.m. – and then pushed back to 9 p.m. – on account of the oppressive hangovers everyone was reeling from.

'Probably because they don't need to any more,' I replied. I had my camera off, and hoped my voice didn't sound quite as bad as I felt. 'They've got their tokens, and they pumped the price up to more than 50X what they paid, so they've got no reason to post about us any more.'

'If they don't post about us, we're doomed. The token price isn't going to go up by itself. And as more and more unlocks happen, it's just going to go even lower. What the hell are we supposed to do?'

'Well, a few of the smaller guys *might* write something. But it's uncertain,' I said.

'Fuck the smaller guys.' Archie turned his camera on, and revealed himself lying in his bed, wearing the same clothes from the night before, with his signature vape laying on his pillow beside his head. 'We don't want those shitkickers. It's embarrassing. Something will come up. We're still at a 50X increase, don't forget.'

'Yeah, but fat lot of good that's going to do us. We haven't got any tokens to sell. By the time our team tokens get unlocked, we'll be at zero.'

Miles was right: for good optics, and to reassure buyers that we wouldn't mercilessly dump on them, we had imposed a hefty lock-up period on our team tokens: twelve months, which, by industry standards, is a lifetime. They wouldn't be funding our retirement any time soon. Of course, there was always the community development pot, from which Miles had sold tokens in yesterday's launch melee. While their value had almost halved from when Miles had put the sell order in, there was still over $2 million in there. However, as tempting as it was, we couldn't really touch those. We had to be cautious, as the launch frenzy was now over and volumes had dropped. This meant any sells we made would impact the price far more than they did on launch day. It also meant it would be easier for observers to spot us selling from project wallets, as there were fewer transactions to wade through, and people were watching the blockchain like hawks following the accusations of us being a rug. If we were caught with our hands in the till, we'd be finished.

So while we had each made a considerable amount from the launch, we wouldn't be sailing off into the sunset anytime soon. We needed the token price to remain buoyant, long enough for our team allocations to come unlocked.

But, even as we were planning ways to keep our token above water, another opportunity altogether dropped into our laps. One so lucrative, it had the potential to render the whole Portent Protocol project redundant.

The morning after the team call, I awoke to five missed calls from Archie, nearly a dozen messages and an email, all telling me to call him as soon as possible. It was 7.10 a.m. Before even getting out of bed I returned Archie's call. He answered on the first ring.

'Mate, I told you something would turn up, and it bloody has.'

'What is it?'

'I should've checked yesterday, it was pretty stupid not to, but the whole day was a bit of a write-off. I've just been clearing my Twitter DMs and email inbox, and I've got a shit load of messages from projects who are asking for help with their marketing.'

'What do you mean?'

'I mean, people saw the TENT pump, and now want us to help them market their own coins. They'll probably pay through the teeth for it, as well.'

At this point, I leapt out of bed.

'That's definitely interesting. Who are the projects, and what do they want us to do specifically?'

'A lot of them are contacts of mine, who were keeping an eye on the launch. Hard to tell what they want at this point. Come round to Miles's flat, and we'll get a plan in place.'

An hour and a half later, I found myself drinking coffee as thick as tar in Miles's shoebox-sized kitchen. After a brief recap of how the TENT token was performing – it wasn't looking good: we were down to $12 now, around 66 per cent off our all-time-high – Archie and Miles gave me the rundown of their contacts who were looking for help with marketing. So as not to overload us, and to make sure we weren't biting off more than we could chew, they had whittled down the dozen or so requests they had received to just two.

The first project was called ArtBlocks and was run by a middle-aged Geordie called Richard. A close friend of the cousins, alongside ArtBlocks he was also the founder of a VC fund, Silver Crest Capital, which had written a $50,000 cheque to Portent Protocol for a private round allocation.

After being in the VC game for the past several years and seeing time and again how much money there is to be made launching tokens, Richard decided to try his hand at setting up a project himself. ArtBlocks was looking to construct a 50m² mosaic, intended to commemorate the creation of blockchain technology. Richard had commissioned an artist – who was supposedly quite well known in the world of mosaics, although I had certainly never heard of him – to produce this so-called 'tribute to technological disruption' at his studio in Detroit.

But Richard wasn't just stopping there. The unique selling point of his creation – and the way in which he was incorporating crypto and, most importantly, a token launch – was that the mosaic would have a digital counterpart, hosted in the metaverse.

The 'metaverse' is a broad and loose term for a 3D digital space in which people are able to interact with one another through avatars. There is no real stipulation on what that 3D digital space needs to be to constitute a metaverse, nor what form a person's avatar needs to take. A metaverse can, for example, be a digital re-creation of a real place in the physical world – for example Greater London, or the Ritz Hotel – and an avatar can be a virtual facsimile of the person it is supposed to represent, with similar facial features, hair and clothes. However, a metaverse can also be modelled to look like a fantasy landscape, or outer space, and the avatars populating it can resemble mythical creatures or sci-fi characters.

While the term 'metaverse' owes its admittance into the mainstream vernacular to the crypto bros, who at the height of its usage were slapping it onto every half-baked project that they were looking to raise funds for, the metaverse itself wasn't an invention or a product of the crypto industry. The popular battle royale video game *Fortnite* can be classified as a metaverse, as it involves online avatars interacting with one another. As can *Runescape*, the massively multiplayer online roleplaying game. However, while it didn't invent the metaverse, the crypto industry did very much claim it as their own. In the industry's unceasing search for ways to give tokens use cases and applications, crypto was the only logical form of currency to use in digital-native metaverses. Many people drew parallels between cryptocurrency and the gold used for bartering in *Runescape*, and there was even a vocal contingent of crypto evangelists who clamoured for Jagex – the makers of the game – either to create their own in-game token, or to incorporate one that was already on the market.

It was April 2021 when all this was explained to me – long before the word 'metaverse' had become the hackneyed conversation killer we know it as today. It would be another six months before Mark Zuckerberg's disastrous and clout-chasing rebrand of Facebook to 'Meta', which was arguably the point at which the metaverse reached both peak recognition and peak cringe.

This made Richard's ArtBlocks project one of the first movers in this emergent corner of the cryptosphere. However, it wasn't the only player; several other projects beat it to the punch. Most notable among these was Ethermon: a *Pokémon*-style game, where players catch, own and fight digital monsters. Ethermon was launched in 2017 and rose to astonishing popularity in 2021 as blockchain gaming and metaverse narratives started catching on. Ethermon had its own token, which could either be bought on a decentralised exchange or earned through gameplay. It was used to make in-game purchases, such as upgrading battle equipment or entering tournaments. It also had a series of NFTs, which represented ownership of the monsters that users would play with.

If the game itself sounds childish, the price tags attached to its NFTs certainly weren't; at their height, even an entry-level Ethermon NFT would fetch tens of thousands of dollars. The most sought-after monsters, with the most desirable traits such as high battle strength, could easily fetch north of six figures.

'A metaverse, are you serious?' I asked Miles, when he had finished bringing me up to speed. 'With goblins and dragons and all that shit?'

'Yes to the metaverse, no to the goblins. It's just to give his project a bit of an edge. The artwork is the main aspect of it. The metaverse is just a bit of fun – it makes it a bit different.'

'Yeah, plus,' Archie added, 'metaverses are going to be hype. Ethermon is pumping, lad. Soon everyone's going to jump on the bandwagon. No one can see prices like that and ignore it for long. It's inevitable.'

'Yep, exactly,' Miles said, nodding his head as if that settled things. 'But, like I said, the main aspect of the project is the physical art-work. And the tokens, obviously.'

'So what do his tokens do then?' I asked.

'Ah, that's where things get interesting ... they're governance tokens and, by holding them, you get to vote on where the artwork is displayed. Richard wants to take it on tour, around all the world's great galleries – the Louvre, MoMA, that sort of thing. And token holders decide where the mosaic goes next.'

I was unimpressed, and pretty confident that the New York Museum of Modern Art, which houses work by the likes of Jackson Pollock and Salvador Dali, wouldn't be interested in a massive mosaic paying homage to the creation of the blockchain. But I didn't want to rain on the parade.

'Right,' I said, 'and when is the mosaic going to be finished?'

'Should take around two and a half years.'

'And when does he want to launch his token?'

'It's tentatively scheduled for eight weeks from now. We told him to go sooner, to be honest. The market's pumping right now, and the metaverse narrative is about to fly.'

At this stage, I wanted to point out that it was unlikely anyone would buy a token that wouldn't have even a semblance of utility for at least a few years. But the necessity of establishing a new source of income prevailed, and I changed the subject. I asked about the other project that was looking for help with marketing.

This, as it turned out, was to be far more conventional in nature. They were called Zogo Spin and were setting about to launch a decentralised gambling site. The project had a peculiar pedigree, as it was run by a family friend of Archie and Miles called Thomas D'Invilliers, although he preferred his business contacts to use his formal title: the Marquis of Ashburnham. He came from one of the oldest, most aristocratic families in England, with his ancestral seat being a go-to setting for film and TV producers shooting period dramas.

'So why does he want to start a crypto project?' I asked. 'Surely he has enough money as it is?'

'Yeah, it's more of a passion project for old Ashy,' Miles said, forgoing his formal title in favour of a nickname used only by his closest friends. 'The poor lad has lost so much money betting through dodgy offshore bookies that he's setting up his own shop.'

When I shot him a questioning look, Miles explained in more detail: the Marquis of Ashburnham, he confided, had a gambling problem. Apparently, it wasn't uncommon for 'Ashy' and his pals to descend on his box at Stamford Bridge on the weekends and lay on six-figure bets between them. Sometimes seven figures, if they had partaken of one too many glasses of champagne. And, in fact, his bets were so large and so frequent that ordinary high-street bookies refused to do business with him. It posed too much risk for them, so Ashy had to resort to offshore agents instead.

These less-than-savoury characters were more than happy to facilitate the young marquis' vice, albeit at a cost. They heavily marked up the odds, meaning that when he won, his payouts would be far smaller than if he had bet through, say, Ladbrokes. And that's when they actually paid out anything at all. It wasn't uncommon for these offshore bookmakers simply to refuse to give him his winnings when he hit a lucky streak.

In fact, he spent so much time travelling to places like Cyprus – where a lot of these agents are based – to try to retrieve his money in person, that he came up with an idea for another business venture: a private jet rental company. He had set this up several months prior to entering the world of crypto.

'I see. So he basically wants to get one back on these offshore agents?'

'Yep, exactly,' Miles said, 'and to run them out of business. He reckons there are a lot of other people who do too, and a lot of money to be made from it. He says that his mates have all already promised to route all their bets through his platform, as soon as it's launched.'

Given how much money it sounded like Thomas had, there was only one question left for me to ask:

'So ... how much can we charge him?'

Miles shot me a smile. 'That depends. What do you think we can get away with?'

'Let me think about it and see what I can come up with.'

And, with that, I got to work. I threw some slides together in a PowerPoint template, made up a list of services for each of the two projects, stated how crucial these would be for the success of their respective token launches, and then pulled together some costs that I thought sounded about right.

By 8 p.m., the documents were ready. I recommended charging ArtBlocks $7,000 per month. In return, we would write them a couple of articles and get our media contacts to publish them in the press. I also added some light social media management into the mix, to pad things out a bit. For Zogo Spin I recommended a one-off fee of $25,000, for us to create their brand from scratch and get them set up with all the basics they would need, as they were in a much earlier stage of development.

By 9 p.m., the documents were sent off. And by 9.30 p.m., we received a reply from Richard.

'Fucking hell, I thought you lads would be charging an arm and a leg. I'd have to be a moron not to take you up on $7k per month, for all that work. Let's fucking do it. I'll have the funds with you in the morning.'

Archie, Miles and I all looked at one another. We were seized by a strange mix of emotions. On the one hand, we now knew we had a proposition that could be monetised, and for which there was clear demand. And, within a few hours of deciding to set up an agency, we had our first client. On the other hand, we had seemingly undersold ourselves, and left money on the table. Who knew what the other crypto agencies were offering, if $7k per month for such a slim scope of work was considered cheap. But, regardless, one thing was abundantly clear: we were onto something here, and this could turn out to be a very lucrative venture indeed.

Exhaling solemnly, Miles summed up the mood.

'Well, here we fucking go then, I guess.'

9

The Big Break

Richard's monthly payment gave us a source of recurring revenue. And Thomas's lump sum – all paid upfront before we even lifted a pen – gave us a safety net of cash. This provided a base from which we could build out our operation. We brought on a slew of employees, from graphic designers to social media managers, to help us with the project work. Archie shanghaied a contact of his to spin up a website for us at short notice, and Miles got to work sorting out all the tedious legal and operational hoops that need to be jumped through when setting up a company. As we were a service provider, with no immediate plans to launch some kind of marketing agency token (although we definitely didn't rule it out), we decided to forgo a complicated offshore setup and go down the above-board route of registering with Companies House. Before this, though, we needed to give our enterprise a name.

We set up a Zoom call to hash this out. Having always wanted to run my own agency, I had quite strong opinions on this matter, and decided to go in decisively with an opening gambit:

'How about Mornington Partners?' I suggested

'Are you fucking serious?!' Archie said. 'Where did you even get that from? It sounds like an undertakers or something.'

'Well, this new business is going to be legit, isn't it, so I reckon it needs a legit name as well. You know, something that inspires trust and all that.'

'Fuck that,' said Paul. He was sprawled on a bright yellow sofa, chest hair poking out above the neckline of an Aztec-print tank top, puffing away at something that seemed far too long and conical to be a cigarette. 'Let's just call it Moonshot Advisors, and be done with it.'

I laughed, thinking this was one of Paul's classic ironic quips. The smile was quickly wiped off my face when I saw Archie and Miles both nodding with concentrated approval, as if they were hearing something brilliant for the first time.

The matter was settled: thenceforth, our legitimate, sophisticated UK operation would trade under the name Moonshot Advisors.

While I may have found this ridiculous, our prospective clients certainly didn't. Once we were fully up and running, more and more projects kept rolling in. Word was going round that the team behind the TENT token launch were putting their services out for hire, and they had a proper website and name and everything. Our inboxes were heaving. So much so that, between us, we simply couldn't take on all the work we were being offered. We had to start turning projects away. As much as we hated leaving money on the table, there were only so many hours in the day, and we were rammed. The only projects we were able to take on were those that offered more money than one of our existing clients. At which point it would be out with the old and in with the new.

One project that very much fitted this bill was Plouton Mines. When they approached us to ask for our help, we were ready to drop our whole client list on the spot. Not on account of the project so much as the person running it: billionaire US business tycoon Clint Steele.

We were first introduced to Steele in July 2021. A business partner of Richard's, who was working with him on ArtBlocks, put us in touch. He was impressed with the work we had been doing, making a wholly ludicrous art project sound interesting and relevant, and wanted to connect us with Clint – both as a sign of his appreciation to us, and also as a favour to his billionaire friend who needed help on a crypto venture he was embarking on.

Clint came from an established, old-money family of New York property moguls. He also ran an investment firm, which had purchased and developed billions of dollars' worth of prime East Coast real estate since 2001. He was keenly involved in philanthropy and was certainly no stranger to scandal; his acrimonious, five-year divorce suit was the talk of the tabloids when it was settled in 2016.

Gossip columnists from coast to coast were split over the judge's decision to award the $22.5 million Park Avenue duplex, and $12 million art collection, to his ex-wife.

'Fucking hell, this is it then, is it? This is when things really start taking off.' Miles and I were heading for lunch, and his excitement about our upcoming call with Clint Steele lent his movements an erratic edge. He nearly got run over twice trying to cross the road, taking a few steps off the pavement and then scurrying back to a chorus of horns and jeers.

'Bloody hell, what's wrong with you?'

'Look,' Miles said, casting sharp glances either side of him before launching a third attempt at the road, 'what's the deal with Clint anyway? What's he all about, and why's he getting into crypto?'

'Richard's guy didn't say. But he told me the name of Clint's project – "Plouton Mines" apparently – and I looked into them.'

'What do they even do?'

I gave Miles all the context I had. From what I could see online, Plouton Mines had links to oil mines in Alaska. Initially, I thought they were some sort of oil-backed stablecoin. These were projects that launched tokens onto the market equal to the value of a given commodity. Paxos Gold was the most notable example of this; it had a market cap of around half a billion at the time, with each of their PAXG tokens being equal to the price of 1 troy fine ounce of gold. This equivalence with the price of gold was maintained through bullion, which Paxos held in secure vaults, for which users could theoretically redeem their tokens any time they wanted.

However, Plouton Mines weren't tokenising the value of a commodity like Paxos were. They were tokenising an entire oil mining company. They were what's known as a security token: quite an uncommon form of cryptocurrency, which seeks to create digital forms of traditional assets such as stocks or bonds. Security tokens are somewhat rare to come by, because launching them requires highly stringent regulatory oversight.

As we've seen, it's a great convenience for project founders that crypto tokens don't confer any ownership rights to the investors who buy them. Not only does this enable founders to raise funds without having to give away any control or equity stake in their project, but it's also one of the primary reasons why it's so difficult to regulate cryptocurrency; without ownership rights attached to them, it could be argued that crypto tokens resemble something far closer to commodities than securities. This is a classification that many in the industry lobby hard for, as commodities are subject to far less regulatory scrutiny than securities.

Indeed, since 2020, the US Securities and Exchange Commission – the body that regulates securities – has been fighting a hostile court case with Ripple Labs, the company that launched XRP, a token used for payment settlements and remittances. The SEC is suing Ripple Labs for selling over $1.3 billion in an 'unregistered, ongoing digital asset securities offering'. Ripple Labs are fighting the case, claiming their token isn't a security. And they're prepared to spend a fortune to win; in May 2023, their CEO, Brad Darlington, claimed that, by the time the case is over, Ripple Labs will have spent over $200 million battling the lawsuit.

A lot is at stake, therefore, in the argument over whether a cryptocurrency is a security or not. However, it's a fight that security tokens have no interest in; they claim from the offset that they are, in fact, securities and, as such, need to submit copious reporting requirements to the SEC. This is a difficult avenue to go down, with myriad hoops to jump through and a labyrinth of complex regulations to navigate – but Plouton Mines seemed up to the task. They had a team full of heavyweights backing them; as well as having Clint as their chairman, their board of directors and C-Suite were stacked with Wall Street veterans and Magic Circle lawyers. Their CEO alone – a man by the name of Bill Johnson – had more than three decades of experience trading securities and managing investments.

'Blimey. So they're a serious operation then?' Miles asked, when I had finished my rundown.

'Looks like it. But when I was researching, I came across some pretty weird stuff.'

'What kind of stuff?'

'There's some vile stuff about them online. Like really awful, personal stuff. People photoshopping Bill and his family into scenes from porn films, that kind of thing.'

'Bloody hell, his family too! Why are people so pissed with them?'

'I couldn't tell for sure. Looks like the project was active back in 2017 and screwed over their investors somehow.'

'They must've done some properly bad stuff. Most people who were buying shitcoins in 2017 aren't even in crypto any more. Let alone holding grudges against specific projects.'

'Well, we're speaking to them in an hour. Let's try find out what's going on.'

We bought two falafel wraps from a vendor with a stall in the street and headed back to our office. We had recently moved into an abandoned building in Bermondsey, just by the river. Some of Archie's friends had leased the upper floors, to open a bar on the roof, and kindly offered us a couple of rooms to set up shop in.

The floor we were on was one big room, divided by smeared glass partitions, which presumably demarcated the different offices that used to occupy the space. By the looks of things, no one had set foot in there for decades. The faded, once-functional blue carpet was soiled and torn in patches. The windows were set in yellowing frames, didn't open any more, and looked like they might fall out into the street at any moment. A damp, musty scent hung thick in the air. We loved it straight away. We thought the grittiness of it lent our operation the air of an authentic startup. So we bought some beanbags, rounded up the motley selection of office equipment we found scattered about, moved it all into one of the smaller, less dingy glass-partitioned rooms, and ran our operation from there.

Miles and I got back just in time to have lunch and join the call. A few minutes in it became obvious to us all that neither Clint nor Bill, the CEO, was particularly clued up on crypto.

'So I'm sure you guys have already done your research, but I thought I'd better say a few words about what it is we're doing with Plouton.' Bill was sitting in the driver's seat of what looked like quite a flash sportscar. Racing-style seats were clad in white leather upholstery. The convertible roof was down, revealing a cloudless blue Californian sky. His headset picked up the light breeze blowing through the car, making his voice somewhat difficult to hear.

'Essentially, what we're trying to do here has never been done before.' Miles and I raised our eyebrows at one another from across the desk. By this point, we had heard dozens of projects claiming to be the first of their kind for one thing or another.

'We've bought a mining company out in Alaska, and we're looking to conduct a token sale instead of an IPO.'

This was in line with what we had discovered during our research, and it certainly wasn't unique. Token sales, as we know, are the crypto equivalent of IPOs, and the majority of projects conduct them. However, where Bill had a point was on the size of the Plouton Mines operation; whereas most companies that IPO are large, highly developed firms that have been around for many years, the typical crypto project that floats a token publicly often hasn't even learnt to crawl. Token launches essentially take startups public, which leads to a great many problems.

Very often, not only do the projects in question have no profit or revenue streams, but they actually incur significant operating losses. Eventually, these losses either turn positive, as the company begins monetising, or they get so severe that the startup runs out of any funding they may have raised. Once this happens, they're left with no choice but to shut up shop. Unsurprisingly, in the case of most crypto projects, the latter situation is more common. However, because they're publicly traded, it isn't just the team and the funders who get burnt: it's the token investors as well.

'We're probably not going to be doing things in the same way as your other clients,' said Clint Steele, speaking for the first time since the call started. He had a smooth, deep voice, and was sitting in a large boardroom in front of a floor-to-ceiling window. The skyline revealed him to be somewhere high up, overlooking Manhattan.

'We're not tokenising the value of oil,' Clint continued, 'we're tokenising the value of a highly profitable company. The oil mining gives the company revenue and value, and that's what's backing the token. Just like equities get their value from the earnings of the company which issues them. And we're going to provide dividend payments to token holders, so they have a share of the profits from the mining company.'

'Right, got it,' I said. 'You're a security token.'

'Yes, exactly. And that means we're going down the compliance route and doing everything by the book. We're registering ourselves with the SEC, and everything we do is going to be under a lot of scrutiny. We don't wanna end up like the last guys who ran this company. No way.'

'Out of interest, Clint,' said Miles, 'what *did* happen back in 2017?'

'Well, I suppose it's better you find out now from us rather than later down the line. It seems the owners were into some very bad stuff. They're being accused of selling a whole bunch of tokens which didn't exist, to a *load* of investors. And, apparently, they used the money on some pretty extravagant purchases.'

'What do you mean by extravagant, Clint?' asked Archie. 'Like houses and holidays and stuff like that?'

'Ha! If only. The stuff these guys apparently spent their investors' money on is incomprehensible. To give you an indication, I heard they spent nearly a million dollars on a solid gold cast of Nelson Mandela's hands, to adorn the lobby of their office.'

Our faces were every shade of confusion and bewilderment imaginable.

'And you say they sold a load of tokens – can you tell us exactly how many?' I asked.

'About $36 million worth.'

'Blimey. Why did you buy the company at all, with that stuff going on?' I asked.

'Well, for one simple reason: despite their incompetence, the previous owners had set up some top-notch mining deals in Alaska. Obviously, with all the other stuff they were doing, the investors didn't believe they had the oil to back up the tokens they issued. Basically, they didn't think the company or the mining was real.'

'But it is all real,' Bill cut in hurriedly, 'and we wanted to come in and pick up where they left off – but doing everything by the book. And we want to make their investors whole again, because it's the right thing to do. So, when we launch, we're going to give them all the tokens they should've received the first time round.'

After this agitated assurance from Bill, we wrapped up the call, said our goodbyes and left. We weren't convinced by what we had heard. We didn't fully trust Bill and Clint's declared motivations, or their intentions towards their company's conned investors. But, after a brief deliberation, we decided to push ahead with them. Partly because we wanted to give them the benefit of the doubt; if what they had told us was a lie then, between us, we couldn't think up a single other reason why they'd buy a floundering project with its reputation in tatters. But also – and primarily – because these guys looked primed to be our big break. And not just because of their money.

We figured if we had a real, old-money billionaire on our client list, it wouldn't just be the dime-store projects run by get-rich-quick crypto bros who'd be knocking at our door. It would be the heavy hitters, too. We'd have blockchain luminaries lining up round the corner, along with every TradFi firm trying to attract younger, tech-ier customers by delving into digital assets.

With all the weight of Clint's name and prestige behind us, we'd be a beacon of trust and reliability in an intimidatingly inaccessible industry. In short, we'd be quids in.

We discussed how big we should go on the proposal, and eventually landed on a figure of £20,000 per month. For services that didn't amount to very much at all: some rudimentary social media management, a couple of puff media pieces every month, and some basic graphic design. We couldn't do any influencer marketing, as they had the SEC sniffing around them. Best to keep it low key, at least for the time being.

Within 2 hours of the call they had our proposal with them. Later that evening, while we were having pints on the roof of the bar and discussing our plans for expansion should this deal come through, we got a reply from Bill.

'Change the pound sign to a dollar sign, and we have a deal.'

We looked at each other for a fraction of a second, all nodded our approvals, and then rushed back downstairs to get our first invoice over to them.

'Well,' Miles said, looking gleefully at the three of us in turn, 'I guess we're in fucking business then.'

10

Dropping the Ball

Just like we thought, once word got out that we were working with an illustrious billionaire, A-list clients started rolling in. And, with our sense of self-confidence approaching a zenith, and our team expanding faster than ever, we welcomed the work with open arms, whether we were able to accomplish what they wanted us to or not.

Many of these A-listers were large, traditional brands who saw what was going on in the crypto space, both from a financial and a brand-building perspective, and wanted to get in on the action. The first of these opportunistic firms to come our way was a large, internationally renowned American football team – one of the biggest in the world – with a fan base topping 9 million dedicated supporters. A few months before they approached us, their season had just finished, and they had performed especially well. They now wanted to launch a series of NFTs to commemorate their spectacular form. The problem was, we had never worked on an NFT launch before. We had no track record in this area and no idea how to sell NFTs. But we were willing to give it a shot, given how much money was up for grabs.

It was autumn 2021, and the buzz around NFTs had been crescendoing for months. Our last encounter with this formerly niche area of the crypto space had been when we approached the NFT card game Horderz for a partnership with Portent Protocol back in April. In the six months since then, NFTs had become all anyone in the industry could talk about. And, more than that, it wasn't just crypto punters who were caught in the throes of NFT mania; the mainstream, too, had started to take notice.

In March 2021, digital artist Mike Winkleman – better known by his alias 'Beeple' – made history with the landmark sale of his NFT artwork *Everydays: The First 500 Days*. The piece was a collage of Beeple's first 5,000 sketches and animations, with subjects ranging from pop figures to lewd political illustrations. The artwork was auctioned by world-renowned auction house Christie's. Founded in 1766, Christie's has a long and highly distinguished history; over the centuries, some of the greatest expressions of human creativity have changed hands under its roof. Works by every eminent artist you've ever seen hanging in a gallery – from Picasso to Modigliani and even da Vinci – have gone under the hammer of Christie's auctioneers. And now they were jumping on the NFT bandwagon, too.

Beeple's collage was the first purely digital work of art ever offered by a major auction house. However, it was the figure it fetched that captured the world's attention: the NFT sold for a record $69 million. Overnight, Beeple went from relatively obscure digital doodler to the third most valuable living artist, after David Hockney and Jeff Koons. And he brought the entire NFT industry into the limelight with him.

The industry's flagship collection, Bored Ape Yacht Club (or BAYC for short), launched one month after the Christie's auction. It consists of 10,000 NFTs, all featuring a cartoon ape, but in each individual piece the ape wears different items of clothing, with no two NFTs having the same accoutrements. While it may sound like a simple, even infantile, concept, BAYC obtained unfathomable prominence.

The collection had none other than Guy Oseary – talent manager to the likes of Madonna and the Red Hot Chili Peppers – doing its publicity. BAYC's inclusion on Oseary's star-studded client list was enough to convince *Rolling Stone* magazine to overlook the project's complete irrelevance to the music industry and splash a cigar-smoking ape across the front page of a special issue profiling the collection. After that, every celebrity from Justin Bieber to Jimmy Fallon could be found sporting a Bored Ape as their social media profile picture.

And, with publicity on that scale, it didn't take long for the money to start rolling in; by the time we were approached by the American football team, the 'floor price' of the collection (i.e. the price of the cheapest NFT up for sale) was hovering at around 40 Ether, or $130,000. For a single digital picture of a cartoon monkey.

The way we saw it, the hype surrounding NFTs was akin to the IDO craze we had been witnessing for the past several months, and the ICO era of crypto back in 2017. NFTs were the flavour of the month and, if we didn't get in on the game – and get in *quick* – we'd live to regret it. It was with great zeal, therefore, that we told the football team we'd be delighted to market their NFTs for them. However, when we got into the nitty gritty, and it came to negotiating the terms of our engagement, we received a rude awakening: the football team, we learnt, didn't just want us to promote their collection. They wanted us to create it from scratch, put all the NFTs up for sale, and do everything in between.

As inexperienced as we were in the NFT game, at least we knew what an NFT actually was. Which, as we discovered, was far more than could be said for the football team. As it turned out, their director of marketing had been persuaded to launch a collection by our landlord Patrick Chalker – Archie's contact, who owned the bar above our office. Chalker was an old friend of the marketing director and, one night, when he was in town on a business trip, Chalker started showing him how much money sports brands could make in the crypto racket. And, to demonstrate this, there was no better case study than NBA Top Shot.

NBA Top Shot is an NFT marketplace that allows basketball fans to trade digital collectibles of their favourite NBA 'Moments' – short video clips of the most iconic moments in the NBA's history, each represented by a unique NFT. While each NFT is distinct, the same Moment might be made into multiple NFTs – a bit like more traditional baseball cards, which might have many cards featuring the same player. And, like baseball cards, some Moments are more desirable than others, and fetch higher prices. Among the most expensive Moments ever sold was a video of a dunk by LeBron James from a 2020 finals game. NBA Top Shot produced sixty-nine of these Moments and, in August 2021, one was sold for just over \$230,000. Nearly a quarter of a million dollars, for an NFT of a 17-second video clip.

NBA Top Shot was launched in October 2020 and, by September 2021, the marketplace had over 1 million registered users, and just under \$1 billion worth of NBA NFTs had been traded on it. To this day it remains the most commercially successful sports NFT project ever launched, and it played a major part in the development of the NFT sector as a whole.

The morning after this was explained to him, the marketing director got in touch with us. He wanted to know how much it would cost to launch a set of NFTs for his football team. In no time at all we had a signed contract in place, and we got to work figuring out how, exactly, we were going to pull this off.

First things first, we had to work out the logistics of the collection – no easy task, given how many different types of NFT are available, all offering different functionalities and serving different purposes.

As we know, at their core NFTs are simply a one-off entry on the digital payment ledger that is the blockchain. However, this seemingly straightforward premise can be put to a dizzying amount of uses. For example, there are NFTs that represent objects in the physical world. Nike, in December 2021, designed a line of trainers and gave each pair a corresponding NFT. The NFT allowed people to verify ownership of the shoes; if someone stole them, they wouldn't have the matching NFT in their wallet, so the theft would be detectable.

However, most NFTs – and, indeed, almost all of the well-known collections like BAYC – are simply 'digital artworks'. These are also known as 'pfp NFTs', with 'pfp' standing for profile picture. These NFTs exist primarily to be used in lieu of a headshot on social media (in other words, they serve no purpose other than allowing their owners to flex). When these NFTs go on sale, the individual pieces form part of a 'collection' – a group of NFTs, each containing variations of the same image.

We needed to decide, therefore, how many NFTs the collection was to be composed of. Over a brainstorming call, I suggested 1,111 pieces. When quizzed on why, I had nothing to offer other than I thought the number sounded good – it was distinctive, but not wholly round, so it could lead people to think there was some kind of purpose or reason behind having so specific an amount of items up for sale. This seemed to suffice, and my suggestion was given a unanimous green light.

The next item on the agenda – deciding how the sale, or 'the drop', to employ some industry vernacular, was to be conducted.

There is no set, prescriptive way to drop an NFT collection. However, there is something of a formula that most projects tend to abide by, which bears similarities to the way in which ordinary tokens are launched. Typically, projects will spend a number of weeks or months building out a whitelist of future buyers, with those on the list given the (ostensibly) guaranteed opportunity to 'mint' an NFT on launch. 'Mint' just refers to the process of buying an NFT, during which the token itself gets assigned to a specific piece in the collection and entered onto the blockchain ledger.

At that time, without a whitelist, it was unlikely a drop would perform well. Investors had long ago gotten fed up with not being able to take part in NFT drops for the hottest collections, so they started refusing to even try to participate in a sale without a spot on the whitelist. However, there was no guarantee that potential buyers would end up minting an NFT even if they did obtain a coveted whitelist spot. So, in a bid to counteract this, and mitigate high dropout rates, projects began oversubscribing their whitelists.

The optimal oversubscription amount varies, but our rough rule-of-thumb guidance to the projects we went on to advise was that they should aim for between 500 and 1,000 per cent oversubscription. So, if they were looking to get 1,000 people from their whitelist minting an NFT, they should aim to get 5,000 people minimum on the whitelist itself. Should this criterion be met, projects could be reasonably confident that their collections would sell out on launch.

However, back then, green as we were in the ways of whitelist chicanery, we imprudently neglected this crucial ingredient. In our haste to get this project off the ground, and to dive into the marketing as quickly as possible, we decided to forgo the faff of setting up a whitelist, opting instead to take our chances and rely exclusively on the demand that we expected we would receive on the day of launch. This was our first mistake. Our second came in the form of the sales platform we were – or, rather, *weren't* – using.

Over many calls and email exchanges with the team's director of marketing, we implored him to conduct the sale through a custom-made site. At the time, this was the most commonly used medium through which NFT sales were conducted. We presented him with numerous examples and case studies of highly successful sales to have gone down this route, including BAYC themselves. And yet, somehow, he had convinced himself that the optimal sales tactic would be to list the NFTs directly onto OpenSea, in the hope that fans would buy straight from there.

OpenSea is the largest marketplace for NFTs. At its peak in January 2022, the platform recorded $4.87 billion in trading volume in that month alone. It dominates the NFT space, so much so that getting featured on the OpenSea homepage is widely regarded as the best publicity a project can get. Of course, that degree of prominence is primed for exploitation by those on the inside looking to make a quick buck. In May 2023 it came to light that one of the platform's product managers had been using his privileged knowledge of which assets would be featured on the coveted homepage to buy the NFTs in question, selling them shortly afterwards for profit. He was promptly prosecuted and convicted for fraud and money laundering in the first ever case of digital asset insider trading.

And yet, despite the dominance of OpenSea, we advised the football team that listing their NFTs for sale directly on the marketplace would be a disaster. For starters, the process for buying NFTs through OpenSea at the time was highly convoluted, and only allowed users to transact in a token called WETH, a version of Ethereum's Ether token, which enabled transactions to be pre-authorised, and executed them automatically at a later point in time. Without WETH, a buyer would have to wait for the person selling an NFT to accept their offer and authorise the transaction before the sale was able to go through.

While transacting in WETH wouldn't be an issue for seasoned blockchain users, we envisaged that the kind of people who would want to buy a football NFT would be unfamiliar with crypto. We couldn't imagine many of the team's faithful rushing to send their money to a trading platform, buy a load of Ether, send this to a crypto wallet, go onto Uniswap and exchange this for WETH, and then use this WETH to purchase one of the NFTs on OpenSea ...

And this issue led us into the third flaw in our plan, which was arguably the most insurmountable of all: trying to get fans of the football team interested in NFTs in the first place. Not only would we need to convince them that NFTs were worth buying, and show them how to make purchases, but we'd actually need to get them up to speed on what, exactly, an NFT even was. Up to now, all of our marketing had been targeted towards people who had at least a vague interest in crypto. Now, however, we were marketing to American football fans, many of whom would be at best clueless or indifferent, and at worst actively opposed to the concept.

However, these were all problems to deal with further down the line. We were still in Q3, and we weren't looking to conduct the drop until late Q4. And what we needed right now, before we could cross those ill-boding bridges, was to create the NFTs themselves. This meant designing the artwork, which was Paul's domain.

'Yeah, so look, I'm a bit tied up at the moment. The design team's pretty stretched. Until we bring someone new on board, we won't have bandwidth to tackle this.' Paul was tall, easily over 6 foot, with long gangly limbs and a round, protruding paunch. He was deliberately zany, with a wardrobe consisting almost entirely of loud Hawaiian shirts, which he wore all the year round, and which all had some kind of novelty print on. Today it was pineapples.

'So what do you suggest then?' I asked.

'We've got some freelancers on standby. We can use them if we need to. If we go through this guy I've been speaking to on Fiverr, it should save us a bit of cash as well. He's based in Africa somewhere – Nigeria I think – so should be cheap as chips.'

Fiverr is a marketplace for digital freelancer services. Through its site, you can hire anyone from graphic designers to copywriters and social media managers, all on an affordable hourly rate. It's an effective tool for startups that need a quick boost to their capacity, for low-level tasks. That use case, effective as it may be in certain situations, isn't quite applicable to NFT projects, which are marketing themselves as high-quality digital artworks or collectibles, with price tags to match. And yet, it's an all-too-common occurrence for projects to procure the services of Fiverr freelancers, pay them the bare minimum, and then sell their work on to 'collectors' with several extra zeros tacked onto the end.

'Right. How much is he?'

'How many NFTs do we need?'

'One thousand, one hundred and eleven.'

'Hmm. It'll take too long to make all of those from scratch. How about this: we do five variations, and say that the NFTs are split into four tiers of exclusivity. We make a one-of-one, a set of ten, another set of a hundred, and then a set of a thousand. That way, we can do all that rarity stuff which people like, but we only really need to make five separate images.'

'Not a bad idea, actually. How much would it cost for your guy to make five NFTs?'

'I'll have to get a quote, but reckon he should be able to knock up five images for a couple hundred bucks. How much are we selling them for?'

'Haven't worked out specific prices yet, but the Yanks are looking to make around eighty or ninety thousand from this. More or less. We're getting ten grand for the artwork, and I need to price up the marketing costs later.'

'Well, I'll keep all that quiet when I'm speaking to the freelancer!'

With this, I was about to wrap up the meeting and shepherd

everyone to the bar for a well-deserved beer, but first I wanted to get Archie's take on everything. He hadn't said a word for the 2 hours we had been speaking. Instead, he sat glued to his phone, typing eagerly, and dashing out of the room multiple times to make calls.

'Archie, mate, any thoughts from you at all? This is a big deal, our first major household name brand ...'

'Yeah, nice. All sounds good to me. Great work, team.'

'Right. Anything else to add at all? If you have any objections to what we've said you'd better raise them now before we get started.'

'Yeah, one thing to add actually,' Archie said, chucking his still-vibrating phone down onto the table, 'two words for you chaps: crypto conference.'

11

Blockchain Bingers

Crypto conferences are a cornerstone of the industry. Ostensibly, they exist to provide a space for the industry's leading proponents to come together and share ideas, with conference organisers proudly proclaiming them as providing a platform for thought leaders to shape the discussion around the industry's most pressing issues.

In reality, they're an excuse to have a piss-up.

Many companies in the industry have more marketing budget than they know what to do with. And, over the past few years, many firms decided that their surplus cash could be put to good use sponsoring the revelry and largesse of others, all while showing their investors that they were 'increasing brand awareness'. And, for the organisers, conferences were a great money spinner.

Archie's idea for us to host our own crypto conference would provide us with a potentially significant source of diversified income. It would also bring a huge number of cash-rich crypto projects right into our laps. If we put on a good event, and showed them a good time, they'd be lining up to do business with us.

We decided to waste no time, and scheduled the event for early November – just two months from initially coming up with the idea. We got straight to work on monetisation: the first thing we did, after coming up with the name itself, was to create a sponsorship deck. This outlined the different levels of promotion that projects could procure, what would be included in these, and how much they would set companies back. In no time at all, the first payments started rolling in. Just as we predicted, projects with exorbitant treasuries, acquired during the bull run, leapt at the opportunity to have their names up in lights at what we were telling them was going to be the biggest crypto conference the UK had ever seen. Within seven days of Archie coming up with the idea, we had taken over $50,000 worth of sponsorship, with much more than that in the pipeline.

We monetised every facet of the event imaginable. As well as the standard aspects of an event for which sponsorship would be expected – main stage sponsors, for example – we created sponsorships for the lighting, the sound system, the drinks and canapés, the VIP dinner that we were hosting the evening before the event, and everything in between. If there was something we were spending money on, we would devise a way to offset this with a sponsorship package. We would've had a sponsor for the air in the room, if we thought anyone would go for it.

And companies were lining up round the block to offer us their money. They even offered us suggestions for additional areas we could create sponsorship packages for. If we told them the main stages had already been earmarked, they would ask if they could plaster their logos around the entrance of the as-yet unprocured venue, and be the official 'lobby sponsors'. When the lobby was no longer available, we had projects asking if they could put some banners outside and be the 'exterior sponsors'. And, when every square-inch of pavement had been taken, we had people asking if they could be the official bathroom sponsors.

Miles, who by this point had assumed the title of Moonshot Advisors CFO, was projecting we would make anywhere from $300 to $500,000 on the event.

'Not bad, eh?' Archie said after work one day, when we had congregated around our favourite table on the roof for some celebratory cocktails. 'Aren't you chaps glad we decided to do this, and do it bloody quickly?'

We nodded our agreement, and Archie continued: 'We can't take our eyes off the clients though. This event is going to be a nice little earner for us, but we need recurring revenue. Don't forget, we're mainly doing this to get more clients.'

'Exactly,' agreed Miles. 'We're already on track to make a mill in our first year, not counting the event. And that's just from the clients we have now. If we take on new ones after we smash the conference, who knows what we could be in for.'

'But if we don't retain our existing clients, we're just moving one step forwards, two steps back. How're we doing on that front?' Archie addressed this question to me. As the only one of us to have ever worked in an agency before, I had fallen into the roles of general manager and head of client services, as well as running the content and press teams.

'Yeah, everything ticking along nicely. Happy customers all round, I'd say … except for Viaduct, of course.'

'Eugh. Not those guys. Most boring people I've ever worked with. Why are they even in crypto? They should be accountants, or some shit like that.'

Viaduct Capital was a relatively small client of ours. They couldn't afford to pay us a premium rate, on account of the issues they were having with fundraising: in essence, they just weren't glamorous enough to attract the top VCs. They were building a platform that would allow companies to tokenise real-world assets and use these to access liquidity from DeFi protocols. Basically, firms that struggled to raise money from banks could put their assets up as collateral, and then take out loans from decentralised lending platforms against those assets. Through the Viaduct platform, for example, a shipping company could take a loan out against the value of one of their boats. They would be matched up with a lender, who would send them a portion of the ship's value in crypto. Should the company default on their loan, then Viaduct would repossess their boat, sell it off and use the money to pay back the lender.

At the time, I thought this was a relatively solid concept (that is, compared to some of the other projects we were working with). I was quite taken by the real-world applications of the product – shortly after we started working with them, Viaduct announced a partnership with a company that issued student loans. Through the deal, the student loans company would be able to go onto the Viaduct platform, borrow a given amount of crypto from a DeFi lender, convert this into regular money, and issue this to Masters and PhD students who need to finance their degrees. Not all of my colleagues, though, were as interested as I was.

'What's wrong with those bean counters now then?' Archie asked. 'Do they have an interview coming up, and need our help growing a personality?'

'They're launching their token.'

'Good. It's a good time for it. Although I don't know who the fuck they think is going to buy it.'

'Yeah, it's a good time, except they're not doing it this month. They're looking at November. Early November, the same time as our event.' Paul exhaled melodramatically to my left, while Archie narrowed his eyes and started tapping his vape aggressively against his own temple.

I shared their sentiments. Token launches were a lot of work. They involved at least one of the founders grafting almost round the clock in the run-up, along with a host of other team members from virtually every department in the company. This was mainly because our clients, despite what they might have their prospective investors believe, either didn't know how to do most of the required tasks themselves or were simply unaware of just how much work there was to do in the run-up to a token launch. However, in the case of Viaduct there was a silver lining, which would provide us with ample incentive to tolerate the additional workload: for the entirety of our engagement with them, we had been taking 30 per cent of our fee in project tokens.

This was an arrangement we leapt at whenever the opportunity arose. It was beneficial to all involved. For clients, it lessened the amount of cash they had to pay us upfront, which was always welcomed by early-stage startups who might not necessarily have raised substantial funds yet. For us, it provided highly sought-after private sale allocations. We obtained exposure to the huge upside potential of new tokens being launched onto the market. In addition, we insisted on all the tokens we received through these arrangements being fully unlocked – meaning we could sell them all as soon as they launched.

This was a prevalent practice that marketing agencies and crypto services providers engaged in, and a highly lucrative one. In the case of Viaduct Capital, we were owed around $30,000 in tokens, at the private sale price. Because the private sale price is always lower than the price at which a token is listed, it meant that, even if their token only appreciated by 500 per cent from their listing price – which, in those days, was not difficult to achieve in the slightest – we would be set to make around $200,000.

'Thing is,' asked Paul, as I finished giving my co-founders a rundown of our projected profits, 'if we sell them all straight away, won't that piss off Nomisma?'

'Yeah, maybe,' replied Archie, 'but after the conference, we'll be done with them. We want to be going after the biggest protocols in the game, not the shitcoins they send our way.'

Nomisma Labs was a VC, and another partner of ours. They were a small team, made up of three or four affable Welshmen, based jointly out of Cardiff and Singapore. They differed from other VCs in that they actually provided some degree of guidance and support to the projects they invested in. Beyond just writing them cheques, they helped secure partnerships with other service providers and paired them up with launchpads, exchanges and the like. And a select few projects, in which they saw the most potential, were put onto their 'accelerator' programme.

This was essentially an incubation, but with some additional perks, such as having the director of the Nomisma accelerator, Cillian, join the project team on secondment until their token or platform launched. Cillian was a boy of just 22 years of age. He had joined Nomisma as an intern after leaving school and worked his way up the ladder. He was widely regarded by those who knew him as one of the most effective, hard-working and unpleasant people in the industry. He was a real hatchet man. His day-to-day tasks involved whipping service providers into shape, putting the fear of God into projects' junior team members (and senior team members, for that matter) and handling the more clandestine components of token launches. He was a big asset for the accelerator projects he joined, and a big pain in the arse for us.

Our problem with Nomisma, however, wasn't Cillian. We could deal with him. Far more fundamental was that all their portfolio companies – even those that made it onto the accelerator programme – were of a laughably low quality. Take Stamped and Sealed, for example – this was a particularly half-baked venture they backed, which sought to create 'rare stamp NFTs'. Their plan was to issue NFTs that each represented ownership of a valuable, collectible stamp. Stamped and Sealed would hold onto the items for their owners, supposedly in secure bank vaults, so that they were kept in good condition. The value of the NFT was supposedly tied to the stamp so, as the stamp appreciated in price over time, so did the NFT. Holders could also choose to cash in their NFT (or 'burn' it – an industry team meaning to permanently destroy) and take delivery of the rare stamp whenever they wanted, to do with as they pleased.

This was, by all accounts, a highly tenuous proposition, which was made all too apparent to us on our initial call with them. The CEO of the project, Alfred, proudly described himself as an avid 'philatelist': which just means stamp collector – and told us that he had been dying to find a way to combine this with his other great passion in life – technology. Crypto, and NFTs specifically, gave him the perfect opportunity to do this, so he joined up with the Nomisma team and launched Stamped and Sealed. However, once we got down to brass tacks, the enthusiasm with which he recounted his project's backstory was quickly stamped out.

We started quizzing Alfred about the viability of Stamped and Sealed, and he fell at the very first hurdle: he couldn't think up a single reason as to why anyone would want to buy an NFT of a rare stamp, as opposed to just the stamp itself. When pressed, he all but admitted that the NFT angle was only there to tap into the hype that surrounded them at the time, and that it would actually be easier – and likely cheaper – for people to just buy the items through the usual channels ...

'Heads up, Alfred isn't with Stamped and Sealed any more. Don't message him about anything, that fucker's dead to us.'

Thus read a message we received from Cillian, the day after our call. As it turned out, Nomisma had not only invested in Stamped and Sealed's token, but also in the project's equity. So much so that they held a controlling stake and, shortly after our call, they fired the stumped stamp collector. By acknowledging that his project was nothing more than a cash grab, Alfred had unwittingly committed the cardinal sin of crypto – so Cillian sent him packing.

In their efforts to salvage their investment, and dress up what was clearly a useless, ill-thought-through idea, Nomisma then paired up Stamped and Sealed with a 'project advisor' – a high-profile individual who is given free tokens or NFTs in exchange for promotion. In this case, the project advisor was a social media influencer and alleged millionaire entrepreneur from India, called Ravinder Menon. Boasting over 2 million followers on Instagram, 27-year-old Ravinder had recently been featured in the Forbes '30 under 30' list, and ran what he claimed to be a number of highly successful tech companies.

Nomisma added him to a number of WhatsApp groups with the Stamped and Sealed team and us, to coordinate the publication of various articles in outlets that Menon occasionally contributed to – including the likes of *CoinTelegraph*, one of the industry's leading publications with around 3 million readers per month, and also *Forbes* itself. However, the grade-A coverage he promised never came to fruition, which set alarm bells ringing. And yet the consternation at Menon's media ineptitude was nothing compared to a discovery made later by Cillian: as it turned out, Menon had recently been denounced by a number of prominent YouTubers and news outlets as a complete fraud. There was a wealth of evidence revealing his lavish lifestyle, which he so ostentatiously bragged about across social media, to be nothing but a facade, and his businesses to be complete non-entities.

Over the course of several years, Menon had made a number of outlandish claims across his social media platforms, and in interviews with high-profile media outlets. Among these included an assertion that he was personally mentored by none other than the billionaire visionary behind Apple: Steve Jobs. Menon claimed Jobs approached him to 'harness the power of the app store'. However, when grilled on this in a later interview with a prominent scam-exposing YouTuber, Menon backtracked on his story. He admitted that he merely *considered* Jobs a mentor, because he had watched inspirational videos of him on the internet. Menon's confession continued, and he eventually yielded that 'the internet is [his] mentor'. When confronted about the interview, Menon tried to claim that the author of the original piece had manipulated the information he had provided her with. And yet, even to this day, the article remains live on the outlet's website, along with all its spurious content.

Keen to avoid any reputational damage that could arise from an association with someone so publicly exposed and excoriated, Cillian kicked Menon off the project, retracting his project advisor role – although, in a manner typical to his character and way of oper- ating, Cillian didn't feel it was necessary to take the time to inform Ravinder he was off the project. He simply stopped replying to any of his messages and ordered us to do the same.

'If that prick messages any of you, just give him the fucking silent treatment.' Cillian had a permanently blocked nose, which lent con- siderable menace to everything he said. I couldn't help but wonder if his nasal congestion was on account of regular physical alterca- tions, or just an unhealthy lifestyle spent indoors glued to screens. Needless to say, I never had the temerity to ask.

'Complete radio silence,' Cillian continued, reinforcing his point. 'We don't want to touch Menon with a bargepole. He was supposed to make a sizable investment in the project, so if he still wants to do that, we'll take his money, but that's it. No public association whatsoever.'

But Cillian needn't have worried about a public association – the Stamped and Sealed project didn't last long. They were unable to meet their soft cap fundraising target and closed down shortly after we created their website, rebranded them, and billed them thirty grand for the work. They paid up and sent what money they had left back to their disgruntled investors. It turned out that even crypto VCs, with their notoriously high threshold for nonsense, wouldn't give such a shoddy project their stamp of approval.

But, this notable failure aside, Nomisma did send a lot of business our way. And not all of their projects were consigned so hopelessly to failure. Some – like Viaduct – actually stood a chance, slim though it might be, of seeing some reasonable token price appreciation. If they got their marketing right. Which, with the amount of money we stood to make, I resolved to ensure they would.

12

Liquidity

As our conference drew ever nearer, the workload we were dealing with began to spiral out of control. Along with all the logistics around the event, which was the domain of Archie and a pair of newly hired events coordinators, Bradley and Claire, and the launch of the Viaduct token, which was my domain, we had around ten or eleven retained clients to service, along with a slew of ad hoc project work on the go. And, to top it all off, we still had the American football NFT launch to think about, which was scheduled for only a few days after our conference. Meaning that, even after the big event, there was no reprieve in sight. Safe to say, we were all feeling the strain. Beanbags had been acquired en masse, and it quickly became the norm to come into the office in the morning and find at least one person asleep on them, having not gone home the night before.

And then, to make matters even worse, a few days before the conference was due to start, we received the details of how Viaduct were planning to launch their token. It was scheduled to take place in just three weeks, so they really hadn't done us any favours by leaving it this late to tell us. Or, for that matter, by the platform they had chosen to launch on.

Rather than going down the tried-and-tested route of selling tokens on a launchpad, and then following this up with a centralised or decentralised exchange listing, Viaduct were trying something new: an LBP auction.

'LBP' stands for 'liquidity bootstrapping pool', and it was supposedly a fairer way to launch tokens onto the market, and to set subsequent exchange listing prices. Essentially, they were a variation on a 'Dutch auction': a type of auction in which the price starts high and gradually gets lower until a buyer is found. LBPs put a spin on this by having the price jump up again every time a buy order is put in. There is also a constant downward pressure on the price, meaning that, if no buys get put in, the price will constantly decrease until either a level of demand is found, the auction ends, or the price reaches zero. A project conducting an LBP would put a given number of their tokens on sale and set a starting price. This would then slowly and consistently decrease, until someone buys some of the tokens. When they do, the price jumps up in proportion to how many tokens are bought, and then continues to decrease. After a given amount of time – which the project sets – the auction ends. Whatever level the price is at when the auction ends is the price at which the token gets listed onto a decentralised exchange.

LBPs were a novel concept at the time and, like everything new in the crypto space, there was a considerable buzz around them. At the time Viaduct was looking to launch their token, not many of these auctions had taken place. And the few that had taken place all saw tremendous levels of uptake. Take Mask Network, for example. They're a browser extension, allowing users to send both crypto and encrypted messages through social media sites. In February 2021 they launched their token via an LBP. By the time their auction had finished, they had raised $39 million, and their token had surged in price by over 200 per cent.

However, with this much money up for grabs, LBPs inevitably caught the attention of scammers. In late October, less than a month before Viaduct were scheduled to launch their token, a now infamous project called AnubisDAO held an auction of their own. The team behind the project was fully anonymous, with their main developer known only by the alias 'Beerus'. By some accounts, Beerus and his team had only come up with the idea to launch a project two days before their auction. They saw an opportunity to capitalise on the hype, not just around LBPs, but also the dog-themed token fad – fuelled by the likes of Dogecoin – which was engulfing the industry at the time. They spun up a brand in a mere two days, featuring the Ancient Egyptian, canine-headed deity Anubis, announced their existence to the world, and got their LBP auction under way.

The sale was scheduled to last for 24 hours. Within 20 hours they had raised $60 million. And within 21 hours they had pulled the rug. The developer, Beerus, removed all the funds from the auction and sent them to an unknown wallet address.

'Who the hell is sending their money to a project that only went public on the actual day of their token launch?' Miles asked, as the co-founders and around half a dozen of our team stood round my screen in the office, reading a news article about the scam.

'Yeah, bloody hell,' Paul chuckled. 'Imagine how much they could've rugged if they'd bothered with a website. And that logo ... looks like it was designed in Microsoft Paint!'

'Nah, fuck that,' said Archie, with severity in his voice. 'Anyone sending money to a project run by a bloke called Beerus deserves to get rugged.'

I didn't find any of this particularly funny. Even if people had been foolish to buy into a project with so many red flags, a lot of money had been stolen. I just wanted to discuss business.

'How do we think this is going to affect Viaduct's launch then?' I asked, trying to make my impatience as clear in my tone as it was in my expression.

'Bloody hell, here he is,' smirked Paul. 'Had a punt on Anubis yourself, did you?'

'Don't worry about Viaduct,' Miles said, batting Paul's elbow away for me. 'The $60 million rug is a good thing. Shows there's demand in these LBPs.'

'Yeah, but do we not think people are going to be a bit wary of using the platform now? As in, there could be some anxiety around LBPs after people lost so much money.'

'Look, fuck it,' said Archie, strolling back to his seat. 'This is Cillian's problem. Let's see what that little nutter has to say about it all, and just leave the decision with him.'

We raised our concerns with Cillian, but he dismissed them with typical curtness. He said that the potential upside of an LBP was limitless, and no one was going to care that one or two projects had rugged. People in crypto expected that kind of stuff. In fact, it would look weird if projects *hadn't* run off with funds. It would show that there was no interest in LBP launches.

We didn't push the point. We didn't challenge Cillian on his conclusion that scams were a bullish indicator of the popularity of a launch platform. After all, he was running the show. For once the onus wasn't on us alone, and if things went badly it would be Cillian's head which would roll.

With the Viaduct situation decidedly out of our hands, I allowed myself to turn some of my attention back to the conference. While Archie had largely been holding things down on that front, the reality of how big the event was shaping up to be was beginning to dawn on us.

We had initially envisaged it would be a nice little earner for us, and nothing more. But it seemed we had underestimated just how much demand there was for these types of events. On every front – from sponsors, speakers, media partners, attendees – our estimates were getting knocked out of the park.

It was all hands on deck. So I rolled up my sleeves and got to work.

13

The Grifter's Gavel

After weeks of round-the-clock grind, the day of our event finally rolled round. Or, that is to say, the *first* day of our event. In our zeal to bring in as much sponsorship money as possible, we realised, around a month before the event, that we had sold too much of just about everything. We had sold more attendance tickets than the venue had capacity for, more speaking slots than there was time for, and more sponsorships than there was wall space for.

To correct for this, and to make sure we didn't have a horde of crypto founders demanding their money back, we had to make our event a two-day affair. The first day was to be completely virtual – partly because we were in tech, and doing things online was expected, but mainly because, with a virtual event, we could host more speakers and display more logos.

The first day of the event passed largely without incident. Barring a few minor hiccups – a couple of sponsors losing internet connection during their keynote speeches, and a few speakers not turning up – the day was largely a success. Through a herculean effort, in the run-up to the event we had managed to transform our office into the crypto equivalent of Broadcasting House.

The room we normally worked out of had been put to use as a storage space for all the surplus gear we had ordered for the second day. Almost none of the tattered blue carpet was visible beneath the mountains of cardboard boxes. At the far end of our floor, a long, narrow room was being used as a command centre. Rows of monitors had been lined up against the glass partition, displaying the dozen or so panels taking place at any given time. Two small and particularly squalid rooms in the middle of the floor were being used as studios, for the members of our team who were giving talks.

Prior to the conference we had only ever entered these rooms once. After that first foray we decided they were too rancid to step foot in again. But now wasn't the time to be squeamish, so we held our nerve (and our breath) and got on with it. By the time the panel I was moderating had finished, I had mastered the knack of asking questions while breathing as little as possible, and only ever through my mouth.

When the day came to a close, even with the makeshift setup of the whole situation, we were extremely pleased with ourselves. We had lawyers, investment bankers, media personalities, prominent entrepreneurs, politicians, and even former Cabinet ministers all taking part in our conference, sharing their views on crypto with the thousands of watchers tuned in. And, in their eagerness to position themselves as being at the forefront of the hottest trend in finance and tech, many of these luminaries even braved the rank tumult of our office and gave their talks from HQ.

For me and my co-founders, this was all a massive trip. We felt like we were leading the media arm of a resistance movement, running a pirate TV station that was broadcasting the revolution to legions of dissidents – our blockchain brothers in arms – all ready to bring down the system.

It was with these fanciful ideas swirling round our heads that we left our office and headed out for the main event of the day: the VIP dinner.

While the livestreams and virtual panel discussions had been borne from necessity, and very much made up on the hoof, the dinner before the main event had been in the planning for a long time. In fact, it was one of the main reasons we were hosting the conference. We had long spoken about getting all of our most valuable contacts in one place, to showcase to current and prospective clients how prominent and influential our network of connections was.

We had been looking forward to it for weeks, and no expense was spared for the occasion. We booked out a large, swanky central London restaurant, filled up their 150-person capacity with our top contacts, ordered the choicest menu options they had to offer, and an excessive quantity of their finest wines to wash it all down with. Truth be told, it was a bit lavish, but the way we saw it no one would want to do business with us if we didn't go at least a bit over the top. Crypto is a gaudy game, and nouveau riche crypto bros appreciate when events are a bit flashy. Plus, we had an image to project: we wanted to make the prospective clients there that night think that we were making so much money we could take or leave their business. They'd go mad for that.

Or, at least, those were the reassurances we rattled off to each other in moments of panic when we needed to justify dropping twenty grand on a dinner.

Our largesse, however, was vindicated a few days prior to the event when we received an email from Nereus, a 'layer 2' network (basically a network that sits on top of another network like Ethereum, which is supposed to make it easier to transact on layer 1). They got in touch to say they'd heard about our dinner and were keen to sponsor the whole thing. Whoever said that there's no such thing as a free lunch – or dinner in this case – clearly never worked in crypto.

Not only did we recoup the full twenty grand, but we even managed to make a profit. All in exchange for plastering the Nereus banners around the restaurant. We didn't think they'd be too fazed by this fee; they were a carbon copy of another, larger layer 2 network (or, in industry parlance, a 'fork' – a project that copies another project's code, for its own use). Their copy-and-paste code base had recently achieved a $150 million valuation, with minimal work required from the Nereus team. So the money they sent our way was probably just pocket change to them. The best part was, their team was based in India, so we didn't even have to give up any seats for them. We couldn't have hoped for a more ideal outcome.

The only downside to an otherwise triumphant evening was the oppressive headache to which I awoke the next morning. But, barring that, and a slightly parched throat, I didn't feel too bad at all – well rested, even, which came as a pleasant surprise. However, after picking up my phone and checking my messages, I realised with horror why this was: I had slept through my alarm, by no less than 4 hours. I was now late for my own event.

After I had showered, drunk my bodyweight in coffee, and eaten a near-fatal dose of paracetamol, I stormed across town to the conference. It didn't help that I lived in the depths of south London, and the venue was in the north, meaning I had to traverse the entire diameter of a heaving capital to get there. Luckily, I was afforded one avenue of distraction from the vice-like grip of panic throttling me: as of 10 a.m. that morning, the Viaduct auction was under way.

Sitting on the dank, crowded bus, getting increasingly agitated at the glacial pace at which it crawled through London's congested streets, I caught up on that morning's proceedings. It didn't take long for my mood to liven as I learned the sale had got off to a phenomenal start; in just the first 5 minutes of the auction, Viaduct had sold $50,000 worth of tokens. And in the next, this had jumped to $300,000, as a single buyer put in an order for nearly a quarter of a million dollars' worth of their DUCT token. And then, from what I could make out, things started going insane.

Their auction seemed to have caught the attention of the Count of Monte Crypto, one of the most highly regarded influencers in the space (in spite of the name). He was a figure held in the utmost esteem by his multitude of followers, for the sound investment advice he gave and the halfway decent research and analysis he carried out on projects. Compared to most of the grifters in the space, he was something of a breath of fresh air.

The auction caught his eye organically. Neither us nor the Viaduct team had paid him to promote it (and, as rumour had it, he was one of the only influencers in the space whose influence couldn't be bought and sold). The morning of the sale, he was hosting a YouTube livestream, where he gave Viaduct's auction a shout-out. He didn't even mention the project by name; he simply said there was an LBP going on, which he had heard of and was interested in. That was all it took to change the game for Viaduct.

Within literal seconds of the Count mentioning the auction, Viaduct received a windfall of bidders. The line on the chart displayed on my phone screen, indicating the price the token was being offered at, had shot up. It was a vertical wall, which rose higher and higher by the second. After about 10 minutes, it plateaued slightly, curved into a peak, and then straightened out. By the time the frenzy had subsided, Viaduct had sold just under $9 million of tokens. All before I had even rolled out of bed.

Despite my monumental fuck-up, the second day of our conference was off to a blinding start. And I hadn't even made it to the venue yet.

When I finally arrived at the event, my hangover had subsided slightly. But, when I saw the conference in full swing, with scores of people standing around on the steps leading up to the entrance, the panic returned. The drama of the Viaduct auction had kept it at bay, but now it was back, and it was even worse than before. I rushed into the imposingly large foyer of the conference venue in a state of visible distress. This was quickly exaggerated as I moved through the bustling crowd, trying to get my bearings in a venue that I had never been to before. I looked around, trying to find someone I knew.

It was Alice I encountered first, which came as a huge relief. Alice was a new account manager we had brought in, around the time we decided to host the conference. A former teacher in her late twenties, Alice had realised that, after three years on the Teach First programme, she had no desire to spend her working hours surrounded by a room full of screaming children, and wanted to work with adults instead. Why she thought crypto would be any better was beyond me, but she was a huge asset to the firm: she was eminently sensible, and often acted as a calming and rational influence on the boisterous crypto bros. Last night, however, had been an exception.

Alice had been at the penthouse of Silver Crest Capital co-founder David, on which around two dozen of us had descended the previous evening after dinner. When I took my leave in the early hours of the morning, she was still going strong, and showed no signs of calling it a night (or a morning) any time soon. The last I saw of her, she was doing laps of David's rooftop pool, loudly proclaiming herself to be some sort of tropical fish. She would, I therefore hoped, be somewhat sympathetic to my sorry state. I imagined we would smile guiltily at one another, lend each other some mutual words of reassurance, debrief over last night's antics, and join forces to find the rest of our team, blagging our way through our late arrivals.

'Bloody hell, you look like shit.' Alice gave a quiet laugh, which seemed to stem from self-satisfaction rather than any amusement.

'What time did you get here?'

'Been here since 8 a.m. Caught the opening speeches, spoke to some clients and did some good networking. It's been great. I suppose anything's easy after you've had to teach thirty children on a hangover.' Alice was still laughing, louder now. She looked as if last night hadn't even happened.

'Have you seen the others?'

'Course I've seen them, I've been here all day. Oh yeah, they're looking for you by the way.' What little colour I had in my face drained straight out as soon as she said this.

'Right. Did they say why?'

'No idea, but they seemed pissed. Well, not pissed, more scared. Think something's going on. Don't know what, though, sorry.'

Alice drifted away into the crowd, and I set about trying to find one of my co-founders. I pushed my way to one of the walls of the foyer, outside the crowd, against which sponsors had their booths set up. I began working my way around the perimeter of the room, hoping to get a better vantage point by being out of the fray. As I neared the end of the first wall, I spotted Archie sitting at a trestle table in Viaduct's booth, with two of their team members sitting either side of him, and several more huddled around. They were all staring fervently into a pair of monitors hooked up to a laptop.

None of them seemed to notice me making my way over to them. When I got to the table, no one looked up. I pinched Archie's shoulder, but he still didn't turn around.

'Archie, you all right, mate?'

He glanced up reluctantly, but then on seeing me stood bolt upright.

'Fucking hell, here he is. Where the fuck have you been?'

'Um, you know, been around. Networking mainly.'

'Look, something's happening. We need your help.' Archie pulled one of the Viaduct team members out of his chair. He was a thin, rakish boy who looked like he was fresh out of uni. Despite being manhandled out of his seat, he didn't take his eyes off the screen. I was then thrust into his chair.

'What's going on?' I asked, turning to Konrad – Viaduct's COO. He was an unassuming man in his early forties, from somewhere in central Europe; I never bothered to find out where exactly. Sporting a buzz cut, nondescript glasses and a green plaid lumberjack's shirt, he looked like the kind of guy you might see nosing around a public library in the middle of the day. But, despite his mundane appearance, I had suspected for some time that he was more sly and cunning than his ready-salted exterior let on.

He spoke without looking away from the laptop: 'Hey man, good to see you. Great event.'

'Yeah, thanks. What's going on?' I asked again, with more insistence this time.

'Ah, a bit of a problem, man. You know we've got this auction going on?'

'Yeah, I checked it about an hour ago. Doing bloody well!'

'Eh? Man, it's not doing so well now. Something's happened, and it isn't good.'

'Shit,' I said. The first thought that crossed my mind was that people had started selling back their tokens and withdrawing their funds. 'Don't worry, I can get some more influencers posting. Give me a second.' I went to pull out my laptop, but Konrad grabbed my arm.

'No! Brother, don't do that. It's not because people aren't buying. Basically,' Konrad took a breath, and pinched his nose, 'basically, man, one of our developers has been selling tokens into the auction.'

'Shit.'

'Yeah, not good. And people have noticed, and they're pissed.'

At this point I looked at the screen. The $9 million they had raised so far had been slashed in half. The graph on the screen looked like an upside-down V.

'So, fill me in, why's he doing this? And how has he even got tokens to sell?'

'You know we've been using an outsourced dev house?' I didn't, but nodded anyway. 'Well, one of the developers says we haven't paid him what we owe him.'

'Ah, right. And have you?'

'Well, no. But man, that's not the point. We were going to. As soon as the auction was done.'

'How much has he sold? And where did the tokens come from?'

Konrad looked like he was in physical pain. 'So, basically ... all the project's tokens are fully unlocked.'

'What the fuck.'

'Yeah, I know, but brother there's a reason we had to do that. It's a technical issue: we couldn't lock them up before we minted them. So we were going to lock them after mint. Or just mint them and not touch them. Same thing.'

'Bloody hell. And how much has he sold?'

'Umm, I don't know, man. I need to check.' Just then, Cillian marched up to the table. He was talking into a phone, which he was holding up to his ear with his right hand, and was typing on another phone with his left hand.

'Here's Cillian, he'll know. Cillian!' Konrad said, waving. Cillian looked at him, finished typing, and came over. 'How much did he sell?'

'One second,' Cillian said into his phone, then turning to Konrad. 'What?'

'How much did he sell?'

'Fucker sold ninety grand.' He looked down at me, lifted his chin curtly as a greeting and, in an almost pleading tone, said: 'But we didn't even owe him that much. We only owed him thirty.'

'Yeah, thirty; it's nothing, man,' said Konrad.

'Ninety is nothing either,' said Cillian sharply, 'but to these fucking investors, it seems like a lot. But that's not the point. They've all looked at the seller's wallet. It's holding all our tokens. They know it's someone on the team.'

'Shit,' I said.

'Yeah, and there are enough tokens there to drain all the funds in the auction, if the dev wanted to.'

I rubbed my eyes. 'So, what's the plan?'

'I've been speaking to the dev. He's on the phone now actually.' There was a clatter of chairs, as Konrad and the rest of the Viaduct team all rushed to their feet.

'What's he saying?'

'Man, tell him to put the money back.'

'Ask him what the fuck he's playing at.'

'Look, shut up. He hasn't said anything for 20 minutes. I've been trying to talk to him, but he isn't replying with anything.' Cillian looked over at me. 'He's autistic,' he said, as if this was essential information needed to get me up to speed. I stared back at him, scowling and shaking my head. 'What?' he said. 'That's not offensive. He's genuinely autistic.'

'Cillian, man, pass me the phone,' said Konrad.

'Fine, you speak to the guy, I've had enough of him anyway. Been on with the fucking guy for an hour now.'

Konrad took the phone and headed for the exit.

'Okay, look,' I said. 'Let's assume he puts the funds back. We need to do something as soon as possible afterwards.' I pointed at the screen. 'Before everyone else withdraws.' The right-hand side line of the inverted V was now noticeably lower than it had been 10 minutes ago, when I first looked at it. Even more money had been flowing out of the auction.

'Well, what do you suggest?'

I looked at Cillian for a moment and, without saying anything, started bashing out a statement explaining that the developer had sold the tokens in error, and that they had now all been returned, and all investors made whole again. The statement went on to say that all the unlocked tokens in the dev wallet would be sent, as soon as possible after the auction had concluded, to a custodian.

Custodians are regulated third parties that control a crypto project's treasury funds to ensure no embezzlement or misappropriation can take place (needless to say, custodians aren't used by the vast majority of crypto projects).

When I was done, I showed the statement to Cillian. 'Like it, mate, like it,' he said. 'What's that shit about a custodian, though?'

'If you want people to continue contributing to the auction, you'll need to say that.'

'Fucking hell. But what about if we just send all our tokens to an exchange, once we list on an exchange, and tell people that they're now with a custodian?'

'What you do with your tokens,' I said, 'is your business. I can't exactly stop you, if that's what you're planning to do.'

Cillian seemed placated by this and walked off with a look of concentration on his face.

An hour passed, and we remained huddled around the laptops in the booth, watching the funds steadily drain out of the auction, and the anger steadily rise in the Viaduct Telegram group. There was around $4 million left when Konrad returned. He was holding his phone triumphantly in the air as he strode over to us.

'All sorted, he returned the funds.' Konrad had almost a crazed look about him, as if he were riding on a massive high.

'Bloody brilliant! How did you do it?' gushed the person to my right, in a Viaduct hoodie.

'Ha! Brother, I'll tell you, it was easy. I just told him, I said, "Look, man, you need to put these funds back. If you don't, we know your address. We know where you live in Wales. You don't want Cillian showing up at your house, do you, brother? Would be a nasty surprise for your mum!" He still lives with his mum, can you believe it?'

'And that was it?'

'And that was it. He said he's done it, just said that now. Can we check?'

Sure enough, the funds had been returned. I took a screenshot of the transaction, inserted that into the document with the statement, and then sent it out on Telegram. Straight away I opened the tab that had the graph showing the funds in the auction. It had shot up. Viaduct received just over $1 million in inflows within 20 seconds of the statement being posted. We watched as the funds climbed back up, passing 5 million, then 6 million, until eventually reaching the level they had been at before the dev's sale was noticed. And then they surpassed even that. All within the space of under 10 minutes.

'Well, that's that then,' Archie said. 'Market seemed to like the statement. Well done, mate.' He gave me a congratulatory thump on the back.

'Let's see how much we make from this then,' said Konrad. I looked at him, and saw he was literally rubbing his hands together with excitement.

I shut my laptop, stood up, and made my way out of the booth. Konrad began moving in for an embrace, but I shot him a thin-lipped smile and walked off.

I wanted to be outside. I needed some air. To digest what had just happened and ruminate on my part in all of it. I felt dirty, and I wasn't sure why. I needed to think.

14

Pay Day

The rest of the event passed by in a blur. Speeches were made, panel discussions were held, and Archie wrapped things up with a suitably enthusiastic and trite closing address on the main stage. After a lengthy ovation and a short debrief with our team, the conference attendees descended en masse to the after-party. We had hired out the entirety of a large, four-storey bar in Holborn for the occasion. With three dance floors, a 500-person capacity, as many free drinks as could be quaffed and a licence to stay open until 4 a.m., the venue was a huge hit with everyone in attendance.

I stayed until the bar closed, but didn't join the fifty or so revellers who decided to keep the party going at an after-hours club in Soho. One of the event speakers claimed he would be able to secure us a table for at least another 3 hours. Instead, I headed for home. Despite it being the early hours of Saturday morning, I had to do at least half a day's work on waking up – whatever time that may be – as well as a full day on Sunday. So I said my drunken goodbyes, hailed a cab, and asked the driver to stop at an off-licence on the way so I could pick up a nightcap.

I awoke the next day just after midday, with a pounding headache and a bitter taste in my mouth – partly from the recollection of what had occurred with Viaduct the day before, but mainly from the booze. Having been out on both Thursday and Friday night, I was now facing the first and second day of a hangover simultaneously. But I had too much on my plate to mope around feeling sorry for myself. The first item on my to-do list: speak to Cillian and get him to send over the tokens we were owed. I would then have to perform the mind-numbing task of manually selling these off in batches, over a period of several hours, so as not to impact the price too much. It was a prospect I was dreading.

After making myself a cafetière of coffee as thick as tar, I called Cillian. He answered on the third attempt and sounded as bad as I felt.

'What's up bro, why are you calling me this early? I only went to bed an hour or two ago.'

'Sounds like you had a good night. Well, sorry to bother, but I just need to get those tokens. I've sent you our wallet address on Telegram, so if you're able to ping them over now, I'll let you get back to sleep!'

'Huh, what tokens?'

'We agreed 30 per cent of our monthly fee would be paid in tokens, at the private sale price. Did it as a favour, to bring your monthly fee down when you didn't have much money.'

'Oh, right. Yeah, that, got it. What was the vesting on those, again? Private round?'

'No vesting. We agreed fully unlocked.'

'Ha! Yeah right. How many tokens are you owed?'

'502,343.'

'Yeah, look man, that's not happening.'

'We agreed with Konrad, before we even signed the contract.'

'Is it in the service agreement?'

'It should be. Let me check, bear with.' I put Cillian on hold and dug out the contract we had in place with Viaduct. My heart sank, as I realised that we hadn't actually specified in writing that our tokens were to be fully unlocked. Viaduct was one of our earliest clients, before we had any proper legal support in place. The contracts we used back then consisted of a generic template I had found online, which I'd then tailor to each individual client. I have never had a scrap of legal training in my life, so these contracts were about as watertight as a sieve.

I picked up my phone, unmuted it, and held it to my ear. Cillian seemed to be making some kind of gurgling noise, which I pretended

I didn't hear. 'Okay I just checked. It's not in there. But we definitely agreed. Maybe in an email somewhere, but probably just on a call. It's our standard terms.'

'If it's not in the contract, I can't do it. How much money is half a million tokens worth?'

'Let me check.' I pulled up their price chart and opened the calculator app on my phone. '502,343 tokens, trading at $0.82 dollars right now ... should be worth just over $411,000.'

'Fucking hell. There's no way I'm sending you that. If people see you selling that much, it'll fuck the whole project.'

'I won't sell them all, only some, and I'll do that in batches.'

'It's not happening mate, forget it.'

'We're owed those tokens, Cillian.' I tried my best to sound resolute.

'Look, man,' Cillian said, quite calmly, as if fully aware of the position of power he was in here, 'maybe I can send you 10 per cent. Maybe. And then the rest on the private vesting schedule, of 10 per cent a month.'

'Twenty-five now, twenty-five each month. How does that sound?'

'That would still be a $100,000 sell. No way.'

'I told you, I'll sell it in batches.'

'Yeah, that's what everyone says. Even the ones who start off doing that give up after a while, 'cos it's fucking long.'

'I'm not going to just get fed up and dump them all. Not least of all because you then just wouldn't send us the rest.'

'You're right there. But still, it could mess up the price, even in batches. How about this,' Cillian said, after pausing for a few seconds, 'we have almost 15 million in the bank. I'll just send you the cash for 25 per cent of the tokens. And then, from next month, the tokens themselves.'

'That could work.' We then entered a protracted price negotiation – it was a tradable token, in a market that doesn't close on weekends, so the price was fluctuating while we were on the phone, and would likely continue to do so while Cillian got the funds ready to send. We finally settled on a price: $0.89 per coin, meaning we would take away just over $110,000. Our biggest ever single payment to date, and the first time we would have cleared over 100 grand in one go.

I hung up, after assurances Cillian would send the money as soon as he had got a bit more sleep. He didn't trust himself to send a six-figure transaction while still not sober from the previous night. I didn't blame him, and even appreciated his caution.

Sure enough, a few hours later, as evening approached, my phone pinged. It was a notification from our wallet app, informing us we had received tokens. This was followed straight away by a Telegram message from Cillian: a winking emoji, and the words 'enjoy boss x.'

I opened the wallet app and looked at the balance. With Viaduct's payment and the funds we already had in there, our balance was well over $375,000. And that was just one wallet. We had several set up, plus three or four bank accounts. I put my phone away and, with an ear-to-ear smile etched on my face, I carried on with the task I had been doing before the funds came through: typing out an email to the American football team we had been hired by.

Celebrations for our milestone payment – and, indeed, for the overall success of our event – were short-lived. We needed to turn our full attention to the football NFT launch, due to take place in just two weeks' time. We were straight out of the frying pan and into the fire. We had never marketed an NFT before and were stressing out about it – although our concerns were mitigated by the team confirming they would promote the drop on their official Twitter account, which had over three-quarters of a million followers.

And yet, reassuring as this was, we didn't want to bank on it too much. The way we saw it, the overwhelming majority of their followers and fan base not only wouldn't care about the launch, but would be actively opposed to it. Examining the comments on their first post announcing the collection confirmed our predictions:

'What the fuck is an NFT?'

'Better watch out or the rivals will right-click save the collection' (an allusion to the fact that, even though the team was claiming to be selling unique items, anyone could download a visually indistinguishable copy of the jpegs).

However, all of these were preferable to the outright condemnation that made up the bulk of the comments:

'Oh ffs, the greed is getting beyond belief. This is downright reprehensible.'

Knowing we couldn't rely on the fans alone (or, in fact, at all), we resolved to adapt our standard repertoire of marketing tricks. We sourced NFT-specific media outlets and influencers, commissioning promotions from as many as we could. During this process we discovered, to our delight, that NFT promotions were, on the whole, far cheaper than typical token promotions. The NFT space was still in its adolescence then, so the prices hadn't become too badly inflated.

Our efforts, it seemed, were paying off. We managed to drum up sufficient interest among the fan base that the hosts of the team's unofficial podcast channel invited Archie onto their show. Given its popularity among the fan base, this was a key promotional opportunity in the run-up to the drop. I spent hours preparing a thorough brief for Archie, with all the requisite talking points and key pieces of information. He hadn't been too involved in the project so far, so was in need of a primer. I didn't have time to join Archie on the podcast but, given the comprehensiveness of the brief, I had confidence he'd be able to sell the project sufficiently well, and build up even more hype around the drop. Archie could sell sand to the Saudis, so I thought no more about it, and got on with my other tasks.

My confidence, it transpired, was completely ill-founded. Five minutes into the podcast – which was being broadcast live – I received a text from Archie:

'Mate, what the fuck do these NFTs do??'

I sighed and put my head in my hands. Archie hadn't read the brief. I began typing, as fast as I could. I spelt out the details of the collection – how many NFTs, what their prices would be, and everything else Archie needed to know there – as well as the reasons why fans and NFT investors should buy them.

My efforts to salvage the podcast, however, were in vain. Archie was flustered and, even with the info I sent him, he still wasn't able to sell the project convincingly. The comments on the episode spoke for themselves:

'The boy did a really poor job of selling us on it. Sounded like he didn't know what an NFT was himself.'

'Great idea to get someone on to explain this, but I think he might've been the wrong guy to do so. I honestly think I could've done it better.'

'NFTs in general seem like a massive scam.'

As bad as this was, the podcast shambles was only the start of our problems. The next, and far more substantial, issue arose the night before the launch. And it came as a consequence of the football team's ill-advised decision to list their collection directly on OpenSea.

Back then, the functionality of OpenSea was far from optimal. We already know that they were only able to facilitate payments in the niche currency WETH. But, on top of this, they also had no ability to 'batch mint' NFTs. This meant that, to list an NFT collection directly onto the marketplace, every single item would have to be uploaded manually. Other projects circumvented this by conducting their sales on their own platforms. For us, though, this wasn't an option. So we had to assign a member of our team the Sisyphean task of manually uploading 1,111 NFTs to OpenSea.

Needless to say, he did not complete the task; after a few hundred, he gave up. Not out of laziness, but sheer exhaustion – it had taken him over 12 hours to do this amount. After so much work, we eventually reached the conclusion that the task was actually impossible. Based on how long the initial batch had taken him to upload, to get them all uploaded to OpenSea in time for launch, he would have had to start weeks ago.

We debated our next move. Delaying the launch was off the table. Not only would the team refuse, but they'd never want anything to do with us again if we pushed them into that decision. And they would likely badmouth us throughout the industry to boot. After much deliberation, we decided to push ahead with only a few hundred items on OpenSea. Most of the funds from the sale were due to come from the auctions anyway. And we could always just upload more NFTs if the ones on OpenSea sold out.

And so, on the morning of 22 November, the sale went live. The team announced this across all their socials. They also sent the news out to their email mailing list of tens of thousands of people and put an article up on their official website. The announcement went out at 10 a.m. but, to our utter disbelief, the sale actually started several hours earlier than this. Certain eagle-eyed watchers were able to find their OpenSea page before it was announced, saw it had NFTs already listed for sale, and started buying them. Despite only a few NFTs being sold ahead of the official launch time – and all of those being the cheapest ones on offer – we took this as a good omen.

At 10.01 a.m., my co-founders, Alice – who was the account manager for the campaign – and I were sitting in the office, waiting with bated breath for the sales to start rolling in. At 10.06 a.m., the five of us were on our feet, literally jumping for joy. Not only had we seen several thousands of dollars' worth of sales already, but all bar one of the big-ticket NFTs that we had put up for auction had bids on them.

As the day wore on, the buys kept flying in. By midday, we had sold all the NFTs that had been manually listed on OpenSea. We had to set an intern to work uploading more, as fast as he could, on the promise of a considerable bonus if he worked quickly enough. All the auction NFTs not only had bids, but *bidding wars*. Multiple users were vying with one another to get their hands on them and were driving the prices up. The rarest NFT in the set, which granted the lucky buyer the privilege of having lunch with the whole team of players, had a top bid of $25,000 on it – a figure that got higher and higher every minute, as around a dozen investors kept sending in new bids. The team's marketing director was delighted, sending us hourly emails telling us that he was going to recommend us to all his contacts, and that he would ensure even the owners heard about this phenomenal achievement.

When all was said and done, and all the proceeds had been tallied, the team had bagged well over six figures on the launch. Compared to some of the other projects we had worked on, this wasn't a very big fundraise at all. And it would hardly affect the fortunes of the team. But it was a big sum for an NFT launch. There weren't a huge number of projects on the market yet so, given the size of the overall sector, a hundred grand mint was not to be scoffed at. Plus, we had generated a more than 500 per cent return on investment for the team, who had spent just under $20,000 in total on bringing their NFTs to market (all of which was spent on us at Moonshot).

'Cracking work, guys, couldn't be happier. Let's enjoy our success, and then reconvene next week to discuss the next launch. Now that we have a proven track record of delivering, I can look to get more budget from the CFO. I want to double down on NFTs, hard.'

Miles, Archie, Paul and I sat round my laptop on the rooftop bar, our glasses brimming with Bollinger, reading this email from the team's marketing director.

'Well,' said Paul, 'I guess we go again. Let's make sure to get the same Nigerian freelancer for the next drop. His art went down an absolute treat.'

'Nice,' said Archie, 'just make sure you don't let slip how much we raised through this sale, though.'

'Ha! Come on, mate, any more silly comments? No danger of that, don't you worry.'

'Nice,' said Archie.

15

Cagey Customers

Several weeks on from our conference, our names were firmly on the map. And we were beginning to reap the rewards. We had more requests for work than we had ever had before. And, thanks to our most recent success, our confidence was at a new peak. We upped our prices across the board, and began pitching – and winning – clients of a previously unseen calibre. And, in no time at all, we discovered we didn't even need to pitch: these operators started knocking at our door.

Among the influx of new projects we took on in the wake of the football NFT drop was Cage Clash. We weren't sure how they had got our contact details – whether a mutual contact had passed them on, or whether they had heard about us through word of mouth or social media. But that didn't matter; as soon as we read their message, we knew they were a project we wanted to work with.

For starters, their team had extraordinary credentials. The founder, Malcolm, was also on the founding team of a high-profile project that was setting out to create the first feature-length film funded entirely through an NFT sale. It received a huge amount of press coverage, on account of one of its other founders having previously worked as a producer on a major film by Martin Scorcese.

Not only that, but Malcolm had also recently made a noteworthy purchase of a 'Crypto Punk' – one of the first NFT collections to ever launch, and one of the industry's 'blue chip' projects (a term appropriated from traditional finance, which refers to the biggest, safest and most reputable stocks on the market). Crypto Punk sales were closely monitored, and always generated a lot of attention, owing to their astronomical floor price. At the time Malcolm made his purchase, each one of these coveted jpegs was retailing for around 90 Ether. This was when Ether was trading at around $4,500, meaning the cheapest Crypto Punks on the market were fetching over $400,000 apiece.

Beyond just the founder's credentials, and his impressive collection of six-figure cartoons, Cage Clash was also a proper operation. They were incredibly well organised, with a good minting strategy and all the logistics of their collection nailed down – it would be a 10,000-piece drop, all with unique traits and rarities. And, to top it all off, they were *cool*. Or, that is, they appeared cool to the crypto community.

For an NFT enthusiast, they ticked all the right boxes. They had good artwork, which was very much on brand for crypto participants: anime-style cartoon animals, sporting various quirky get-ups and accoutrements. They even had a few 'legendary' NFTs – the highest tier of rarity – which they were planning to gift to influencers, to encourage them to post about the project for free. For the highest-profile influencers, they even took the trouble of making completely bespoke 'honorary' NFTs, specifically for them. These were in the legendary tier of rarity, but they weren't computer-generated like the others. They were hand-drawn, by some artist who was friends with Malcolm. This was a common practice that savvy NFT projects employed, to increase the likelihood of crypto celebrities posting about them on social media (or, if they were lucky, using the NFT as their Twitter profile picture).

And we soon discovered that Cage Clash's relevance and appeal to NFT collectors went even further than this. They weren't stopping at just a pfp collection: they had plans to tap into the booming 'GameFi' market by building a *Fortnite*-style battle royale blockchain game.

'GameFi' stands for gaming finance and, back in November 2021, it was all the rage. It first rose to prominence with Axie Infinity, whom we met earlier as the victims of a $650 million hack by the North Korean state-sanctioned Lazarus Group. But Axie was in the limelight well before this; some four months prior to the hack, in December 2021, Axie Infinity reached its peak $9.8 billion market cap. They were able to obtain a valuation bigger than Ubisoft, makers of the *Assassin's Creed* and *Far Cry* franchises, by being the leader of the 'play-to-earn' movement that swept the industry – a gaming model in which users got paid in crypto tokens simply for playing.

At the height of its popularity, Axie Infinity had 2.7 million daily players. At the time of writing, that's more than the combined number of people who have played the top ten games on Steam in the past 24 hours. This army of players was predominantly based in lower-income countries, such as the Philippines and Venezuela. The players there saw Axie as a lucrative source of alternative, or even primary, income. But, when trying to make a living from the game, these poverty-stricken players came across an obstacle: three NFTs were required to even access the game, and starting prices were around $150–200 for even the most basic ones. Axie was simply inaccessible to the people who wanted – or indeed needed – to play it the most.

To circumvent this, many players in the Philippines set up 'guilds' – groups of players who clubbed together to rent the equipment needed to play the game. And, sadly, when the more exploitative grifters in the crypto industry saw the vulnerability of Axie's core user base, they were quick to pounce.

The opportunistic individuals who lent NFTs to guilds would often take a percentage of the guild's revenues as repayment for the NFTs, often as high as 75 per cent. These crippling fees would often continue long after the cost of the NFTs had been fully repaid. If the guilds stopped sending funds, the NFT owners would reclaim their items. And, if that happened, then guild members would have no means of accessing their source of income, which often went towards providing the most basic living necessities for the players and their families. They were left with no choice: they simply had to keep handing over the lion's share of their revenue to the feudalistic NFT owners.

However, for the project founders watching the success of Axie Infinity, these shameful practices didn't matter. They saw the game's $17.5 million daily revenue and dreamt up ways of entering the highly lucrative play-to-earn space themselves. Many were highly successful, with *Lion's Den* being a particularly notable case. This was a play-to-earn game, hosted in a safari-themed metaverse, which rewarded players for taking risks. Founded by an anonymous developer, known only as 'The Lion Tamer', the game featured deliberately low-res, pixelated avatars, which were divided into lions and boars. Which animal a user played as depended on the NFT they minted when the project launched; 90 per cent of NFTs were boars, and 10 per cent lions. The objective of the boars was to deposit their NFTs into a barn, which then earned them in-game tokens, called BACON. The lions had to steal the BACON, but could be held at bay by boars paying them taxes in the game's token.

Despite the gameplay looking and feeling like it was concocted by a stoned student in a hazy 1990s dorm room, the game was an instant hit. The Simba-inspired NFTs dropped at the particularly juvenile price point of 0.6969 Ether. Within five days, the floor price had pumped to over 3 Ether, more than $13,000 at the time, and the collection had a trading volume of over $53 million. The highest price someone had paid for a lion NFT was 20.5 Ether, or around $85,000.

Its success was due in no small part to the promotional efforts of an influencer who went by the name of Mufasa. Mufasa was one of the leading figures in the world of NFTs at the time; he ran a 'VC' fund called HFSP Capital (with 'HFSP' standing for Have Fun Staying Poor – a common, and incredibly conceited, acronym in the space. Crypto proponents would deploy it against against any naysayer brazen enough to call into question the legitimacy, utility or purpose of the nascent asset class). Mufasa had built up an audience on Twitter of tens of thousands of the most invested and fanatical NFT community members. This meant he wielded tremendous influence. A single tweet from him was enough to sell out a mint or send a collection's floor price through the roof.

He was an early investor and advisor of *Lion's Den* and promoted it so hard across his Twitter that many in the space speculated that he was the anonymous Lion Tamer who had set the project up. Of course, this was little more than conjecture at the time. But what was certain was his role in the success of the project. Thanks to him, *Lion's Den* became the hottest GameFi project to launch since Axie Infinity itself.

By building in this thriving section of the space, Cage Clash were looking to tap into the strong narrative surrounding play-to-earn games, and to replicate the results of Axie and *Lion's Den*. We considered it a shrewd move, and we were in no doubt that it would generate a tremendous amount of hype around their launch. Or, that is to say, a tremendous amount *more* hype. Cage Clash's artwork, strategy, positioning and team credentials had caught the attention of institutions.

At this point in the market cycle, traditional brands on the trendier end of the spectrum were all looking to break into the NFT space. They wanted to dip their toes into this latest consumer fad. Some organisations, like the football team we had recently worked with, achieved this by launching their own collections. Others opted to go down an easier, albeit more resource-intensive route: they found 'cool' NFT projects and acquired them outright.

This was exactly what Vanguard Holdings did with Cage Clash. Vanguard was a Canadian firm which invested in gaming companies – mainly casual, free-to-play mobile games. They saw what was happening in the blockchain gaming space with the likes of Axie Infinity and wanted to get in on the action. So, in October 2021, they announced that they were going to purchase Cage Clash, to gain a foothold in that sector. They paid Canadian $800,000 upfront, and further remunerated Malcolm and his team with 6 million shares in Vanguard Holdings itself. At the time, these shares were valued at around Canadian $0.7 a piece, which gave Cage Clash a roughly $4.2 million stake in the firm. It was a $5 million deal in total, to purchase a crypto project that, as yet, hadn't launched, had no revenue or user base, and did nothing at all – such was the hype around play-to-earn games, and around Cage Clash itself.

Given all these factors, we thought success was all but in the bag. Little did we know that we couldn't have been more wrong.

'What the fuck is going on, guys?' Malcolm was sitting in his car – a high-end four-by-four, judging by the interior – and was absolutely seething. His oval, slightly lopsided, face had been getting redder and redder during the 10 minutes we'd been on the phone with him. His internet connection wasn't great but, even so, I was able to discern a pixelated vein protruding ever more prominently from his left temple.

'Look, Malcolm,' Archie said, with the slightly irritated, slightly conciliatory tone he often adopted when clients were angry with us, 'these things take time. We've only been going for a week. You can't expect results that quickly.'

'Launch is in two weeks!'

'Yeah, I know that. But have you considered whether you're spending enough money? You don't have a massive budget. We're used to working with more budget than this.'

'You've spent $120,000. In seven fucking days. How much more budget do you need?!'

Despite our initial assessment of Cage Clash as a sure-fire sell-out, our marketing efforts hadn't had *quite* the effect we were hoping they would. Our initial round of influencer marketing, on which we had spent $25,000 of Cage Clash's money, had virtually no effect at all. We were aiming to get 15,000 people into their Discord (a social media messaging app used pervasively in the NFT space). We ended up with a fraction of that. And the ones that did land didn't sign up to the whitelist.

In spite of this, though, failure on this project didn't seem like a possibility. It was unconscionable to us. We knew they'd be an unmitigated success if we just stepped up our game. So, in this mindset of hopeful delusion, we doubled down and set our sights on the next tier of paid promoters: celebrities.

Over the past few months, we had been revamping our influencer offering. It was a big money-spinner for us, and something every project wanted. As part of our expansion, we developed partnerships with several highly specialised influencer marketing and brand ambassador agencies. This was no mean feat; many of the firms we approached ran for the hills as soon as we told them we wanted their talent to promote blockchain investments. However, crypto money is difficult to turn down and, eventually, we managed to strike up deals with several top outfits.

One of these, in particular, was a goldmine for big-name celebrities. They were called Plug Promotions and had been catering to crypto clients for some time already. Their influencer list read like the gossip pages of the *Daily Mail*. They had everyone from 50 Cent and Lindsay Lohan to Chris Brown, Kevin Hart and even Kim Kardashian on their books. Needless to say, names like these didn't come cheap; Lindsay Lohan was $35,000 for a single 140-character tweet (these were the days before Elon Musk's takeover of the platform, and the overhaul of their notorious character limits). Chris Brown was $160,000. And the fee for the likes of Kim Kardashian wasn't even disclosed; instead, the classy line of 'price on application' was given.*

So far, we hadn't had the opportunity to try out our new celebrity marketing capabilities – those price tags were prohibitive, even for cash-rich crypto projects. We were itching to test them out, so we pushed them hard to Cage Clash. After some hesitation from Malcolm, we managed to tempt him into commissioning a tweet from a well-known US rapper, boasting around 1 million followers on Twitter. We pitched it as an ideal fit: he was just a tad too niche to be a household name, so didn't command quite as significant a fee (and, in fact, at $8,000 per post he was something of a bargain). But he was actively involved in the crypto space, and had promoted some successful projects in the past, so had established a substantial, trusting audience of crypto natives.

At the appointed hour, he sent out a post advertising Cage Clash to his 1 million Twitter followers. He evoked nostalgia by comparing them to Tamagotchi and Digimon – late ninetie to early noughties Japanese video games – while also alluding to Cage Clash's potential to become the next big viral sensation. Needless to say, it wasn't marked as 'ad', and he didn't even bother with the stock 'do your own research' disclaimer that most influencers tacked onto the end of posts promoting projects they themselves had clearly not researched.

By all accounts, it looked like an organic tweet discussing a project he was genuinely interested in. And his followers took note; hundreds of them reshared the post, and even more flocked to Cage Clash's Twitter profile, with their account seeing a few thousand new followers in the immediate aftermath of the shill. But

---

* In October 2022, her fees came to light in a $1.2 million lawsuit that the SEC filed against her for unlawfully touting cryptocurrencies on Instagram. She was paid $250,000 for a post promoting a token called EtherumMax, a so-called 'cultural token' which made vague promises about lifestyle perks for its holders.

when the initial surge in interest had died down, the results were disheartening. People took a look around their profiles, engaged with their recent posts a bit, and then left just as quickly as they came.

It seemed the crypto community was fed up with pfp projects. That was the only explanation we could come up with. So, instead of reassessing and restrategising, we went further still. We figured that we just needed to spread the word wider than we had done and lean into the play-to-earn side of the project rather than focusing too much on the artwork. We threw another $25,000 at influencers. And another. And another. Only to find that the results were the same each time. After we passed the $100,000 mark, we changed tack, and threw $20,000 at our best media contacts for some top-notch coverage. That ended up having even less effect than the influencers.

Thus we found ourselves in the situation we were in now.

'Look, Malcolm,' I said, desperately trying to think up something to say. 'We do know what we're doing here. We've sold out NFT drops before. Big ones.'

'And how the hell does that benefit me?'

'Look, Malcolm ... Have you considered postponing launch?'

'If that's your bright idea to salvage this launch, I'm firing you here and now. It'd probably save me a fortune if I did.'

'Okay, well, how about this ...' Panic had started to creep into my voice, and I was on the verge of despair, when inspiration suddenly struck: 'Mufasa! What about Mufasa?'

'What about him?'

'If we could get him on board, for promotion I mean, that could be a game-changer.'

Malcolm scoffed. 'Well, yeah, sure, but how the hell are you going to do that?'

'Leave that with us, Malcolm.' I said, trying hard to feign self-assurance. 'We'll get him on board, no issue.'

'Right. Whatever. I need to go. Stop spending our money: the taps are off.'

'What is the offer?'

I sat staring at Mufasa's Twitter DM in a state of disbelief. As soon as I had composed myself a bit, I sent a screenshot of it to Malcolm. It was past midnight, but three dots appeared at the bottom of the WhatsApp chat as soon as the picture was delivered. Barely 30 seconds later, I had received the terms of the offer Malcolm was willing to make: 10 per cent of the mint proceeds (around 40 Eth if it sold out, worth $120,000 at the time), plus $100,000 worth of advisory shares across Vanguard Holdings and NFT Investments, plus the promise of future 'incentive packages' for promoting those companies if all goes well with the drop. All in exchange for one or two mentions of the project on his Twitter.

I sent Malcolm my reply: 'Nice. Quarter of a million, for some social posts. Surely he won't be able to turn that down.'

Mufasa replied the following day, turning the deal down.

'I think it's just because he's a multi-millionaire,' I wrote to Malcolm, after sending another screenshot of Mufasa's rejection. 'Maybe we can double it?'

'Hold on 2 minutes.'

After less than 90 seconds, Malcolm messaged again.

'On the phone to Vanguard now. 10 Eth upfront. $500k in Vanguard stock. 15 per cent of the mint. 50 per cent of trading royalties for the first two weeks. High-value consulting for NFT Investments and Vanguard on top – $100–200k per year for a few hours per month, that kind of thing.'

'Fucking hell. No chance he's turning that down.'

I quickly tallied the figures in my head: just shy of three-quarters of a million for a couple of tweets. And yet, sure enough, Mufasa refused. Or, that is to say, I inferred his refusal; he simply didn't respond. He was our silver bullet to turn this launch around. Without him, we had no other option but to continue with what we had been doing up to now, and hope that, somehow, something different would happen.

In hindsight, however, his refusal was a blessing in disguise. Less than two months after my brief exchange with Mufasa, he was accused of being a grifter by JPEG Janitor, a prominent Twitter account that investigated and publicly called out NFT scams. They revealed his real name, as well as posting excerpts from an online bio of his in which he boasted of his complete lack of work ethic and his pride at never having held a real job.

JPEG Janitor then went on to accuse the influencer of everything from fraud to masterminding pump-and-dumps, providing an abundance of damning evidence and case studies to back up their claims. In light of this, the NFT community was quick to cancel their former frontman. *Lion's Den* distanced themselves, as did the other projects he had invested in. His fund, HFSP Capital, was forced to shut up shop. Mufasa's days as the Midas of NFTs were over, and his reputation was in tatters.

That wasn't the end for Mufasa, though; after a hiatus from social media, he returned and rebranded himself as a straight-talking crypto pundit. His self-professed redemption arc seemed to win people over, and he was welcomed back with open arms. To this day, he posts regularly on social media, giving plaudits to projects he likes and issuing warnings about those he's wary of. In the collective consciousness of crypto, reputational ruin is easy to forget and forgive, especially when the grifter in question makes early calls on projects that go on to prosper.

At the time of trying to bring him on board to Cage Clash, though, Mufasa's demise and resurgence hadn't come to pass. He was in his prime, with his influence at a zenith. So his refusal to work with us was a big blow. We did the only thing we could: spend another forty grand of Cage Clash's money, and hope for the best.

Launch day came, and Cage Clash had around 300 people on their whitelist, out of a publicly announced target of 2,000 (and an internal target of 10,000: enough to cover every NFT in the collection, just from whitelist mints). And yet, despite these bleak prospects, and their indignation towards the amount of their money we had spent, they were having a launch party in their Holborn offices, to which we had unexpectedly been invited. In crypto, not even financial ruin can get in the way of a good party ...

At 8 p.m. on 30 November, Archie and I, and Alice – who, after a stellar performance on the football NFTs, had been assigned to project manage Cage Clash – stood outside a large townhouse, just off Russell Square. It looked more like the vacant home of a non-dom rather than the offices of a tech startup. After double-checking the address, we called Malcolm and told him we were outside. He came outside, a bottle of Dom Pérignon in one hand and Veuve Clicquot in the other. Thrusting the Dom into my chest, he nodded towards the door and told us to come up.

Their office was a plush, palatial apartment that they had converted into a workspace. It belonged to the parents of one of their developers (who, it turned out, were in fact non-doms after all). Hanging from the high-vaulted ceiling was a crystal chandelier, incongruous with the row of monitors set up on desks beneath it. More desks and monitors lined the far side of the room, flanking a floor-to-ceiling bay window out of which three people were leaning and smoking. The stucco walls were plastered with anime posters, and there was hip hop blaring from what looked like club-quality speakers.

'This is sick,' Archie said, turning to me with a glint in his eye. 'We need to get a setup like this for our office.'

'Might look a bit out of place among the mould and water damage.'

Before Archie could respond, the hip hop was abruptly cut off.

'Guys, Moonshot in the house! Cheers to them!' Malcolm exclaimed, raising the bottle in his hand and taking a drink. Foam splashed out of his mouth and ran down his cheeks. A cheer erupted throughout the cavernous room, echoing faintly off the parquet. I turned to Alice, and she mirrored my bemused look. She was as clearly taken aback by the high spirits and warm welcome as I was. We had wasted a $150,000 of their money, and they were toasting us. Archie, on the other hand, didn't seem to find it odd in the slightest. Quite the contrary, in fact: from his proud smile, raised chin and puffed-out chest, he gave off the distinct impression that he had expected such a welcome.

The music resumed, and Archie strutted off to inspect the posters. Alice and I went over to chat to the people by the window. We had barely introduced ourselves, however, when a cry went out: 'T minus 10 minutes to launch guys! Let's get ready.' The smokers flicked their cigarette butts into the street and scurried to their seats.

After what felt like a lifetime, the sale got under way. And it was even more painful than I anticipated. Not only did hardly anyone from the whitelist even bother trying to buy one of their NFTs, but the people who did try were hindered by a glitch on their sales platform. Every time someone went to mint an NFT, the 'gas fee' came out at around $12,000. That wasn't even including the price of the NFT itself.

After being shouted out by a red-faced Malcolm, the row of sweating developers by the window managed to fix the bug. But it was too late by that point. Whatever ember of demand there was to buy one of Cage Clash's jpegs had been irrevocably stamped out. No one tried to mint, even after we announced that we were slashing the prices in half to reward early buyers. Malcolm resorted to buying up the NFTs himself, from multiple different wallets he owned, to make it look like it wasn't a complete washout. Although just who he was trying to fool I wasn't quite sure.

From then on, the mood turned sour. The music was shut off, and no one spoke. Everyone stared sullenly at their screens, sighing and rubbing their foreheads. Archie opened the fridge door to get a beer, and Malcolm slammed it shut, mumbling something about needing to save the beers for another time.

The three of us looked at each other and, without saying a word, made for the door. We slipped away, without so much as a goodbye to Malcolm or anyone else.

'Fucking hell, that was awful,' Alice said, stepping out into the lamplight and the brisk November air.

Awful was an understatement. It was our worst performance to date. Our first total failure (although certainly not the last).

As bad as it was, though, what was in store for us, and for the entire industry, would have us looking back fondly on that disastrous night.

16

Snowball Effect

We resolved to put the whole sorry affair with Cage Clash behind us and move on. Despite fumbling the bag on one of the most promising launches we had ever worked on, we had done remarkably well from their influencer procurement frenzy. This gave us something of a golden parachute, to soften the blow of them firing us – which they did, before our heads hit our pillows that night. It also meant we were going into year-end with a very healthy balance sheet.

We had more cash on hand than ever before. And, not wanting it to just sit stagnant, we racked our brains as to how it could best be put to use. In the midst of our deliberations, inspiration struck: we decided to try our hand at the crypto media racket.

This was an area a lot of the big crypto players had made moves in. Digital Currency Group – the conglomerate that owns an array of crypto trading, lending and financial service firms – purchased CoinDesk for $500,000 in 2016.* In April 2020, Binance snapped up CoinMarketCap – the industry's largest data and information service – for $400 million, in the largest crypto acquisition to have ever occurred up to that point. And in February 2022, Binance announced it was making another move into the media realm: a $200 million investment in Forbes. The announcement came less than two years

---

*   In July 2023, amid a liquidity crisis at DCG fueled by insolvencies in a number of their lending platforms, they entered talks with a consortium of investors to sell CoinDesk for $125 million.

after Binance sued Forbes for defamation, after the outlet published a story claiming Binance 'conceived of an elaborate corporate structure designed to intentionally deceive regulators'.

The motivation behind crypto's obsession with owning the media was obvious: why buy the news article, when you can buy the newspaper itself?

Controlling some of the industry's most well-known and familiar outlets afforded crypto giants an unfathomable degree of influence and expanded their hegemonic control over the narrative production line. It was straight out of the Rupert Murdoch playbook. And we wanted in.

With megalomaniacal visions of a *Succession*-style media empire in our minds, we started reaching out to contacts of ours at some of the smaller outlets we worked with, hoping that one of them would be open to an acquisition offer. After drawing blanks on the first few feelers I put out, I hit on a stroke of luck. The CTO of Leopard Labs – the VC that incubated Portent Protocol (which, at this point, seemed like a lifetime ago) – also happened to run a news site, unimaginatively named news-of-crypto.org. It was a dingy little website (as the '.org' domain would suggest), but nothing that a bit of elbow grease wouldn't spruce up. And, best of all, the current owner seemed positively desperate to get rid of it.

The Leopard Labs CTO was a Hungarian techie called Boris. Sporting a ponytail and goatee, and wearing the same nondescript beige short-sleeve shirt in every meeting I ever had with him, Boris looked like a character straight out of a cheesy 1980s porno. He was a thin, etiolated man of about 40, but his smooth, taut face made him look no older than 25. No doubt his flawless complexion was due to a lack of sunlight; he used to tell us with pride that he seldom ventured out of his basement office. He was regarded by those who knew him as one of the hardest working (and certainly the most stressed) people in the industry. As well as running the technical side of Leopard Labs, he was involved in a number of other projects, and also alluded to doing a bit of freelance copywriting and content consulting. And, as we had just pleasantly discovered, he also ran a news site.

'It's really nothing special,' he said to us on a call I arranged to discuss the acquisition, putting on a deliberately monotonous intonation to reinforce his point. 'I once did some consulting for the guy who owned it. He retired and gave me the site for free. To be honest with you, it's become a bit of a burden. I want to get rid of it, but I feel a bit of nostalgia for it. The owner was my first content consultancy client. He was almost like a friend to me, I suppose.'

'That's great, Boris. Really great.' Boris creeped me out slightly, and I was always a bit on edge when I spoke to him.

'Yeah, it is great. Not the site, I mean. The site is a bit of a shithole. I meant the history of it,' Boris said, sighing as he spoke.

'Well, don't worry. We'll take good care of it.'

'I know you will. That's why I want to give it to you.'

'Yeah, brilliant, that's what I wanted to discuss. How much were you looking to get for it?'

'No, you don't understand. I want to *give* it to you. For free. I just want the site to keep running, but I can't keep running it myself.'

I tried not to betray my elation. We had set aside a considerable sum for acquiring a news site. And now it looked like one had dropped right in our laps.

'I completely understand where you're coming from, Boris. You can rest assured, we'll take great care of it! We'll polish it up, give it a whole new look, and get fresh content on there daily.'

'That's exactly what I wanted to hear. Thank you, man. Consider it yours. I'm just glad it's behind me,' Boris said, with all the solemnity of a grieving relative delivering a long-expected eulogy.

'Great, cheers Boris! Get some sleep if you can – you look bloody awful.'

This was a big step forwards for us; not only did it mean we could manufacture as much media coverage for our clients as we could churn out, but it also meant we could start selling article placements to other projects. We could also run ads, hold awards ceremonies (a common money-spinner for crypto media outlets, with projects paying to win whatever award takes their fancy), or any number of other monetisation avenues. It had the potential to be a very nice auxiliary revenue stream for us. To show our appreciation to Boris, and out of the sheer kindness of our hearts, we offered him a revenue-sharing deal: we would keep 80 per cent of all funds generated by the site, and he'd get 20 per cent. He was over the moon with this arrangement and offered to write a few articles every month about our clients.

As exciting as the news site was, we knew it was nothing more than a side hustle and didn't want to expend too much time and effort on it. We had much bigger things in the pipeline, which demanded our attention.

As the year drew to a close, and with Portent Protocol circling the drain, we decided it was high time to launch a new project.

Portent hadn't been floundering so much as freefalling; every day the token price achieved a new all-time low. The long-awaited prediction platform – the whole reason the project even existed – launched back in August, and actually saw some good usage for a while from community members who had long waited to put their increasingly worthless tokens to use. After a while, though, this died down, as the novelty wore off and users realised they didn't really care about predicting the future price of bitcoin on our shoddy little platform. They sold their tokens, and likely moved over to trading on one of the big exchanges.

For a while, we tried to stimulate demand in the token by offering presale allocations in other projects to the biggest TENT token holders. We thought it would be a great cross-collaboration between Moonshot and Portent; Moonshot clients who were approaching their token launch would put a certain amount of their presale tokens up for grabs to the Portent Protocol 'whales' (an industry term, meaning the biggest, richest holders of a particular asset). That way, the clients got to raise some additional funds and receive some exposure to known crypto investors, the Portent community got access to presale allocations, and the TENT token got a use case. However, this initiative was rather short-lived; people stopped participating in the presales after the first dozen or so got fatally dumped on by VCs and influencers. We tried to breathe some life into it by offering allocations in NFT launches. However, we were hindered by access; at that time, all eyes in the industry were on NFT launches, and projects were reluctant to give their coveted jpegs to such a relatively insignificant community.

While this was disappointing for Portent, it gave way to our next bright idea: an NFT launchpad.

As far as we knew, there were no other NFT launchpads on the market. Token launchpads were ten a penny, but there were no products out there that made NFT launches more accessible. So the way we saw it, an NFT launchpad was a necessary product; investors were getting tired of not making it onto rigged whitelists and missing out on huge gains in the booming NFT space.

We decided to call our product Aquarius Drops, and we factored into it the prediction element of our last project. Essentially, the way it worked was projects would give us a load of their NFTs before launch, and users would then make predictions on some aspect of the collection after it launched – what the floor price or the trading volume would be 24 hours after launch, for example – and the closest predictions would then win an NFT.

We thought it was a good concept, and so did the VCs who we started soliciting for fundraising. We filled up our seed round within a week of having a pitch deck prepared. Quite a considerable feat, given the size of the raise we were aiming for. We realised with Portent that we had set our sights too low and hadn't raised enough money to do anything interesting or meaningful. We simply didn't have a long enough runway to improve our product, or to play around with it and experiment. So with Aquarius Drops we aimed higher and set ourselves a $5 million pre-launch fundraising target. Enough to have some fun with.

And, as 2021 gave way to 2022, and the fundraise continued to bear fruit, Aquarius Drops started to become a major area of focus for us. We increased the cross pollination of our businesses by signing our new project up as a client of our agency, which provided a great route to channel the VC funds Aquarius Drops raised out of the scrutinised, publicly viewable project treasury and into our own pockets, whilst shoring up the cash flow figures of Moonshot Advisors in the process.

Yet even with all the VC money flooding into our coffers, we didn't rest on our laurels; we continued to broaden our horizons, looking for other sources of new funds. And it didn't take long to find an untapped well: other crypto projects.

Back in those days, all the major layer 1 blockchains had set up 'grant foundations'. These were quasi-charitable (or, rather, pseudo-charitable) organisations, which issued funds to startup projects looking to build on their network. Ostensibly, this was done to foster adoption of blockchain technology and expand the industry as a whole. However, beneath the PR narrative there was only one real reason these networks were giving out free money: to get builders and users onto their chains.

Despite all the noise that decentralised finance projects made, and all the media coverage they bought, it was an open secret that nobody actually used DeFi applications. People speculated on the tokens and couldn't really care about what the projects that issued them actually did. Because of this, layer 1 blockchains found themselves with vastly inflated token prices, but no actual users on their chain. Take Near, for example. At its peak, it had a valuation of just under $12.5 billion. But this figure was completely uncorrelated with usage. Official figures of how many users are active on a given network are misleading as the teams 'spoof' them: they send money back and forth between their own wallets – or get their market makers to do this – to massage the daily volume and payment settlement figures, thereby giving a false picture of health. However, we heard from contacts of ours within the Near Foundation – the entity that created and controls the project – that there weren't more than a couple of thousand people using the network each day, and only a few dozen projects were actually building anything. So, to counteract this, Near launched an $800 million grant fund, which they would award to projects developing products within their ecosystem. They wanted to attract builders, in the hope that users would follow.

Arguably the most renowned case of this was Sweatcoin, a leading player in the 'move-to-earn' sector of the crypto space. This was a particularly bizarre phenomenon, which started as an offshoot of the 'play-to-earn' model popularised by the likes of Axie Infinity. The first move-to-earn protocol, and the project that sparked one of the strangest fads in the history of crypto, was called Stepn. It promised users a source of passive income, simply by staying active and moving around. Users had to buy an NFT, which took the form of a digital sneaker, and, after that, they would start to generate the project's native token based on how many steps they took each day. There were different tiers of sneaker NFTs, available at varying price points, with the higher tiers generating more tokens per step. In early 2022, the hype around Stepn was palpable; between 9 March and 19 April – a period of just forty-one days – the project's token GMT pumped in price by 34,000 per cent. At its peak, the project claimed to have over 4 million monthly active users, and in the second quarter of 2022 it reported a profit of $122.5 million. This would put them just outside the Fortune 500 for earnings that quarter.

Stepn was built on the Solana blockchain, which, at its peak, had a market cap of around $75 billion. Near had seen the success of both Solana and Stepn and wanted to replicate the results of their far larger competitor. They saw getting more users onto their chain as the key to unlocking their potential and, for this, they would need to stamp their mark on the thriving move-to-earn sector.

So, in a bid to get in on the latest fad and take on Solana, they partnered with Sweatcoin, a fitness app that had been around since 2016. They already had over 100 million users around the world, who Near figured must be dying to be introduced to the benefits of blockchain tech.

Initially, Sweatcoin provided its users with an in-app currency based on how many steps they took per day, which could be used for purchases and discounts on products within the app itself. However, in July 2022, Sweatcoin took on funding of $13 million from a consortium of crypto firms, including the Near Foundation, to launch a token on the Near blockchain. App users would be able to convert their existing in-app balances into Sweatcoin's new SWEAT token, which could then be traded like any normal cryptocurrency. And the result of Sweatcoin's pivot into the crypto space was exactly what Near were hoping for: the launch of the SWEAT token added 13.5 million new participants to the Near network, as Sweatcoin users downloaded crypto wallets to receive the tokens they had been promised.

These somewhat desperate tactics, which essentially amounted to layer 1 blockchains paying people and projects to use their network, very much worked in our favour. We were building on Avalanche, another layer 1 network, which at the time had a valuation of around $21 billion. They had just launched a $220 million grant fund, specifically targeting decentralised finance and NFT projects. Given that we were positioning ourselves as catering to both of those market segments, we reckoned that a grant from Avalanche would be all but in the bag. So we sent off our application and waited for a response.

All in all, we considered our decision to build on Avalanche a stroke of brilliance. When we were making our selection, we started with a list of around half a dozen layer 1 networks. Avalanche was very much the underdog: it had a smaller valuation, fewer projects and, overall, a much lower profile than the other contenders. This benefited us greatly, as their underdog status meant that Ava Labs – the entity that owned and ran the project – put more time, effort and resources into bringing new projects and users onto their chain.

And, for that matter, so did the other projects already on the network. We were soon to discover they were always up for partnership discussions, and readily handed out advice and insight into the ecosystem. They were quick to connect us with all the essential promoters and tastemakers across the network, and even plugged us to their Telegram and Discord communities. They wanted to form a tight-knit community, reasoning that collaboration and friendliness would likely pay dividends in future. After all, it couldn't hurt to be owed some favours. In this industry, you never knew when you might need them.

This was all well and good but, for us, there was another factor to consider with Avalanche. It excited us more than anything else about them and was ultimately what tipped the scales in their favour when it came to decision time.

They were about to host their inaugural global summit, and it looked set to be like nothing the industry had ever seen.

PART THREE

17

Crypto Continental

The Avalanche summit was due to take place in March, in Barcelona. The timing for this was perfect. The market was in high spirits, with the overall industry market cap hovering just shy of $2 trillion. Bitcoin itself was trading at around $40,000, with a market cap in the $800 billion range. And there had been a slew of new rising stars entering the scene and contributing to the general exuberance. Most notable among these was a project called Terra Luna. Created in January 2018, it started really taking off in summer 2021, appreciating in price by over 1,200 per cent before the year closed. This netted a great number of people extraordinary gains and, as 2022 got under way and the rally continued, Terra Luna was one of the main factors contributing to the general euphoria in the air.

The industry was flourishing, and everyone thought the party would never stop. And Avalanche – themselves one of the industry's darlings – wanted to take centre stage and bask in the limelight of the crypto summer.

This was to be their first global summit, and they were pulling out all the stops. Armed with what could essentially be regarded as an unlimited budget, they hired the entirety of the Poble Espanyol for their summit venue – a sprawling 50,000m² open-air museum, reminiscent of a medieval castle or fortified town, comprising 117 separate buildings, each replicating a famous cultural landmark of the Iberian peninsula. The rumour we heard was that they spent a cold hard million just to secure the venue itself. And that's not to mention all the extras.

They had just signed a big-ticket sponsorship deal with Formula E, the electric vehicle branch of the Formula 1 franchise, for an undisclosed figure. No doubt they would be making a big song and dance about this, and likely jetting their Formula E stars out to Barcelona for some promo opps. They were also highlighting perks to be found at the event, such as their 'zen' area, where guests could unwind to live music in a yurt, get massages and even permanently commemorate their attendance at the summit by getting a tattoo. All in all, there were over 3,500 people due to attend, each paying up to $600 for a ticket. We didn't need to worry about this, however; through our recently acquired crypto news site, we were able to secure press passes, granting us VIP access to all areas of the event. This was a complimentary gift Avalanche were offering to members of the crypto commentariat in a bid to get them over to Barcelona to write about the event.

The way we saw it, the summit was a big opportunity for us – both to drum up new business for Moonshot Advisors, and also to make some useful connections from the Aquarius side of things. All the major VCs in the industry would be in attendance, along with just about every project building on Avalanche, so it was a goldmine for striking partnerships and raising funds. About a month out from the event, we decided that we needed to make as big a splash as possible. In a bid to draw attention to ourselves, and to help us stand out, we put the Aquarius treasury to good use and started planning a side event.

We hired a bar set in a leafy Catalonian park, just a short walk from the Poble Espanyol. The venue had an intimate feel to it, while remaining within walking distance of the main event. The bar itself was large and modern, with marble floors throughout and French doors running the whole length of one wall, offering a panoramic view of the Barcelona skyline, including the Sagrada Família. It was set to be an event to remember so, pulling out all the stops, we even gave it a theme, 'drink 2 earn', with cash and NFT prizes on offer to the people who could prove they had drunk more than the other guests. It was a gimmicky concept, but it seemed to go down well; a few days after launching our Eventbrite page and sharing it around in the main Avalanche community groups, we had a couple of hundred signups.

It was with great optimism, therefore, that we jetted out to Barcelona for what looked set to be the event of the year.

There were six of us attending the summit in total: me, my three co-founders, and our two event managers, Bradley and Claire. We were staying in the centre of the city, opposite the Casa Batlló, the former home of renowned Catalan architect Antoni Gaudí, and famed for its surrealist design and iconic wavy blue facade. We had booked a large six-bedroom apartment for the weekend, which boasted two living rooms, a dining room, a drawing room, and all the bells and whistles that its aristocratic Spanish owners could kit it out with. We figured that if we were going to do this weekend, we may as well do it right.

After settling in and catching up on emails we had missed while we were travelling, we headed to the summit. We knew we were nearing the event before the venue was even in sight. Avalanche banners adorned the broad, leafy boulevards. Crowds of people marched in unison, all headed in the same direction, and sporting garments emblazoned with Avalanche logos and slogans. They were all the same shade of bright blood red, Avalanche's signature colour. Pulling up to the castle gates, the crowds thickened and stalled, all bobbing and fumbling to get through the portcullis. Stepping out the cab, we spotted a smaller door to the side of the main gate, roped off and attended by half a dozen burly security guards. The VIP entrance. We approached and informed them that we were with news-of-crypto.org, hoping they wouldn't scoff or say they had never heard of it. They retained a professional indifference and pointed us towards a kiosk where we could claim our press passes. We were in.

With our passes secured, we made our way through the site's narrow, labyrinthine passageways, treading carefully over the cobbled faux-medieval lanes, and gazing around at the asymmetrical stone buildings that loomed precariously over us. Every now and then, incongruous glass-fronted shops and restaurants reminded us that we were walking around a tourist attraction, and not an actual historical site. They all had hosts outside, like you might find on the strip of a Mediterranean party island, beckoning you to come in.

'No thanks,' we said politely as we were approached for the fourth time in the space of as many minutes.

'Are you sure?' asked a red T-shirted Spanish hostess, with a look of questioning bemusement on her face. 'Everything's free.'

We stopped in our tracks. 'What's that?' asked Paul.

'Everything on the menu's free. A-b-alanche,' she said, accenting the final syllable, 'have paid ahead for everything, for the weekend.'

We looked at one another. With raised eyebrows and piqued interest, we stepped into the restaurant. It was a steakhouse, which had clearly gone to great pains to replicate the quaint feel of the outside passageways; we stooped under two exposed brick archways as we were led to our table, walking over slightly uneven grey slate floor tiles. But its modernity was betrayed here and there by an ambient LED light, a not-quite-distressed-enough leather upholstered chair.

We took our seats and were handed some menus. It only had a handful of items. We weren't sure if it was because of the touristy nature of the place, or because of what the quality of the food would be, but there wasn't a single dish available for less than three figures. We ordered a chateaubriand each, and two bottles of 2014 Pomerol to wash it down with, which came highly recommended from the sommelier.

We finished eating, waited a while after the waiter cleared our plates to see if a bill was going to materialise, and took our leave when we were satisfied it wouldn't. We stumbled a few steps down the street and were beckoned into a tequila bar by another host. With why-the-hell-not shrugs abounding, we entered the bar. Twelve shots of Patrón Silver later, we emerged and resumed our search for the main hall, resolving to flat out ignore any other hosts we may cross paths with.

Forty-five minutes – and several *cervezas* – later, we were in the main room. It was hosted under a vast marquee, packed to the brim with red-clad crypto bros, all sloshing Estrellas that they had obtained free of charge from one of the five dispensaries dotted around the tent. At one end, a bright red Formula E car proudly stood on a raised platform, flanked gratuitously by two tanned, smiling, athletic-looking girls with platinum blonde hair and Avalanche-branded bikinis. They were the only women I could see in the whole marquee. A noticeable number of tipsy, geeky men weren't even trying to hide their leers.

On the other end of the tent stood a large stage, with a projector screen above it running its entire length. Someone was standing centre stage, holding a microphone to his mouth. He seemed to be delivering a speech. It could hardly be heard over the general din of the crowd, and no one seemed to be paying him any attention. Like us, most people seemed focused on trying to orientate themselves, and take in their surroundings. It was quite reassuring to see that we clearly weren't the only ones taken aback, and more than a little overwhelmed. We decided to do the only sensible thing we could think of – grab some free drinks, get out of the melee of the main tent, and explore the rest of the venue.

After some aimless walking, we came across a footpath winding up a gentle hill. Despite it being the middle of the day, the path was lit by torches that lined its sides. We decided to follow it up. When we neared the end, we saw what looked like some kind of church. A tourist information sign just in front of its manicured gardens informed us it was a replica of an old monastery. We entered the garden, navigating some imposing cypress trees and manicured box hedges, and approached the main building. Before we got there, we were stopped in our tracks by two burly security guards. We were told this was a VIP area, and we could only gain access if we had the right sort of clearance pass. Or if we worked for Chikn.

Chikn was the flagship NFT project in the Avalanche ecosystem. It was a 10,000-piece collection, all featuring, as the name would suggest, variations of a digital, photo-realistic chicken. It would almost look lifelike had it not been stylised through iridescent colour schemes. These, along with various novelty accessories like sunglasses, thick gold chains and cartoonish moustaches, indicated the rarity of the piece. At the time, these Chikn NFTs were selling for several thousand dollars each. Partly because, beyond just the artwork, the NFTs 'laid' EGG tokens if the owner staked it.

These EGG tokens had their own value and, as well as being trade-able, they could themselves be staked to generate FEED tokens. These could then be 'fed' to the Chikn NFTs to grow them, resulting in increased production of EGG tokens when staked afterwards. It was like a farcical version of the old Facebook game Farmville, except with thousands of dollars required to play. But this novel idea paid off and, soon after launching, Chikn found themselves as the leaders of the Avalanche NFT market, with millions of dollars' worth of their NFTs traded in just a few weeks.

Of course, this was also due to their marketing efforts, which is how I first came across them just before the summit. I had seen on Twitter that they had paid a person in the US – who went by what turned out to be the very appropriate name of 'Alfredo the living advertisement' – to get one of their Chikn NFTs permanently tat-tooed on his chest. And it wasn't some small, discreet little tattoo. It took up a lot of real estate, commanding a significant chunk of his right pectoral. Scrolling through his social media feed, it appeared Alfredo saw a big opportunity in this line of work. After Chikn, he proceeded to get more NFTs tattooed on himself. Among them was a giraffe wearing a baseball cap on his upper abdomen and a pink hole-puncher just below this. Together, these two tattoos took up the whole of the left side of his stomach. I didn't know what I found more disturbing: Alfredo's willingness to sell his skin as advertising space, or the fact that someone thought it would be a good idea to launch a series of NFTs depicting cartoon stationery.

Intrigued, I began to make enquiries about Alfredo, and sought to find out how much it would cost to get an NFT tattooed on him – just to satisfy my own curiosity, as I didn't envisage any of our cli-ents would be inclined to promote their project like this (although I couldn't be sure). Eventually I was informed, by someone who had supposedly met him quite by chance at a crypto pool party, that his going rate was around $1,500 cash – this varied according to the desired location of the ink, which seemed fair enough – but his preferred form of remuneration was a given number of the NFT that would subsequently, and irreversibly, adorn some part of his body.

The fact that Chikn had been able to get a hugely successful, viral marketing stunt (as well as a permanent walking advert) for no cost, other than one of their own NFTs, was either testament to their marketing nous or to the general delirium surrounding the NFT space at that time. I was intensely keen to be admitted to their VIP area and meet some of their team.

We flashed our press passes to security, hoping they would be sufficient to grant us entry. After a brief conversation with their earpieces, the guards let us pass. The monastery building itself was closed, but walking down a side path led us to a rear garden, where a marquee had been set up. It was small in comparison to the main tent, but still spacious enough to fit two cocktail bars, three cream leather seating areas, an ice sculpture of a giant chicken, and a small dance floor.

Besides the furniture, the space was practically deserted. The only people in sight were the half-dozen bartenders manning the two bars, three of whom were doing shots of an indiscernible black liquor with the only other attendee in sight. Thinking he could be a member of the Chikn team, I walked over.

His face was still wincing from the shot when I made my introduction: 'Hey, great space you've set up here.'

The liquor-induced wince morphed seamlessly into a look of confusion. 'What are you on about?'

'I mean, I'm a big fan of your work. Think what you guys are doing over at Chikn is great.'

'Oh, right. Yeah, sorry bro, I'm not with Chikn, I'm with Particle.'

I had heard of Particle. Everyone involved in Avalanche, or NFTs for that matter, had heard of them. In May of the previous year, they had purchased at Sotheby's Banksy's famous 'Love is in the Air' artwork, the black spray paint stencil of a balaclava-ed youth hurling a bouquet of multicoloured flowers, for $12.9 million – 250–400 per cent higher than the piece's estimate of $3–5 million. They then split the piece up into 10,000 NFTs, in a process called 'fractionalised ownership', and sold these off one by one. Each holder of a Particle NFT would 'own' a piece of the Banksy, and vote on where it was displayed.

Particle planned to sell the 10,000 NFTs for $1,500 a piece, which would've netted them a profit of just over $2 million. Unfortunately, they vastly overestimated the demand for owning 0.01 per cent of a Banksy; not only did the collection not sell out, but the NFTs that did sell then started retailing on the secondary market for far lower than their initial $1,500 price tag. To date, the collection has had a total trading volume of 24,950 AVAX tokens. Even taking the all-time high price of AVAX, $144, means that they only sold around $3.5 million worth of NFTs – a $9.4 million loss.

But that's not all. Some astute members of the art world began looking into Particle in more detail – specifically, the terms and conditions of their Banksy NFTs. Buried in the fine print was a clause that stated that buyers of the Particle NFTs would not each actually receive 0.01 per cent ownership rights over the artwork. Instead, all 10,000 NFTs together represented ownership of 0.01 per cent of the artwork. The remaining 99.99 per cent would be held by the Particle Foundation itself. This meant that each particle NFT owner was actually buying 0.000001 per cent of a Banksy.

I wrapped up my conversation with the person from their team, whose name I never bothered getting, and rejoined the others. We ordered a round of espresso martinis and moved on. The Chikn team had flown the coop, so there was no point hanging around talking to a lame duck.

After a few more laps of the castle grounds, various rounds of tapas and additional cocktails, we decided to head back to the apartment. We were all a bit the worse for wear at this point and needed to sleep or shower off the booze before our side event that evening. We shuffled through the swaying crowds loitering around the castle gates, toppled into a cab, and headed back to Casa Batlló.

A few hours later, and displaying all the symptoms of early onset hangovers, Paul, Miles, Archie and I drove towards our event venue. Bradley and Claire had gone ahead of us, sacrificing snoozes and showers to ensure everything was set up and ready to go once the guests started arriving. We pulled up to the park in which the bar we had hired was located and strolled over. The waiters on the door mistook us for early guests and eagerly offered us glasses of champagne and some sort of vegetable-based canapé. We didn't bother correcting them, as the day's drinking was still languishing lightly over us. Instead, we accepted their offerings and stepped inside.

When the guests eventually started to arrive, they did so en masse. The 150-person venue was quickly at capacity, and the soirée spilled out onto the balcony, into the park, and just about everywhere within eyesight of the venue (and walking distance of the bar). Despite the multitude of guests, the evening passed largely without incident. That is, notwithstanding one rather bizarre, and seemingly foreboding, encounter.

As I caroused with our attendees, trying to acquire some useful leads for Moonshot, I was approached by a group of four girls. This immediately struck me as odd as, up to then, I hadn't spotted any other girls at all at the event. They were all short, barely topping 5 foot, all of Asian extraction, and all dressed head to toe in black. But not just that: on closer inspection, I realised they were all wearing the exact same clothes. Black shoes, black jeans and black hoodies with a yellow logo in large print across the front. It was a company I hadn't heard of before: Perpetual Partners.

'Hi, are you with Moonshot?' one of the girls asked me. She spoke with an international accent, the kind that borrows heavily from the American, and was clutching what looked like a professional handheld camera.

'Hi. Yes, I am. Why?'

She looked around at her companions with a smile of excitement. 'We're your new clients!'

'Oh, right. Okay. Sorry, who are you?'

'We're from Perpetual Partners! You know, the derivatives exchange.'

'Ah, got it. Perpetual Partners. Of course.'

'We can't wait to start working with you, We've heard such great things.'

'Sorry, just remind me: what's Perpetual Partners again?'

'We've been speaking with Aidan for the past few weeks. About Moonshot doing our marketing. We'll be working together from next week.'

'Right, got it. Yes, of course. Perp Partners, how could I forget?' Aidan was our sales manager. He had been signing so many contracts recently that it was difficult to keep up. This one had clearly slipped through my net.

'That's why we came to Barcelona,' said one of the other girls, this time with an English accent. 'We wanted to meet you face to face, before we start working together. Next week.' She stressed the final words, as if picking up from my confused expression that I had no idea who they were, let alone that we were to start marketing for them so soon.

Slightly embarrassed, I made a bit of small talk with them, mainly around how they were finding Barcelona and what they thought of the summit today, before making a polite excuse about needing to check on something in the kitchen. Promising to return soon, I went in search of Archie.

I found him on the balcony, talking to a young, tall man with long blond hair, dressed as a Viking. Shaking my head, I went to ask what the frankly ridiculous get-up was in aid of, but suppressed my urge and addressed Archie instead. 'Mate, I need to talk to you.'

'What's up?' Archie asked with irritation, as if I had just interrupted an important conversation.

'I just spoke to some people from a company called Perpetual Partners. Apparently, we're working with them from Monday. You ever heard of them?'

'Shit,' said Archie. He smiled apologetically to the Viking and pulled me to a corner of the packed balcony. 'What did you say to them?'

'Nothing. Just said hello really. Bit of chat about the event. Nothing interesting.'

'Mate, do you know who they are?!'

'Well, obviously not.'

'Look, go back to them, and smooth talk them. Become their best friends. Ask if they want to come to this after-party with us later.'

'Why, who are they?'

'They're an exchange.' Archie said this as if that was all I needed to know.

'Yes, I know that. Why are they so special though?'

'They're our first exchange client. It's a big deal. And it also means they're fucking loaded.'

'How loaded?'

'I don't know. We need to find out. But they're going to be paying us twenty grand a month. Aidan said they didn't bat an eyelid when he quoted them that. No negotiation, no questioning it, nothing. Just signed.'

I glanced back over at the four unassuming girls. They were standing awkwardly by the door leading to the bathrooms, not quite talking to each other.

'All right,' I said, 'I'll go back over.'

'Good man. Remember, smooth talk them. And ask how much cash they have.'

Returning to them with a beaming smile, I asked if I could get them some drinks. I told them the champagne going round was Moët, but we had a stash of Krug in the kitchen that we were saving for our VIPs. They declined. I asked if they wanted to come to an after-party with us later and informed them it was supposed to be the best one of the summit. Tickets had sold out months ago, but we knew the guys running it, so I could get them in. They declined again, saying they had an early flight back to London in the morning.

'Well, if you change your mind,' I said, handing them a small stack of business cards, 'you can reach me on these numbers.' They took the cards and said their goodbyes, apologising for the abrupt exit – but they were already late for a dinner they had booked.

Before I had a chance to stop and ruminate over the encounter, night had descended. The rest of the event had passed me by in a blur of handshakes, exchanged business cards, and greedily drunk champagne. Before I knew it, guests were filing out of the bar, heading to one after-party or another. When the venue was empty, our contingent took its leave. We shunned a cab in favour of walking. It was a pleasant spring night, and we were in no rush. The club we were headed to was only about a mile away, and we felt the night air would refresh us after a solid and consistent day of drinking.

We had scarcely left the park, however, when we were approached by someone clad all in blue, with the logo of Filecoin, a crypto project worth around $3 billion back then, printed on his T-shirt.

'Hey guys, after-party?'

'Yeah, we're heading to the Frens party, in Pacha. You know, the one with Steve Aoki DJing.'

'Oh, no, I meant do you want to come to the Filecoin after-party?'

He was another host, just like in the castle earlier that day. We consulted one another briefly, and decided it was worth popping in; if we could make even a low-level contact with Filecoin, that could prove very fruitful.

We were directed through a nondescript doorway, down a narrow spiral staircase, and through a set of double doors. They opened up into a large, modern space, which looked like some kind of bar or disco. It was almost completely empty. A table next to the doors was stacked with merch. Grabbing some tote bags, T-shirts and a few water bottles for good measure, we went over to the bar. Without asking, we were presented with a round of Sambuca shots. Archie got out his wallet to pay, and the bartender smiled politely.

'Don't worry,' he said, straining slightly over the unnecessarily loud music, 'there's no charge. The sponsor paid already.'

'So the after-parties are all comped as well,' Paul said with interest. 'Good to know. Must cost a bomb, with club markups for drinks.' We ordered a round of beers in bottles and took our leave.

'Well, that was shit,' Archie said. 'Might be worth dropping their marketing guy a message on LinkedIn and tell them they should hire us to arrange their next party.'

Progressing less than 100m down the street, we were accosted by another host. This time, he was standing outside a large, multi-storey nightclub, with a roped-off entry and a queue of around thirty people waiting to get frisked. He tried to beckon us into the queue, but we declined.

'Fucking hell,' Miles said, spotting another host on the other side of the road, 'these projects have lost their heads. Have they hired every club in Barcelona?'

By the time we arrived at the club we had set out for, the answer to Miles's question was obvious: yes, they had in fact hired every club in the city. Every single one had been taken over that weekend by one project or another, all vying to get some exposure at the Avalanche summit. And willing to pay through the nose in complimentary drinks for it.

And, as we discovered the next morning, they didn't just stop at the clubs: nursing quite severe hangovers, we left our apartment in search of some food to restore us to good form. We knew we could get a free meal at the Poble Espanyol, but the previous day's session had left us in dire need of sustenance, and we simply couldn't stomach the trek over to the venue. Taking a few steps from our building, we saw branded promotional flags placed outside a Spanish bistro. The coins and rockets garishly emblazoned on them indicated that they belonged to a crypto project. We stepped into the restaurant and discovered that some GameFi project on the peripheries of the Avalanche ecosystem had hired it for the weekend, as the 'official crypto pitstop' in Casa Batlló. We shook our heads in disbelief, found a table for six, and just told them to bring us one of everything on the menu.

'And six pints of Estrella, *por favor*,' Paul added, to nods of approval from the rest of the table.

The rest of the conference proceeded in much the same fashion: we moved from free bar to free bar, eating and drinking at the expense of others. If token and NFT investors knew that the funds they had handed over to projects were being used to finance international parties, under the guise of increasing brand awareness by gaining industry exposure, perhaps they would think twice about being so cavalier with their capital in future.

And, even with all the fast, easy money sloshing around the industry at the time, I couldn't help but marvel at the lack of foresight from the projects that allocated their marketing budgets to cover the good times of people like me. People who did not care in the least about their 'use cases' or value propositions and were clearly just at their events for the freebies. I wondered what benefit they saw in essentially bribing people to come to bars and clubs that had their logos dotted around here and there. Of course, many of them had more money than they knew what to do with. However, I couldn't envisage anyone being so rich that dropping $100–200,000 on a party that most wouldn't remember the next morning would seem like a good idea. They could, for example, just keep the money for themselves, paying it out as a bonus, as opposed to subsidising nights out for hundreds of people who neither knew nor cared about them.

While this held true for most, if not all, of the projects that ran side events at the summit, the same could not be said about Avalanche themselves. They dominated the crypto media for the entirety of the summit and for weeks afterwards. They even managed to broach the mainstream financial outlets. And not only because they gave free VIP tickets to every financial journalist who would open their emails. They made some big announcements as well.

Chief among these featured Grimes, the US rapper and mother to three of Elon Musk's children, addressing the summit via video link. She announced she would be launching an 'intergalactic children's metaverse book', which would be hosted on the Avalanche blockchain. During the address, Grimes also announced Avalanche would be launching a $100 million creator fund, for art and cultural projects within the Avalanche ecosystem. Grimes's metaverse book, which was aiming to create 'a profound experience for babies that is also deeply meaningful to adults', would be the first project to benefit from the fund. Since making this summit address, however, Grimes has given no further updates on the status of this project, and no information on it exists whatsoever beyond the press flurry that surrounded its initial announcement.*

As for us, the summit was also a big success. Beyond drinking our weight in free booze, we came away with a load of potential new clients for Moonshot Advisors, and prospective investors for Aquarius Drops. And, most importantly, we also made contact with Perpetual Partners, who looked set to take our agency to the next level. If we did a good job and became indispensable to them, we could ride their coattails all the way to the top.

It was the best opportunity we had ever received at Moonshot, and I resolved to make the most of it.

---

* In an interview with *WIRED* in 2023, Grimes lamented the decline of the crypto industry, stating, 'I'm sad about what happened to NFTs and crypto, because it got polluted fast with people trying to make as much money as possible.' In the same interview, she admitted to making more money from selling NFTs than she ever did from music.

18

Bailing with a Leaky Bucket

As soon as our plane touched down in London, I began looking deeper into Perpetual Partners. As Archie had said, they were our first exchange client. But I soon discovered they were much more significant than even that. They were our first client that Three Arrows Capital had invested in.

For a long time, Three Arrows Capital (or '3AC' for short) was regarded as *the* crypto hedge fund. At their peak in 2022, they had around $18 billion in assets under management, making them not just the largest fund in the industry, but one of the largest in the entire world. It was founded in 2012 by two friends from Stanford University – Su Zhu and Kyle Davies – who, after graduating, both went on to work at Credit Suisse. Initially, it was focused on more traditional equity investments. However, seeing how much money there was to be made in crypto, and how easy it was to perform arbitrage by exploiting token price discrepancies across exchanges, Zhu and Davies changed their strategy. They went all in, and never looked back.

As well as trading the markets, they also invested heavily in early-stage blockchain projects, many of which went on to become some of the biggest, most successful ventures in the space. Counted among their portfolio companies were the likes of layer 1 giants Ethereum, Avalanche, Solana and Luna. Such was their artistry at picking winners that industry participants coined an unofficial tagline: '3AC: they never miss.' And now we had one of their projects on our client list.

And it was clear to see why 3AC had backed Perpetual. Their May 2021 token sale raised a cool $20 million, roughly the same amount raised by the behemoth FTX, which Perpetual had the rather ambitious goal of unseating as the leading derivatives exchange in the industry. And their similarities with FTX didn't end at their fund-raise. Like FTX, Perpetual built their exchange before launching their token, and actually conducted their sale on the platform itself. To date, they were the only project I had ever worked with that launched a product alongside a token. So I figured that if anyone had a shot at taking on FTX, it was them. Especially given the background of their CEO, Rupert. He was a former quant fund manager, who left a job as a trader behind in order to become entrepreneur-in-residence at Y-Combinator, a startup accelerator, which helped to grow and develop firms such as Dropbox, Airbnb and Reddit.

Crypto had been on his radar during his fund management days, and when things started heating up in DeFi summer he saw his opportunity: he would marry together the skills he acquired in the arduous training camps of Y-Combinator and the capital markets, and use them to make his fortune in the fledgling battlefield of crypto. And he proved himself highly creative in blazing a trail through the industry.

He figured that Californian tech bros must be dying to get their skin in the crypto game. So under the Perpetual umbrella he spun up an asset management firm: Perp Strategies. They focused on yield farming stablecoins, obtaining better interest rates than government bonds, and with minimal risk. He started pitching to tech firms in California, and quickly amassed over $100 million in assets under management. Seemingly overnight, he had made himself the go-to crypto guy for half of Silicon Valley.

In the nine or ten months or so since his exchange had launched, it had seen several billion dollars' worth of trading volume – a relatively small amount, as Rupert was first looking to expand Perpetual's asset offering. By the time we came to work with them, they had over two dozen tokens available for users to trade. Content with this, their focus shifted to bringing more punters onto their platform. This meant ramping up marketing, which was where we came in.

Perpetual wanted to take things slow at first and devote the first month of our engagement to planning and strategy. This was a breath of fresh air after a year of relentlessly working to unrealistic deadlines for clients who needed everything done yesterday. It was also something of a novelty to be working with a company that actually valued having a solid plan in place, rather than shooting from the hip and hoping they didn't miss. We decided to pull out all the stops. As well as a complete audit of all their marketing materials to date, and a thorough strategy for gaining new users and growing their revenues, we also managed to get them blue-tick verification on Twitter. Back then, this was the Holy Grail of legitimacy for crypto projects.

These were the days before Elon Musk's infamous takeover of the platform, before Twitter became 'X'. It was a time before blue ticks could be acquired for a measly $8 per month subscription. In April 2022, that little blue mark provided genuine validation and social capital. It showed the world that you were someone of note. And there were hordes of crypto projects, desperate to convince the world of their legitimacy, trying to get their hands on one.

Luckily for us, a girl we had hired some months previously as an account manager was something of a socialite. She was called Sophie and lived in Bali, where she worked for us remotely. A part-time fashion blogger and big-time partier, she was part of the digital diaspora who had upped sticks from their dreary homelands spread across the world's colder climes and landed on Bali's tropical shores. She and her set spent their weekends partying in cliffside mansions and their weekdays tapping away at laptops from infinity pool-adjacent sunloungers. Among the cohorts of her fashionable friends, she counted many rising stars in the world of tech, including someone very high up in the Southeast Asian arm of Twitter. When Perpetual came on board as a client, Sophie called in some favours and, in no time at all, I was sitting staring at a message from Rupert asking how, exactly, we had managed to achieve something he had spent months striving for in vain.

The relationship couldn't have gotten off to a better start, and we soon started reaping the rewards. Perpetual told us they were looking to run an influencer campaign, which was music to our ears. However, our excitement was tempered somewhat when they informed us of the nature of the campaign: they wanted Eastern European influencers to promote their 'ref links' on Twitter. The first part of this was straightforward enough: they needed to target

Eastern Europe and other far-flung parts of the world, as they were prohibited from offering their product in the UK.

While crypto isn't regulated here in the UK, there are stringent rules governing derivative products. Perpetual Partners offered incredibly high leverage, up to 10,000 per cent, and had over thirty crypto derivatives available for their users to speculate on. This made them *persona non grata* in the UK, and meant they had to adopt a somewhat complex operating structure. They were registered in the Seychelles, operated out of an office in Canary Wharf, and had a user base mainly consisting of customers in Asia, Eastern Europe and Russia. But this wasn't what we were concerned about. Dodgy domiciles were par for the course. It was promoting ref links that made us wary.

Ref link campaigns are commonplace for exchanges. They involve providing influencers with a link to the trading platform, which they can promote to their followers. If users sign up to an exchange through a ref link, they'll receive a discount on trading fees. Ref link deals are an easy sell to influencers, as typically they're given a percentage of all the trading fees generated by people who use their link. If this percentage is negotiated well, influencers can even be persuaded to promote ref links with no upfront fees. They all wanted a piece of that pie, after hearing stories about people like Carl the Moon. A former supermarket shelf-stacker from Sweden, Carl got in early on bitcoin, bagging a small fortune, and proceeded to turn himself into a crypto celebrity by documenting his progress on YouTube. But it wasn't until he put his newly acquired audience to use, and started shilling ref links for ByBit, that the real money started rolling in.

ByBit was another cryptocurrency exchange and was renowned for being the biggest marketing spender in the entire industry. They had their fingers in every pie, and almost every influencer of note was on their payroll in one way or another. They offered some of the most lucrative deals, often dishing out million-dollar payments to their biggest promoters, as well as 100 per cent of the trading fees generated through ref links. And their splurging extended far beyond the realms of just crypto influencers. In February 2022, they signed a $150 million sponsorship deal with Formula 1 team Red Bull Racing

– the first (but by no means the last) crypto Formula 1 sponsorship deal, and the largest sports sponsorship any crypto firm had ever entered into up to that point.

The depths of their pockets made competing with them almost impossible. On countless occasions, we approached influencers to promote Perpetual – who were a direct competitor of ByBit – only to find ByBit had got to them first and made them sign exclusivity deals. The rumour we heard from Rupert was that their annual marketing budget was in excess of $1 billion per year. For comparison, in 2021 the total advertising budget of Microsoft was $1.1 billion, and they were the third biggest company in the world then, with a $1.8 trillion valuation.

Finding influencers to promote ref links for Perpetual Partners, therefore, would not be an easy task. We figured it was very much a job for Plug Promotions, who had the most extensive list of Twitter influencers that I knew of, many of whom operated in niche jurisdictions.

Our relationship with Jules, the proprietor of Plug Promotions, was flourishing, as we had by now easily sent over a million dollars of business his way. It was somewhat disconcerting the first time we sent him a six-figure payment, given that we only knew his first name, and – barring a single phone call – had only ever spoken to him on Telegram.

Despite this being standard operating practice in the industry, a recently hired head of compliance insisted we at least get a business address for him, before we sent him more money. I obliged, and Jules duly provided an address. A Google Maps search revealed his business was located in a mobile phone repair shop in Kerala, India. I wasn't particularly convinced by this, given the clear New York accent he spoke with on my only ever call with him, and the fact he only operated during US business hours. However, I didn't think the head of compliance needed to be troubled with these irrelevancies and decided to keep quiet about it all. Jules was a great partner of ours, after all.

And the partnership wasn't a one-way street. Jules returned the favour by giving us hefty discounts on campaigns and prioritising our business. The ref link campaign request, though, was an exception. When we approached him with it, we could immediately tell something was off; he didn't respond to our message with his typical greed-induced enthusiasm.

'Yeah, sure thing, guys. I can have a look at this. I might need a few days, even a week, though, to get some recommendations together.'

'Why so long, bro? Just need a quick list of your biggest trading accounts. Should only take a few minutes.'

The reply he gave to this raised more questions than it did answers: he simply sent a link to a Twitter account, bearing the ominous name of Reaper Reconnaissance. I had long been familiar with this account. As, indeed, had everyone in the crypto industry. Reaper was a scam detective: a vigilante figure who investigated and exposed prominent rug pulls. His analysis was incredibly thorough, often not just revealing how scams had occurred, but even unmasking the anonymous culprits behind them, their rap sheets of previous scams, and under what aliases these had been committed. Because of this, he had amassed a colossal – and incredibly devoted – audience. He had around 350,000 followers on Twitter and counted among them was every single person of influence or authority you could think of.

The consequences of all this were simple – and terrifying: if Reaper called you out, and you became the subject of one of his exposés, it spelt the end for your project. You were irredeemably labelled a grifter and were anathema throughout the entire industry.

'Shit. Not that fucking guy. What's he saying?'

'He's going to expose my influencer list. Not good. He has mainstream media journalists following his every move, just waiting to run a big story on crypto scams. They all suck up to him, view him as the industry saviour, or some shit like that.'

Reaper had a particular aversion to influencers, and their wanton use of their followers as exit liquidity. We had had a few run-ins with Reaper in the past; the blatant influencer shilling of the Viaduct Capital token launch, combined with the vast amount of funds they raised and the scandal that plagued their auction, had caught his attention. He reposted some of the promotional tweets we had procured for them, but luckily for us he didn't conduct any more thorough analysis on the project's antics and didn't produce a full-on exposé. Viaduct was able to walk away wounded, but still breathing.

By the way things were going, it seemed highly unlikely that the same would be said of us; to our absolute dismay, things played out exactly as Jules had said. Reaper posted his influencer list, which presumably had been leaked to him by either a disgruntled former client or another vigilante posing as a prospective client. A large, international mainstream media outlet then dutifully picked up on the story, running a major piece about it, which they made a big song and dance about across all their social media channels (their Twitter alone, it's worth noting, had over 1 million followers).

For us, this was nothing short of a disaster. Since we had started engaging with Jules, his influencer list was *our* influencer list. We were white labelling his services, meaning we took all his pitch decks and materials, slapped our own logo on it, and sent it out to clients. The contents, and even the formatting, were exactly the same. Everybody in the industry was going to see this and realise two things: firstly, that we had been outsourcing our influencer marketing to another agency (meaning that the 'admin fees' we had been charging them were completely unwarranted); and, secondly, that we had been applying a hefty markup onto the costs, and the same influencers could have been produced from Plug Promotions for a lot less money. And that's not to mention the reputational damage we were going to incur from being associated with promoters who had been publicly called out by Reaper – one of the biggest stigmas in the space.

I quickly learned, though, that our concerns were not shared by Jules, who had formulated his own damage-control strategy. For reasons none of us could fathom, he decided to lean into the whole affair. He had the effrontery to comment on Reaper's post, mocking him: 'Wow I'm #1 on the list! Too bad prices ain't right' followed by a laughing emoji.

Not content with just this, he also posted screenshots from people who had DM'd him following the leak, requesting his services. 'Wow, after this post I am now getting a bunch of web3 projects asking me for promotion ... @ReaperRecon your influence is working ... how much do you charge per tweet??'

And, soon after this, he posted another screenshot, this time of all the new followers he had acquired as a result of Reaper's post, along with the caption: 'All these followers came from @ReaperRecon little news "leak" ... all you had to do is DM me for my prices man. I would have told you! thanks for all the love & support to my existing followers and welcome all new followers.'

Needless to say, we had no intention of being so brazen. We decided the best course of action was to do nothing and respond to individual complaints from clients as and when they arose. I had a generic statement in my back pocket around using a variety of external specialist partners to ensure the optimisation of campaigns, which I could adapt as the situation demanded.

Fortuitously, however, this wasn't necessary; none of our clients, current or former, reached out to us about the leak.

'Maybe they're used to it,' offered Paul, as we sipped beers on the rooftop bar and discussed coming out seemingly unscathed from the whole fiasco. 'You know, like they expect this kind of stuff.'

'Yeah, or maybe they just didn't see the post,' suggested Miles.

'Look, it's crypto lads,' said Archie. 'People are busy, they don't scroll through Reaper's shit all day. Plus, they expect it. Influencers promote stuff, it's how it works. And we put a markup on their prices, obviously. We've got to eat too, and it took us a bloody long time to find Jules. We should be compensated for that.'

We agreed that Archie's summary of the situation, reheated though it may be, merited a toast. When our glasses were empty, I made my way over to the bar to order another round. As I took my place in the bustling queue, my phone buzzed. It was Rupert, from Perpetual.

'Ha! Get a load of this. New influencer shill list just dropped by Reaper. Had a quick look and saw a guy on there doing retweets for $25. Who the hell is buying that stuff?! Even the good names on there are finished now. Will take them a while to claw their reps back after this – that's if they manage to at all.'

A bolt of panic shot through me, as I remembered those were the accounts we were going to use for Perpetual's ref link campaign. We'd now have to source a whole new list of influencers. I groaned to myself and bid a bitter farewell to any evening plans I had for the rest of the week. The only consolation I could offer myself was that we hadn't sent Perpetual our list yet. That would have been an absolute disaster and eliminated any credibility we had built up with them over the past few weeks (that is, if they didn't get rid of us on the spot).

Carrying a tray of four pints back to the table, I reflected on our lucky break. Much bigger companies than us had been eviscerated by far less significant posts from Reaper. By sheer dumb luck (and either apathy or inattention – or both – from our clients), we had dodged what would almost certainly have been a fatal bullet.

However, unbeknown to me at the time, while we were caught up in a whirlwind of melodrama, far more frightening storms were brewing on the industry's horizon. And, when they hit, they wouldn't so much rock the boat as sink the entire fleet.

19

A Tryst with Terra

Terra Luna had been the centre stage of the crypto industry for months by this point. It was a late-comer to the scene, having only achieved prominence towards the very end of 2021, only to lose half its value in the first month of 2022. However, it rebounded towards the end of February and surged in value. It achieved an all-time-high market cap of over $40 billion in April, and created hordes of new millionaires in the process.

The project was what's known as a 'decentralised stablecoin' – a form of stablecoin not backed by US dollars. These are complex instruments, and in order to better understand them – and just how irrevocably flawed they are – it's first necessary to get to grips with the flaws in more traditional stablecoins. And where better to start than the biggest player in the game: Tether.

For many, Tether represents the dark heart of the crypto industry. And for good reason. They're the issuer of the stablecoin USDT; created in 2014, it has grown to be a dominating force in the crypto landscape. At the time of writing, USDT has a market cap of $110 billion, making it by far the largest stablecoin in that $160 billion sector of the space. This is in spite of the countless controversies and scandals in which it has been mired since its inception.

In its brief history spanning scarcely ten years, Tether has been accused of every financial crime under the sun. Alarm bells first started sounding in 2015 when Bitfinex, one of the world's largest crypto-currency exchanges, enabled trading of Tether on its platform – the first ever exchange listing the nascent industry giant received. Initially, Bitfinex and Tether insisted that the two operations were wholly separate. However, the release of the Paradise Papers in November 2017 brought the truth to light; this vast dossier of dodgy offshore entities blew the whistle on Bitfinex's relationship with Tether, and revealed that two officials from the former had established the latter as a legal entity in the British Virgin Islands. A spokesperson subsequently admitted the two operations share the same CEO.

The blurred lines between the two enterprises is significant, as it represents an immense conflict of interest. This was brought into sharp focus in 2018 when two academic researchers published a peer-reviewed paper alleging that the seismic rally bitcoin enjoyed during the 2017 bull run was not, in fact, caused by organic buyer demand. Instead, it was down to Tether manipulating the market; the paper asserts that, in many instances of new Tether tokens being created, they were promptly sent to Bitfinex, where the price of bitcoin would then pump near-instantaneously. This has led many in the industry to speculate that the true purpose of USDT is to keep the price of bit-coin buoyant, and that without it the market would collapse. So rife is this suspicion that a number of Twitter accounts have been set up, some with follower counts in the millions, to track the new issu-ances of USDT; they send out alerts, and traders rush to buy bitcoin as soon as they see them, in the expectation of an imminent price pump (although this has led others to counter that, whilst USDT may have been behind bitcoin surges in the past, it is now in fact these alerts which are moving the market).

But it's not just conflicts of interest which have raised eyebrows around the Tether team; they've been linked to a litany of crimes throughout their time at the forefront of the industry. And, in many instances, their illicit actions extend well beyond the realm of finance. One of Tether's co-founders is Brock Pierce; a former child actor who starred in *The Mighty Ducks*. In 2002 Interpol raided the Spanish villa in which Pierce was living with Marc Collins-Rector, founder of the failed dot-com-era streaming site Digital Entertainment Network. On searching the property, authorities discovered guns, machetes and, sickeningly, a vast collection of child pornography. Pierce denied any knowledge of the pornography; however, his housemate later pled guilty to sex trafficking five minors across state lines. There are also allegations against Pierce from 2000 which allege he drugged colleagues and pressured them into sexual activities. And, fanning the flames of speculation around his deviancy further still, in 2011 he spoke about cryptocurrency at a conference organised by none other than Jeffrey Epstein.

Beyond the sordid stories surrounding the Tether team, the firm has also been accused of highly illicit business practices on a global scale, stretching right up to the present time. In March 2024, the US and UK governments initiated a joint probe into Russian-based crypto exchange Garantex, which they suspect routed $20 billion of crypto through their platform in order to evade international sanctions against Russia following its war in Ukraine. These transactions were all processed using Tether's USDT stablecoin.

And yet, as egregious as this all is, it is what's underpinning (or, rather, not underpinning) USDT which has received the most scrutiny, and caused the most concerns, throughout the firm's history.

Tether claims that it holds vast reserves of dollars or dollar-equivalent assets, which back up the token. These assets guarantee the stablecoin will be able to maintain its peg with the dollar. However, they have never published any kind of independent audit into their holdings; instead, over the years they've hired firms to produce a number of 'attestation reports'. As the name would suggest, these reports attest to the fact that, on the day the firms were allowed to root around Tether's filing cabinets, they found the stablecoin issuer was indeed in possession of the assets it claimed to have. However, the firms which file the reports do so with some major caveats: namely, that they only review Tether's accounts on the day for which they've been hired. Any activity prior to or after this goes wholly unchecked. This essentially renders the reports meaningless; they simply state that on a given day Tether has a given number of assets on paper. Not where they came from, whether they actually belong to Tether, or whether they vanished 5 minutes after the check.

And yet, for the most ardent advocates of the decentralised agenda, Tether's uncompromising refusal to release a full audit of their

accounts presents no problem at all. Nor does the voluminous catalogue of financial crimes of which they've been accused. Nor even the
sleaze and scandal which surrounds the founding team. For the most
eager evangelists of decentralisation, all of this is irrelevant. Their only
concern is with the assets backing up USDT – not, as you might expect,
the quantity of these, but the fact that they're issued by a central bank.

For the 'DeFi maximalists' (as they're referred to in the industry),
having centrally issued currency backing up a stablecoin is unfor-
givable. It constitutes the cardinal sin of crypto, and renders USDT
a wholly unacceptable underpinning for their new financial system.
The most hardcore crypto bros, as you can see, have their priorities
entirely in order and their heads firmly screwed on ...

Terra Luna was very much in this camp; they weren't enamoured
with the idea of a cryptocurrency being backed by government-
issued assets, controlled by a centralised entity. So when they
launched their stablecoin UST, they decided the most sensible asset
they could use to back it up was yet another cryptocurrency. And not
just that, but one which they themselves had also created: the now-
infamous LUNA. They made each UST stablecoin redeemable for $1
worth of LUNA. The idea was that UST would be kept stable by the
backing of LUNA, and the price of LUNA would be kept buoyant by
investor confidence in UST.

Despite this setup sounding like the crypto equivalent of a circu-
lar argument, Terra Luna achieved huge success – fuelled, no doubt,
by the marketing efforts of Terraform Labs, the registered company
that created and controlled the project. They began by using the
standard playbook of project promotion: they launched a headline-
grabbing grant fund, topping $150 million; they struck major-league,
mainstream sponsorship deals, including a $40 million deal to spon-
sor the Washington Nationals baseball team; and, of course, they
put every influencer and news outlet in the industry on the payroll,
to sing their praises. However, as expedient as all this was to their
meteoric rise, it was Anchor Protocol that really drove their growth.

Anchor was a 'staking' protocol, also built and operated by
Terraform Labs. A staking protocol is basically just a platform where
users can go to deposit their funds and receive interest. Anchor was a
bit like a typical savings account that a bank might offer, in that users

deposit their money and receive interest, except with one big difference: whereas savings accounts offer, at best, mid-single-figure yield, Anchor Protocol gave depositors 20 per cent interest on their cash.

While this may sound like a lot compared to what the banks offer, it paled in comparison to the highest yields on offer in crypto. For many years, the practice of 'yield farming' – which is where punters traverse the world of decentralised finance in search of the juiciest returns – was arguably the biggest, most popular use of cryptocurrencies. Some staking projects were offering users three- or even four-figure percentage returns on their deposit. Contrast this with the 2 or 3 per cent most banks were offering at the time, with interest rates at historic lows, and it's obvious why yield farming attracted so much attention. It wasn't so much a case of yield farming propelling decentralised finance: yield farming *was* decentralised finance. At its peak in 2021, there was over $150 billion sloshing around the DeFi space, most of which was locked up in staking protocols.

As more and more participants entered the scene to get in on the gold rush, the yields started getting out of control. With so many staking protocols on the market, new entrants needed to set themselves apart by offering frankly ludicrous returns. And nothing highlights the extravagance and absurdity of this period in the industry's history better than Alchemix.

Alchemix burst onto the crypto scene in February 2021, with a seemingly impossible claim: they would loan people money that would never have to be paid back. Alchemix saw how much yield was on offer throughout DeFi and, rather than just farming it themselves, they got creative. They built a platform onto which users could deposit their money, with this then being sent out into the DeFi space and used for yield farming. But, rather than just paying people the returns over time, Alchemix gave users all the returns up front. This essentially amounted to a loan that the users wouldn't have to pay back. Thanks to the wonders of Web3, it instead paid itself back.

To use a hypothetical example, if you were to deposit $1,000 into Alchemix, they would instantly give you $10,000. They'd then put your $1,000 to work in the DeFi farms, and simply keep the interest for themselves. When word of this got out, it sent the sector into a frenzy, with thousands scrambling to explore the possibilities of Alchemix. One anonymous user, who went by the Twitter handle 0xDeFi, took out a loan and then immediately used it to buy a $25,000 top-of-the-range speed boat. Through yield farming, the loan repaid itself, and 0xDeFi walked away with a brand-new boat, without ever paying a penny of his own money. Needless to say, when stories like this started to emerge, Alchemix's self-repaying loans exploded in popularity even further. In just two months of it being on the market, users had deposited over $1 billion into the protocol.

However, over time yield farmers were shown the meaning of the age-old maxim 'if it sounds too good to be true, it is'. The reason that many of the farming protocols in crypto were able to offer such unbelievable returns was that they were paying depositors in tokens they had created themselves. Far more often than not, these tokens were backed up by nothing but sheer hope; their value was driven by the belief that their price would either hold or, better yet, increase over time. Clearly, though, this isn't the case, and gradually it dawned on the industry that all the yield in the world meant nothing if the token it was paid out in had no value.

The realisation that months of yield farming gains were capable of being eviscerated by even minuscule market corrections made people increasingly disenchanted with yield farming. Eventually, there was an exodus of liquidity parked in staking pools that paid out interest in volatile tokens. And, conversely, protocols that paid out in stablecoins saw huge capital inflows. Stablecoins were different, because users knew that whatever interest they received was actually going to have value, as the tokens were on parity with the dollar. This was far more desirable than the Wild West system of yield farming that had dominated the industry for so long – but it wasn't without downsides. Because, while the value of the income users received was guaranteed, the yields themselves were much, much lower than those offered by volatile tokens. Often, they barely beat the interest you could get from a regular savings account with a bank.

This is what made Anchor so significant; the hordes of investors who were sitting on fortunes from the bull run were now looking for calmer, low-risk platforms offering guaranteed income, on which to park their funds. Anchor's 20 per cent interest per year fitted that bill perfectly. Very soon, it became one of the most used DeFi applications on any blockchain network, with over $17.5 billion of user cash staked on the platform at its peak. And, as Anchor grew, so did the public profile of the mastermind behind the whole Terra Luna ecosystem: Do Kwon.

Born and raised in South Korea, Do Kwon went on to study computer science at Stanford University. He was quickly recognised as a programming prodigy and, on his return to South Korea in 2016, at the age of just 25, he raised $1 million in angel investment and grants for a peer-to-peer telecoms company he founded, called Anyfi. It was here that he had his first encounters with financial misconduct; in a later investigation, it emerged that some of the grant money with Anyfi received – which came from the South Korean government – had been appropriated for personal expenses. This was a mere flirtation with fraud, though, compared to what was to come.

Do Kwon graduated into the big leagues just a few years later, in 2018, when he founded Terra Luna. This was also the time that he discovered he possessed a particular flair for public relations. When setting up his new enterprise, he realised that if crypto investors were to have any faith in a project, they needed to have faith in its founder. They wanted founders to be cocky to the point of arrogance, espousing delusionally grand ambitions for their projects. So Do Kwon set about fashioning a cult of personality around himself.

He contrived a God complex, styling himself as the 'master of stablecoins', and plastering this epithet across his social media bios. His tweets frequently featured rhetoric that lambasted his rivals; in one particularly theatrical attack, he declared that 'by my hand DAI will die', with DAI being a $9.5 billion competitor to UST.

He also demonstrated a willingness to be as aggressive as needed in his public communications, defending the reputation of his project against even the slightest criticism. In one outburst from November 2021, responding to a thread speculating on how Terra Luna could be susceptible to failure, he wrote: 'Probably the most retarded thread ive read this decade. Silence is a perfectly acceptable option if stupid.'

In all situations, and at every opportunity, he bet big on Luna. This took a turn for the literal in March 2022, when he entered into a million-dollar wager with a prominent social media influencer, known only by the pseudonym AlgodTrading. AlgodTrading was no fan of either Terra or Do Kwon and, in early March 2022, he had a bitter exchange with Do on Twitter. The influencer threatened that, should Luna achieve a new all-time high, he would take out a large short position on it. Do Kwon berated him, questioning how large of a position he could really open, to which AlgodTrading responded: 'Statistically your dunking on 99 per cent+ of your community but all right. Some day your ponzi will collapse, you can't keep fuelling anchor :).'

Do Kwon fired back in his typical fashion: 'Statistically this community bought luna, so they definitely are not poor as your broke ass. Continue in poverty ser.'

Five days later, the bet was made: should the price of Luna be higher in one year's time than it was on the day of the bet, Do Kwon would collect the seven-figure winnings, and vice versa.

It was this unadulterated, unblinking bullishness that crypto investors wanted to see. And it won Do Kwon unfathomable support. People punted more and more of their money into Luna, and staked their life savings on Anchor, safe in the knowledge that Do Kwon was protecting their capital and guaranteeing their fortunes. Of course, despite the unconscionable level of faith and devotion shown to him by millions in the industry, the support was not unanimous. AlgodTrading wasn't his only critic.

There was a small contingent of dissenting voices, who refused to be taken in by his charm, and proved impervious to his charisma. Their criticisms had one key focal point: the suspect origins of the yield that Anchor paid out. They saw that Anchor was the main driver behind Luna's growth and just couldn't get their heads around what would happen if (or, indeed, when) the yield dried up. Of course, Do Kwon shut down these questions with characteristic ruthlessness, and ultimately emerged victorious from the PR battle.

His critics were dismissed as heretics, tinfoil-hatted conspiracy theorists, or simply ignorant of how decentralised finance and blockchain tech operate. Terra continued surging higher and higher, ballooning to its all-time high valuation of $40 billion: a strikingly apposite figure, being nearly the exact same sum of money pilfered by Bernie Madoff through his infamous Ponzi scheme.

And, just like the Madoff Ponzi, in May 2022 the fault lines in Terra Luna began to show. The house of cards upon which Do Kwon's whole empire was built started to collapse. And people began to realise that Do Kwon, like the much-maligned emperor, had no clothes.

'I'm telling you, Anchor is unstable. Get your money out of it now. Like, right fucking now. This is going to be a massacre.'

This was the message Rupert from Perpetual sent me. He forwarded it on from his CTO, who had sent it the weekend before Terra Luna imploded.

It was 6 May, and things were not looking good. For the past few days, social media was awash with speculation. Something bad was happening with Terra Luna. People were bracing for the worst, and the rumour was that Anchor would be the first domino to fall.

But this wasn't the start of the speculation; questions had first arisen nearly two months earlier. The Luna Foundation Guard started market buying vast amounts of bitcoin. This was an organisation 'mandated to build reserves supporting the UST peg amid volatile market conditions' (with its acronym 'LFG' being a nod to the commonly used industry phrase 'let's fucking go'). Their most significant purchase came on 28 March, when they bought 27,000 bitcoins worth around $1.3 billion. They then continued to top up their war chest over the coming weeks, also adding $100 million worth of Avalanche's AVAX token.

This shopping spree was regarded by most in the industry as a bullish signal; Terraform Labs were both shoring up their balance sheet with a diversified range of crypto assets, and also taking large amounts of bitcoin and other tokens off the market, thereby pumping the price. However, the more rational industry observers saw this as odd, and a potential sign that the company was girding itself for some impending and foreseen trouble.

Included among these crypto Cassandras was Galois Capital, a relatively small hedge fund with around $200 million assets under management. And yet, despite their modest size, they were considered to have some of the best traders and analysts on the street. They were frequently on the right side of some of the biggest moves in the market and had a long track record of making accurate calls based on astute analysis. And, for several months prior to Do Kwon's asset purchases, they had been sounding the alarm about Terra Luna. Their founder, Kevin Zhou, gave a series of media interviews, expressing his scepticism towards the mechanism underpinning the decentralised stablecoin. And, in an interview with CoinDesk, he gave his analysis on the LFG's move to shore up its treasury: 'It signalled to the market that they no longer believed in their own narrative.'

Needless to say, Zhou and his like were dismissed as doom merchants, and their cautionary words were drowned out by the short-sighted jubilation that these crypto purchases produced throughout the space.

That is, until they were wholly vindicated in early May.

At the start of the month, vast piles of UST were dumped onto the market and swapped for other stablecoins such as USDC. This spooked investors; fearing that someone knew something they didn't, they started withdrawing their funds from Anchor en masse. Before you knew it, capital flight from the staking protocol was in full and frenzied swing. The exact cause of the UST selloff that triggered the withdrawals wasn't known (and, indeed, still isn't). Speculation was rife, and some in the space even ventured that Anchor and the whole Luna ecosystem was undergoing a targeted attack.

The name that started getting thrown around was Citadel Securities, one of the biggest market makers in the world, which operates in over fifty countries and sees annual revenue upwards of $7.5 billion. The rumour that started spreading like wildfire was that Citadel took the same view as the fringe Terra Luna critics: they believed the project to be nothing more than a Ponzi scheme, so took out a massive short on the Luna token and gradually bought up a huge UST position. They then dumped the stablecoins onto the market in one fell swoop, to try to trigger a 'depeg' – an event wherein a stablecoin loses its parity with the dollar. Were this to happen to UST, the price of its sister token, Luna, would also tank, as the price of one was inherently linked to confidence in the other. Citadel would then be in for a windfall from their short position.

These rumours were wholly unverified, but they were so widespread that Citadel were forced to issue an official statement denying them.

'Well, you know what they say,' Miles said, when analysing the situation later, and discussing whether Citadel were indeed the culprits of the UST selloff, 'don't believe anything until it's been officially denied.'

Of course, this was pure speculation. But whatever the reason for the selloff, and whoever the real culprits were, one thing remained certain: the situation was serious, and investor confidence took a huge blow.

And then, on 7 May, all hell started breaking loose.

UST lost its peg. The mechanism that tied UST's value to the dollar just couldn't cope, as $285 million of the stablecoin flooded onto the market and triggered $2.25 billion of capital flight from Anchor. UST fell to $0.985 per coin. $100 could now buy you 101.5 UST tokens: an untenable situation for a stablecoin to be in.

To counteract this, the next day Terraform Labs sent $750 million worth of bitcoin to their market makers, to defend the peg of UST. The idea was that the market makers would use this money to buy UST, thereby reducing its supply and raising its price back to parity with the dollar. Astoundingly, these defensive manoeuvres, despite being undertaken to salvage the project and avoid disaster, were met with opposition; the more extreme and vocal proponents of decentralisation expressed their shock and dismay at centralised market makers influencing the price of UST. For them, sacrificing the $40 billion Luna project on the altar of decentralisation was a price well worth paying. And if millions of ordinary investors needed to lose out in the process, then so be it.

Terraform Labs paid no heed to their protestations and continued their battle to defend the UST peg. Do Kwon, in a possible attempt at dismissing fear and fortifying confidence in his project, even tried to laugh the whole situation off, in characteristic style. In a profound outburst of cockiness, even by his own standards, he wrote in a now infamous tweet: 'So, is this $UST depeg in the room with us right now? No? I prescribe 24 hours of pegging over the next 7 days.'

The efforts of the Terra Foundation Guard and the market makers proved to be in vain, and Do Kwon's jokes and confidence turned out to be nothing more than a hubristic facade intended to mask the gravity of the situation his project found itself in. The next day, on 9 May, Anchor Protocol saw $5 billion in outflows, and its own native ANC token plunged by 35 per cent. UST, far from regaining its peg, entered a death spiral, dipping as low as $0.35. Investors, having now lost any shred of confidence that parity with the dollar would ever be regained, started offloading their UST into other stablecoins for cents on the dollar. It was at this point that Do Kwon posted what would become an iconic tweet in the crypto industry, which provides endless material for memes even to this day: 'Deploying more capital – steady lads.'

Needless to say, he didn't deploy more capital. Neither he, nor Terraform Labs, nor the LFG, had any left. This was the end for them. And yet, even with the situation as dire and seemingly irrecoverable as it was, at this point a large number of people started placing bets that the price of Luna would rebound – either out of a misplaced trust that Do Kwon would be able to salvage the situation or simply because they didn't understand the severity of what was occurring and saw an opportunity to 'buy the dip'. They soon received a rude awakening: the price of Luna was headed one way only. $65 million worth of liquidations, which occurred as leveraged traders hit their stop losses and were closed out of their long positions, drove home the fatal position Luna found itself in.

The crash continued, and on 12 May Luna, its price already a fraction of what it once had been, dropped a further 96 per cent in a single day. It was now trading at less than 10 cents. A mere week before, it had been worth over $80. And UST was in a similar situation: it went from being worth exactly $1 to fractions of a cent, in a matter of days.

All in all, $58 billion of value had evaporated. And the chaos wasn't confined to just Terra Luna. The swift, dramatic implosion of one of the industry's top ten largest projects dragged the whole market down with it. All in all, it's estimated that $450 billion of value was removed from the crypto markets in the days following Luna's demise. This was the fastest erasure of wealth in the history of finance – not just crypto, but the whole financial sector. Never had anything like this been seen anywhere before.

And, tragically, the losses weren't just financial.

'For Everyone Panicking, Here Are Some National Helpline Numbers.'

This was the headline atop a major online forum run by members of the Terra Luna community. After the project had started to collapse, I wanted to know what everyone was saying about the doomed venture. That headline was part of a post that had been pinned to the top of the page by admins. The text below it read:

> This is one of the reasons why you shouldn't invest money that you can't afford to lose, but even when we tell people not to invest more than what they can afford ... most people look at this as a get out of poverty card.
>
> Here I like to emphasise again, don't invest money you need to survive/live the next weeks/months/even a year. Don't invest in the hopes of having more next month. This is a very volatile market. Nobody knows what's gonna happen. In the long term, it definitely will pay off, but short term it can make you feel like shit and I hope you understand that you are not alone in this.

This missive was followed by an exhortation: readers should reach out for help if they need it. Then came a list of phone numbers – suicide-prevention hotlines in over 100 countries.

I was struck, seeing this post, with a renewed appreciation of just how high the stakes could become when people gambled on crypto. Anyone who has flicked through a financial newspaper in the past couple of years will know that the industry is in a bad way. At times, it has seemed relentless – it's as if, with each passing day, another once great crypto firm is forced to declare bankruptcy. In some cases, firms with billions on their balance sheets have gone bust faster than you can say 'financial bubble'. And, reading these stories, it's all too easy to feel detached from them – to regard them as something that happens over there, to other people. You almost have to force yourself to remember that you can find ruined lives behind every headline. Life savings lost, homes repossessed, mental and emotional distress. Reading reports in the news is one thing. Hearing the stories first hand, from the people directly affected, is something else entirely.

I scrolled down the forum, reading post after post. A lot of people had lost a lot of money, and, beyond the immediate panic and abject distress, was the desperation to understand what had happened. I was captivated by these stories and, at the same time, I felt guilty for being so fascinated, like I was rubbernecking in the wake of a financial car crash. And yet, I couldn't help myself. I had to know the full extent of the damage. I had to know how many lives had been ruined because of this ...

Nobody knows exactly how many suicides followed the Terra Luna tragedy. But from the verifiable sources I could find online, in the immediate wake of the collapse twenty-two people killed themselves because they had lost their life savings.

A young South Korean family – a mother, a father and a 10-year-old girl – were also reported missing in the days after Luna went to $0. Their car was eventually found at the bottom of a lake, with the father still strapped into the driving seat and the mother and daughter drowned in the back. Police investigators, combing through the father's internet history, found he had been searching on his laptop for 'Luna', 'sleeping pills' and 'how to commit suicide' before he and his family went missing. It is thought that he had invested in the cryptocurrency and lost everything.

That forum post, the list of suicide hotlines and the exhortation that investors should reach out for help is still there in the Terra Luna community group. But now you have to scroll down to find it. Pinned in its place is a new post announcing (or, rather, advertising) the launch of a new project within the same irreconcilably flawed ecosystem. Despite the Terra Luna collapse, people have continued to build on its network. Their hope is that the doomed currency will one day make a comeback. There's a reason that the hardcore members of the Terra Luna community came to be known as 'Lunatics'.

To rub even more salt into the wound, the original Terra Luna project has now rebranded itself to 'Luna Classic'. Do Kwon was busy working on Luna 2.0 when he was arrested in Montenegro in March 2023, for attempting to travel with false documents.

Shortly after his arrest, a rumour began circulating that police, after conducting a thorough inspection of Do Kwon's person, found a hard drive concealed in a bodily orifice, allegedly containing millions of dollars' worth of bitcoin. The company which creates the storage devices, Trezor, added fuel to the speculative fire by replying to a Twitter user who posted a photo of an X-ray supposedly showing the device inside Do Kwon's pelvic region. Social media users were quick to commend Trezor for their shrewd product placement.

Rumours aside, following his arrest Do Kwon was charged by a US federal grand jury with eight counts, including securities fraud, commodities fraud, wire fraud and conspiracy.

And then, on 19 June 2023, Kwon and Terraform Labs's former finance officer Han Chang-joon were sentenced to four months' imprisonment by a Montenegrin court for travelling under forged passports.

Do Kwon's plans for a new iteration of his doomed decentralised stablecoin would have to wait.

20

Terra Infirma

In the wake of Terra Luna's dramatic and unprecedented collapse, things were truly desperate. However, where most saw chaos, some of the industry's more degenerate investors saw opportunity. The turmoil in the markets gave them what every trader dreams of: volatility. And it gave it to them in abundance. When Luna was trading at fractions of a cent, it was experiencing astronomical price swings. It could very well pump by 10,000 per cent overnight, only to then dump back down to where it had started in the morning, and then drop a further 99.9 per cent in the afternoon.

One such trader to take advantage of the chaos in the markets was a recently hired employee of Moonshot Advisors, who was only ever known to me by his (frankly ridiculous) Web3 alias: Stone Cold Shiller. Or just Stone Cold, for short. I never bothered getting his real name, partly because pseudonyms were so prevalent in the space, and partly because I had very little contact with him. He was brought on as our new 'NFT executive', to work alongside our design team. However, I was forced to interact with him one morning when I awoke to messages he had sent to our company-wide Telegram group, boasting about the gains he had made in the turmoil following the Terra collapse.

'I've only gone and done it lads. Punted 500 dollars into Luna last night before I went to bed, and got over 50 grand this morning. Fuckin yeehaww.'

I immediately told him to remove the message, remonstrating with him for the recklessness of advertising the gains he had made in one of the most turbulent episodes in the history of crypto. Many of our team had lost money in Terra. My head of content had his life savings in Anchor, and the operations manager of Aquarius was holding eight grand of Luna, which he hadn't been able to sell on time, and had all but a few hundred dollars of his investment destroyed. The last thing we needed was someone encouraging people to trade the chop. Paul, on the other hand, didn't share my concerns.

'What can you do, mate – he's a Shiller by name, and a shiller by nature. It's just what the lad does. Can't begrudge him for that.'

I didn't rise to Paul's idiocy and left his message on read. Stone Cold eventually complied with my instruction and removed his message, but not before encouraging me privately to have at least a small punt in Luna and informing me that he would be leaving five grand in just to see what happens. I declined, and strongly advised him to take his winnings and walk away. I very much doubted he would follow this advice, but felt compelled to give it anyway.

This was my first encounter with Stone Cold since he had joined the company, but it wouldn't be the last. We had brought him on board because of his association with John McAfee, the American software magnate. McAfee Corporation – the eponymous firm that he founded – currently employs over 1,800 people and makes $1.92 billion a year in revenue. The founder himself, however, didn't share in these fortunes. Instead, he had one of the most bizarre character arcs in corporate history, selling his stake in his company in 1994 and launching a series of none-too-successful businesses. By 2009, his personal fortune had declined from $100 million to $4 million.

In 2008 he upped sticks and moved to Belize, to set up an antibiotics company, while swanning around the Caribbean on a six-bedroom yacht he christened *The Freedom Boat*. This latest business venture was short-lived, however, as the company was raided by Belizean police on suspicion of producing crystal meth. They seized his guns – which he had been accumulating since his relocation and which constituted quite the arsenal – shot his dog, and caught him in an amorous act with a 16-year-old girl. When confronted on Twitter years later about his relationships with girls decades younger than him, he responded blithely and shamelessly:

'Yep, I dated a 17-year-old. Dozens of them. All in countries where age of consent is 16 or less. What's your point?'

Things then became even more bizarre, as McAfee found himself at the centre of a homicide investigation. His neighbour in Belize, who was a vocal critic of McAfee and his depraved lifestyle, was found dead of a gunshot wound at his home. McAfee went on the run and took extreme measures to evade the authorities. He physically buried himself in sand for hours on end, and even faked two heart attacks, in a bid to avoid capture. He also unsuccessfully sought political asylum in Guatemala, before being extradited to the US. He was never charged criminally in connection with the murder, but in 2018 he did lose a wrongful death claim and was ordered to pay $25 million to his neighbour's estate.

After running a failed campaign for the 2016 US presidential elections, where he stood as a candidate for the Libertarian Party, McAfee then made the only career decision that could harm his reputation even more: he pivoted into crypto and started promoting 2017 ICOs. He posted regular 'Coin of the Day' and 'Coin of the Week' tweets, touting upcoming token launches that he claimed he was interested in. In 2018, he revealed that he had been paid $105,000 per post for these promotions. He died in June 2021 (despite his girlfriend claiming that he had actually faked his own death and is currently living in Texas); however, because of his involvement in the scene, and the attention he brought to cryptocurrencies, even to this day he's revered as an industry legend and spoken of with great fondness and affection.

Stone Cold knew him from the Caribbean and, at one point, formed part of his entourage. For a notoriously eccentric, drug-addled millionaire, he struck me as an ideal companion: half his hair was dyed peroxide blond and the other half jet black, and his face was covered in so many tattoos, in such disparate styles, that it looked like he had fallen asleep at a party and his mates had done a number on him with the Sharpies.

His career with us, however, was to be short-lived. After just a few weeks at Moonshot Advisors, we realised that he only joined us to use our resources to launch his own memorial token, which was somehow supposed to commemorate the life of his former leader.

Sensing our disapproval of this revelation, Stone Cold tried to bolster his case by showing us some treasured photographs of him and McAfee posing together on the deck of *The Freedom Boat*, holding an array of spectacularly lethal firearms. He seemed to think this would clinch the deal for him; instead, we terminated his contract. It was all just too strange for us to tolerate.

While he may have been gone from our working lives, his memory lived on in much-discussed anecdotes about just how odd his stint at our company was, as well as how unfathomably lucky he had been on Luna. While often serving as a point of great hilarity, discussion of Stone Cold proved to be a touchy subject for Patrick Chalker – our landlord and the owner of the bar above our office. Like Stone Cold, he too had been making bets on Luna after its collapse. However, things hadn't worked out quite as well for him as they had for our former employee.

Hearing about people making astronomical sums off the volatility, Patrick punted ten grand into the failed token. Within an hour he had lost all but a few cents of it, as Luna's price collapsed by a further 99.999 per cent. He withdrew his funds and shrugged off the loss. However, his chagrin was exacerbated by the price movement of the next hour, which saw Luna not only recover, but pump a further 1,000 per cent above the price at which Chalker bought it.

Stone Cold Shiller was very much the exception in terms of traders speculating on Luna, and Patrick was the norm; most who decided to face the chop head on got swept out to sea, losing their stake and staggering away penniless from the experience. However, there were creative opportunities to profit from the collapse to be found elsewhere, and some of the more clued-up, risk-tolerant institutions were quick to spot and capitalise on these. Our client Perpetual Partners was one such firm.

Perpetual's chief technical officer, the one who issued the warning about Anchor being unstable prior to its collapse, was called Lu. He was a reserved, rather meek middle-aged man of Chinese extraction.

Supposedly, and quite in keeping with his unassuming nature, he was one of the best coders and quantitative analysts in the space (at least according to Perpetual's CEO, Rupert).

As we know, Perpetual was yield farming for Silicon Valley firms. Most of their clients' money was parked on Anchor, along with some of their own. Thanks to Lu's warning, Rupert was able to withdraw it all well before the overwhelming majority of people in the industry had even detected a whiff of danger. But Rupert didn't just stop there; putting his utmost faith in the observations and predictions of his CTO, he entered a huge short position on both Luna and UST.

Perpetual didn't normally engage in 'prop trading' – which is where a firm trades with their own funds – but, for them, this was an opportunity too good to miss. And, indeed, when Lu's call came to pass, Perpetual made a killing off the demise of the once great project. Rupert refused to tell us exactly how much, but reading between the lines and extrapolating from his hints he reckoned it to be well over seven figures. Not bad for three days' work, especially considering it was just a side bet for them. It wasn't until the market got much worse and the whole house started tumbling down that Perpetual really started raking it in.

Their CTO Lu noted that some trading platforms were slow off the mark to adjust their price feed for UST and were therefore mis-pricing the formerly stable coin. When centralised exchanges price assets, this is often done inorganically via their own market makers, as opposed to real-time organic market pricing. What this meant for UST was that, after it lost the peg, some platforms still had it priced at $1, meaning you could swap it coin-for-coin with another stable-coin, such as USDC.

Keen to capitalise on this, Lu quickly knocked up an algorithm that bought cut-price UST from platforms that had accurate price feeds and sent this to platforms with artificial pricing. The algorithm then swapped it for USDC at a 1:1 rate, and then sent those stablecoins back to the first platform to purchase even more UST. And round and round the algorithm went, bagging Perpetual more and more profit. They were buying UST for cents on the dollar, and then selling it for a full dollar. It was the arbitrage opportunity of a lifetime, and Perpetual rode it for everything it had to offer. By the time all the platforms they were using had updated their price feeds, and the opportunity ceased to exist, Perpetual had netted themselves a fortune.

However, not everyone was as savvy as them and, for most institutions, the collapse of Terra spelt nothing but disaster. Hedge funds that had drunk too much of the Luna Kool-Aid, and that had made generational wealth off its meteoric rise, saw all their gains eviscerated. Arguably, the highest profile of these blow ups, and the most significant for the wider industry, was Three Arrows Capital: the very fund whose VC arm had invested in Perpetual Partners. Unlike their portfolio company, they didn't see the signs written in the stars for Terra Luna. As well as being an early investor in the project, they had also vastly overleveraged long positions on its Luna token – and not just that, but many other crypto assets as well, including bitcoin and Ether. To open these positions, they borrowed large sums of money from lending firms, including Voyager Digital, a crypto brokerage firm, which at its height had over 3.5 million users and $5.9 billion in assets. As well as offering brokerage services to retail customers, Voyager was also one of the most prolific lenders (and, along with Coinbase, was one of the few crypto companies to be publicly listed on a stock exchange). On 22 June, Voyager announced that they might be forced to issue a notice of default to Three Arrows Capital, as the fund had failed to repay a loan of 15,250 bitcoins and $350 million cash – over $665 million in total.

From there, the rest is history. 3AC went into liquidation, and on 2 July filed for Chapter 15 bankruptcy. Su Zhu and Kyle Davies, the hitherto smartest guys in the room, had blown up their empire. Prior to their downfall, they had just paid a downpayment on a $50 million super yacht – the *Much Wow*, with the kitsch name being a nod to a phrase often used in dogecoin memes. When purchasing it, they bragged that it would be 'bigger than all the richest billionaires' yachts in Singapore' (the domicile in which they were based). Alas, following their bankruptcy, the *Much Wow* went back onto the market. And Zhu and Davies went into hiding. In an interview with Bloomberg, held in an undisclosed location, the pair said they planned to move to the UAE, a country with no extradition treaty with either the US or Singapore. It took over a year to locate Zhu, who was arrested while trying to flee Singapore from Changi Airport. As for Davies, even at the time of writing his location remains unknown.

3AC's collapse was far from an isolated incident. They took the lenders, and many other firms in the space, down with them. Included among these were Voyager Digital, who themselves filed for bankruptcy on 5 July. After a string of other high-profile blowups, the industry finally cottoned on to just how much yield in crypto was derived from Anchor. In the weeks following the catastrophe, it came to light that firms which had been offering their customers 10 or 15 per cent yield on stablecoins were utterly dependent on that one platform. They would send their customers' funds to Anchor as soon as the deposit was made, give them the yield advertised in their own offering, and then bag the difference for themselves. When Anchor fell, not only were they not able to provide their yield farming services any more, but they weren't even able to return their customers' funds to them; they either hadn't been removed from Anchor at all, and were stuck on a platform that had frozen withdrawals, or were removed too late, after UST started crumbling, and were now only worth a fraction of their original value.

And yet, even with all this chaos unfolding, and once great crypto companies folding on what seemed to be a daily basis, for us at Moonshot Advisors none of it really seemed to touch the sides. It wasn't so much business as usual for us; somehow, business was *better* than usual. It was an outcome none of us expected. Although, once we realised the cause of it, we admonished ourselves for ever being so naive.

Seeing the turmoil in the markets, projects were scrambling to get their tokens, NFTs and products live while there was still some remnant of retail interest in the space. They were rushing to market while there was still a market to rush to. New capital was drying up, and there were huge outflows from the space as people either cut their losses or banked their profits and withdrew their funds.

But there was still money sloshing around, and many projects, and indeed investors, weren't quite finished yet. They wanted one last hurrah before the party ended.

We didn't know it yet, but we were witnessing the last gasps of a dying industry.

21

Swan Song of the Swindlers

In all the requests for work we received following the Terra Luna collapse, one theme was prevalent throughout: our prospective clients seemed more desperate and time-strained than ever. And far from looking down our noses, we welcomed this desperation with open arms. It often proved highly lucrative for us; in a bid to get moved to the front of the queue, procure our services before their competitors and fast-track their token launches, projects were offering to throw more money our way than we had ever seen before.

One such project was Paris Pact; they were operating in an emergent niche in the space, called 'ReFi'. Short for 'regenerative finance', ReFi was a lesser-known trend, which sought to provide decentralised services geared towards environmental sustainability. Given that a September 2022 fact sheet compiled by the White House estimated that energy usage for crypto quadrupled between 2018 and 2022, and the total electricity usage of the crypto industry is greater than that of Argentina or Australia, it would seem ReFi projects have their work cut out for them.

Paris Pact supposedly had some serious tech underpinning them. They were recommended to us by a contact of ours who was the head of sales at an outsourced software development firm (or 'dev house'). When founders had an idea for a product, but lacked the technical capabilities to build it themselves, they called in firms like these to build it for them. Our contact, a man named Joshua, told us that his firm had a team of 200 developers working for them in India. They were paid

$25 per hour, and the firm charged its customers $250 for an hour of their time – a 1,000 per cent profit margin. Paris Pact had an unprecedented number of developers assigned to them from this firm, due to the complexities involved in building its platform and token.

The platform was to take the form of a decentralised carbon credits exchange. Carbon credits grant firms the right to emit carbon dioxide and are a regulatory requirement in jurisdictions like the EU. Without adequate carbon credits, firms get fined for releasing CO_2 into the atmosphere. A carbon credits exchange enables firms to buy and sell these allowances, should their manufacturing output necessitate more or less carbon emissions. Paris Pact was never quite able to explain to us why trading carbon credits on the blockchain was preferable to trading them on conventional exchanges, which firms have been using for decades.

And, alongside its inexplicable exchange, Paris was – of course – also creating a token, though with a twist: their token was to be a 'rebase token'. These are complex instruments, yet scratch beneath the code and jargon just slightly and you'll find arguably the clearest, most egregious examples of Ponzi schemes in the entire industry. Essentially, rebase tokens are another kind of stablecoin, which try to maintain a peg with the dollar through a changing supply, rather than a stockpile of reserve assets. If the price of a rebase token increases above $1, then the supply increases. So if it starts trading at $2, for example, then the supply doubles, and users find themselves with two $1 tokens, instead of one $2 token.

Through this, rebase tokens advertise astronomical interest rates, sometimes topping 1 million per cent per annum. The rationale behind these yields is that, as the price of the token increases with new speculators wading in and buying them, the supply will increase, and current holders reap the rewards. The Ponzi economics here are clear as day: the interest rates rely on new investors buying the token, to the benefit of those already holding the token. Once new buyers stop coming in, the yield dries up. And, as the yield is what encourages new people to buy and hold the token, the price will collapse as people ditch their useless assets.

These projects were all the rage during the bull run, with many of them seeing some of the most astronomical gains the industry had ever borne witness to. The best example of this was Olympus DAO, a so-called 'decentralised reserve currency'. They launched a rebase token; however, it received such vast uptake that they abandoned any notion of stability. Not only did the Olympus team give up trying to maintain a dollar peg, they also actively encouraged its volatility:

> **Our initial goal is not to find a stable price.** This may seem antithetical to our currency applications, but we ensure you it is not. Olympus can be tuned to optimize for different things. The main tradeoff is volatility and profitability versus stability and consistency. With volatility and profit comes growth; that is what we want early on.

If this text seems like little more than a string of meaningless buzz-words, that's because it very much is. They were trying to use jargon to distract from a very simple core message: their token was pumping so much that they weren't even going to try to pretend it was stable. Instead, they were going to see how far they could ride this. And looking at the price history of Olympus DAO's token, OHM, it's easy to see why they took this approach.

It was launched with an initial price of $330 and achieved an all-time high price of $1,415. This may not seem like much but, in the context of the token's market cap, it starts to make a lot more sense. Despite the seemingly high initial listing price, the token launched with a market cap of around $30 million. Because of the rebase mechanism, and the changing supply, the price didn't increase that much, but the market cap shot up to over $4.3 billion at its peak. And, at its height, it was offering over 8,000 per cent annual percentage yield. As with all Ponzis, however, it eventually collapsed. At the time of writing, it's currently trading at around $11. That's a 99.2 per cent drop from its all-time high. At the zenith of the mania surrounding OHM, many recognised that it was a Ponzi, but they simply didn't care. CoinDesk summed the mood up perfectly in a frankly staggering article from December 2021 that never should've seen the light of day. Its headline ran: 'Yes, it's a Ponzi scheme. But who cares?'

And yet, nearly a year on from the unequivocal fall of Olympus DAO, Paris Pact was seeking to emulate the deranged experiment that was OHM. Paris was advertising a yield of over 900,000 per cent per year. As soon as we heard this, we tried to convince the Paris Pact team that this was a terrible idea and an awful play. Since Luna had blown up, every eye in the industry was trained on yield farming, scrutinising where the interest payments were coming from. A new industry idiom was even coined: 'if you don't know where the yield is coming from, *you're* the yield.' This didn't make much sense, but the sentiment was clear nonetheless: people were sceptical about yield and, without a clear source, it was instantly assumed that the project offering it was a Ponzi. This was especially true of high yield; even a few percentage points above the Bank of England base rate was enough to raise eyebrows. In light of this, what Paris was advertising was simply laughable. We told them no one would touch them with a barge pole if they advertised that annual percentage yield, but they weren't fazed – primarily because of the type of investor they were targeting:

'We only want to go after the gremlins. The real degenerates. The people sitting in their parent's bedroom, scrolling through 4chan and flipping shitcoins.'

These were the words of Jack, the baby-faced CEO of Paris Pact. When we first met him, we were taken in by his youthful complexion, dimpled cheeks and squeaky voice. We were impressed that someone his age had founded a crypto project. Our usual clients, while not being old by any stretch of the imagination, were often well into their careers when they made the switch into crypto. So we thought there must be something remarkable about Jack for him to achieve CEO status so early.

But first impressions seldom last. We quickly discovered Jack to be not only incompetent, but one of the most odious characters we had ever worked with, who tried to hide his incompetence behind sheer unpleasantness. He had a habit of messaging us at all hours of the night, launching into screaming fits when we replied during normal working hours the next day, and telling us we had better work at 'crypto speed' or he'd find another agency. However, the £20,000 monthly retainer they were paying us, and the promise of six-figure influencer campaigns – both pre and post token launch – were enough for us to tolerate Jack and his short temper. And, indeed, his awful judgement.

The profile he gave us of Paris's ideal investor was met with ardent nods from his lieutenant, Ralph. More than twenty years Jack's senior, Ralph was an ex-military man who made the unconventional career shift into crypto as soon as he realised he could make five times his army salary without having to sleep in a ditch or get berated by a staff sergeant. Now he could get berated by Jack, from the comfort of his home office, which seemed to suit him perfectly.

They were both in agreement; they wanted to target the crypto gremlins.

'Look, that's the plan,' Ralph told us, after we made a last-ditch attempt at convincing him to lobby his boss to widen their target investor profile. 'We're going to go after the kind of people who bought into OHM early doors. The real cretins, they're the ones who're going to pump this thing.'

It wasn't our place to push Paris not to aspire to be like OHM. We had made our case, and that was all that could be done. We could only offer so much advice. And, if that's the route they wanted to go down, then we, as the service providers, had to facilitate it. Even if we all thought it was absolutely mental.

We dutifully compiled lists of influencers who promoted OHM and such similar Ponzi schemes, applied our standard markups, and sent them over. It was a $200,000 campaign, and they signed it off on the spot. This was a lot of money for an influencer campaign at the best of times, let alone in these conditions. And, despite us shooting very much from the hip, procuring the influencers based solely on what projects they had previously promoted, with no test campaign, the launch was an unbelievable success (with 'unbelievable' being the operative word).

Paris managed to sell out all their public sale tokens, raising over $2 million in the process. They used a 'fair launch' mechanism, with no whitelist, and each buyer only being able to procure a set amount of tokens, thereby prohibiting bot buyers and whales from accumulating all the coins and then dumping them. However, we later discovered that the launch wasn't quite as fair, or as successful, as Paris had made it out to be. As it turned out, they had been buying their own tokens, from dozens of different wallets they had set up. Apparently, the first few hundred thousand dollars' worth of token sales were legit, but after that demand dried up. So Jack set about manufacturing the facade of desirability by buying hundreds of thousands of dollars' worth of tokens out of his own pocket.

We had seen this playbook before, with Cage Clash – except, the difference was, Cage Clash had failed to sell out because of an inability to differentiate themselves from the crowd. There were so many projects launching back then that they just couldn't stand out amid the noise. This was a different situation entirely. With Paris Pact, there simply wasn't any demand for their token. They had lent on two distinct narratives: regenerative finance and rebase tokens. Had they employed these several months ago, their fortunes would've been all but guaranteed. However, after the collapse of Luna people simply weren't interested. Liquidity had been eviscerated, and for investors who had been scammed again and again during the bull run, the implosion of one of the biggest projects in the space was the last straw.

But while the prospects were bleak for new projects launching onto the market, we felt somewhat isolated from it all. Paris was just one of many new projects we had taken on following Luna. We were sheltered from the general panic taking place around us – the crashing asset prices, the never-ending procession of insolvencies, and the ominous rumours circulating that the worst was yet to come. We ignored it, telling ourselves that there were still trillions of dollars sloshing around the crypto space, and that, as times got tougher, projects would need our services more than ever. We couldn't imagine for an instant that after this cohort of projects conducted their token sales, which they had long since committed to and which they had been working towards for months, that would be the end of things, and no one else would be foolish enough to try their luck.

We were deluding ourselves – covering our ears to the gasps and wheezes of a dying industry and muttering unconvincing reassurances that we'd be back at an all-time high in no time at all.

And it wasn't just the new influx of clients rushing to market that contributed to our short-sightedness. Our existing clients, too, were adding to our false optimism.

'So, Rupert, how's it all going on your end? How are your plans to become a bank progressing?'

It was October 2022, and Perpetual Partners had long been our most valuable client. Since the collapse of Terra Luna, they had been printing money. In the wake of UST's collapse, many so-called stablecoins had become markedly unstable. This afforded Perpetual ample arbitrage opportunities, as even the major stablecoins were being stress-tested. They were regularly experiencing minor fluctuations in their price, scarcely larger than $0.01 in either direction. While this may seem small, for stablecoins like USDT with market caps in the tens of billions, even these minor deviations from the peg were deceptively significant. And, given the size and the frequency of the orders Perpetual were putting in, these minuscule movements were enough to make arbitrage highly lucrative.

But this was little more than a side hustle for Perpetual. Their trading volumes were through the roof and, as a result, they were raking in fees. They had the unprecedented volatility that crypto was experiencing to thank for this, along with the marketing work we had been doing for them, which allowed them to reach new all-time high user numbers.

While new capital had stopped flowing into the space, and investors had stopped buying into token launches, the traders were still highly active. During the bull run, when numbers were going nowhere but up and newbies could make money blindfolded, speculators who only recently set up their first trading accounts quickly started fancying themselves the new Buffetts or Burrys. The market collapse shattered this illusion, however it didn't deter them; many were chasing their losses, and turning to high-leverage platforms like Perpetual Partners in the hope of making it all back with one good trade.

Perpetual were more than happy to welcome them in with open arms, and part them from their not-so-hard-earned money. They were cashing in on the bin fire, but their most exciting money-spinner by far was coming out of their asset management arm: as well as generating yield for Silicon Valley firms through stablecoin arbitrage, they were now looking to turn themselves into a quasi-bank. Miles was planning to offer high-interest, distressed loans to struggling crypto companies.

'We're speaking to US banks at the moment, to get them to front us the money, which we'll then loan out at higher rates,' explained Rupert.

'I thought you were using the funds in Perp Strategies for that?'

'Ha! No, no way. The dweebs in Silicon Valley would fire us if they found out we were doing that. They're very risk averse, even with the protections we've built in. They're tech guys, not finance guys. Wall Street is the place to go for that kind of funding.'

I couldn't help but smile at the irony of Rupert using the term 'dweeb' to describe the tech bros of Silicon Valley. Today, he was wearing his favourite cat print T-shirt, and was using a virtual background that looked like the inside of a Hobbit house from the *Lord of the Rings* movies. I had a quick scan of the stock backgrounds on Zoom, and they didn't offer that one as standard. He had gone out of his way to add it himself.

'Interesting. But why don't the crypto companies just go to Wall Street themselves?'

'Wall Street wouldn't go within a hundred miles of those guys. We've got relationships with all the banks there, so we can basically act like middlemen. Plus, it's too risky for them. They don't trust these crypto projects, but they do trust us. So the only people who can offer distressed loans are people who are acting as middlemen like us, or people like FTX who have the balance sheet for it.'

Rupert was right. In the aftermath of Terra Luna, industry giants started snapping up failing companies, often at significant discounts. And by far the biggest spender was FTX. The exchange's founder, Sam Bankman-Fried (commonly referred to simply as 'SBF'), saw an opportunity to consolidate his control over the industry, and went on a prodigious shopping spree. Following the collapse of Voyager Digital, for example, he put in a winning bid to acquire their crypto holdings for $1.4 billion, and the company itself for $51 million. He also signed a deal giving him the right to buy bankrupt lending platform Blockfi for $240 million – a fraction of the company's valuation of $4.8 billion prior to the market turmoil. Before this, he purchased Japanese crypto exchange Liquid, and entered talks to buy South Korean exchange Bithumb, along with a slew of other firms. Many hailed him as the industry's saviour, and crowned him the 'crypto king', as his empire expanded exponentially across the globe.

'You're gonna be the next SBF, Rupert!'

'Ha! Well, we'll have to see about that. Maybe in the next cycle. He's cemented his control over the industry, so we can just hope he either blows up, or makes so much money he retires. That's when we can make our move.'

'Well, the way things are going, I reckon a blow up is more likely. Are you coming to the Near event in a couple of weeks as well? It's just round the corner from you, in Canary Wharf. Should be a lot of projects there and, given the state of things, some of them might need some distressed loans.'

'Yes, we'll be popping by. The first couple of banks should give us funding by then, so it'll be good timing.'

'Great stuff. And how about a sponsorship package? OKX will be sponsoring it, along with Near of course. Having Perpetual Partners up in lights next to those heavy hitters would be great exposure.'

OKX was another large crypto exchange. Initially headquartered in China, they were subsequently banned from the country due to its strict and longstanding anti-crypto stance. They were still one of the biggest players in the Asian crypto market, though, and were expanding throughout the rest of the world. Sponsorship deals played a large part of this strategy; as well as sponsoring smaller scale events, like the one we were running for them, they signed some mega marketing deals with the likes of Manchester City FC, to whom they paid $55 million for a three-year contract sponsoring their shirt sleeves, as well as a multi-year deal to be the primary sponsor of the McLaren F1 team.

'Ha! Yeah, I appreciate it, but no thanks. The day I start splurging on conference sponsorships and things like that, that's the day I'll resign as CEO.'

'Yeah, no problem, thought it was worth asking regardless!'

'Plus,' Rupert added, just as we were wrapping up our call, 'we're looking to sign a big deal with a Serie A player. We want him on as a brand ambassador. Should really help us cut through the noise and get the word out about Perpetual.'

Rupert sent me the terms of the deal later, to get my opinion on it: it was a million-pound deal that would see the international football star promote Perpetual in a series of eight tweets and two 15-second video clips over the space of a year. There was also a clause that allowed both parties to extend the deal on mutual agreement, with the possibility of an increased fee and even equity in the company if all went well in the first twelve months.

When he first mentioned this to me on the call, I tried to contain my derision.

'That's no problem, Rupert. There aren't *that* many crypto companies with football sponsorship deals, so I'm sure the market isn't too saturated for you to get some good results out of it. I can get you and your team free tickets to our event, anyway, so don't worry about that.'

I left the call, unsure exactly how to feel. Rupert was bullish, and clearly thought the current slump the industry was in following the collapse of Luna was temporary. For people like him, it was even a positive situation: it afforded him, and the likes of FTX, the opportunity to fill their boots and be greedy while others were fearful.

While I found his attitude reassuring, there was also something in it that I found more than a little repulsive – and not just Rupert's attitude, but that of most people I had been dealing with since Luna collapsed. Everyone regarded what happened as an isolated incident, and painted people like Do Kwon and Su Zhu as individual bad eggs. The general mentality was that crypto was still a force for good and that we shouldn't throw the baby out with the bathwater that a few rogue actors had contaminated. It was the wholehearted belief of most people in the industry that crypto would recover and, now that all the unscrupulous players had left and the nefarious firms had imploded, the industry would bounce back bigger and better than ever before.

Of course, this lie could only be told for so long. Sooner or later reality – and the whole industry – would come crashing down around us.

22

FTX

On 11 November 2022, FTX filed for Chapter 11 bankruptcy.

For days, even weeks, prior to their downfall, rumours had been rife that not all was as it seemed over at the crypto giant's international headquarters in the Bahamas. And, indeed, for those who knew where to look, the first stitch in FTX's tapestry of red flags was woven far earlier than this. Chief among these was the exchange's relationship with Alameda Research, a hedge fund and market maker set up by SBF in 2017. Alameda was the sister company of FTX and was supposed to be a wholly separate entity. To reinforce this separation, SBF appointed a separate CEO to Alameda, Caroline Ellison – his 27-year-old, Stanford graduate, Harry Potter-obsessed former lover.

Ellison joined SBF's outfit in 2018 and, by summer 2020, they were in a relationship with one another. They broke up a year later but kept seeing each other on and off for several months, before ending things for good in spring 2022. All of this was done covertly; however, it was very much an open secret throughout the industry (indeed, it was one of Rupert's favourite talking points on our weekly calls). And this surreptitious affair between two titans of the industry was the cause of many other scandalous rumours – especially when combined with Ellison's open discussion of both performance-enhancing drug use and polyamory.

Writing on Twitter in 2021, Ellison opined: 'nothing like regular amphetamine use to make you appreciate how dumb a lot of normal, non-medicated human experience is.' And in a now deleted Tumblr post from 2020, she espoused her views on the optimal polyamory setup: 'I've come to decide the only acceptable style of poly is best characterised as something like "imperial Chinese harem." None of this non-hierarchical bullshit. Everyone should have a ranking of their partners, people should know where they fall on the ranking, and there should be vicious power struggles for the ranks.'

This naturally led observers to conclude that SBF and Ellison were hosting regular drug-fuelled orgies, in between running the $32 billion FTX and the $14.6 billion Alameda. Commentators surmised that the $40 million penthouse the couple shared with eight other FTX executives, along with SBF's $200 million Bahamian property portfolio, would provide the ideal setting for these amorous escapades.

As salacious as all this was, it was immaterial compared to the far more significant – and far more criminal – rumours that abounded around FTX: namely, that the exchange was colluding with Alameda to the detriment of customers. It had long been known by many in the industry that the biggest market maker on FTX was Alameda itself. Market makers are supposed to be impartial and detached from the firms to which they provide liquidity services. When they're not, the quantity and scale of corrupt actions they can undertake is unconscionable.

FTX's biggest market maker was a firm that had been set up by the exchange's CEO. And it was being run by the CEO's ex-girlfriend. And the executive teams at the two firms shared offices and even homes. And on 2 November the devastating consequences that arrangements like these can lead to were revealed. And the empire that SBF, the poster boy of the crypto industry, had built up over so many years started to collapse.

The starter pistol of FTX's demise was fired by CoinDesk. They published a leaked balance sheet belonging to Alameda Research showing that Alameda held a $5 billion position in FTX's native token, FTT. This indicated that the two firms, which were supposed to be wholly separate entities, had been co-mingling funds.

Co-mingling of funds involves an entity mixing one pool of funds, which are supposed to be earmarked for a specific purpose, with another pool set aside for something entirely different. What the FTT on Alameda's balance sheet showed was that the two firms were colluding with one another. The exchange had given the trading firm a vast amount of its own token, which left onlookers asking three questions. Why did FTX give the tokens to Alameda? What was Alameda using them for? And how deep did the collusion between the two firms go?

The answers to these questions would all come to light in time. However, FTX's rivals didn't need the answers straight away. For them, the questions alone were enough grounds to make moves against SBF's empire. And for FTX's biggest rival, Binance, the leaked balance sheet provided the perfect *casus belli* to take down the competition. It was just the excuse CZ, the founder and CEO of the industry-leading exchange, needed to start dumping his vast supplies of FTT, with a view to putting his former protégé in the ground.

Binance had been an early investor in FTX. When the latter was still just an idea in SBF's head, CZ bought a big prelaunch ticket in the yet-to-launch exchange, snagging himself equity as well as tokens. However, when FTX launched, and quickly started nipping at their backer's heels, the relationship soured. Binance exited their equity position in FTX in 2021, receiving $2.1 billion in a combination of FTT tokens and their own BUSD stablecoin.

Tensions between the two industry giants continued to flare from then on and came to a head in autumn 2022.

'Excited to see him repping the industry in DC going forward! Uh, he is still allowed to go to DC, right?'

Bankman-Fried wrote this in a now deleted tweet from October. His post was a reference to his own influence within the corridors of power in Washington DC – ahead of the US midterm elections in 2022, he donated over $40 million to the Democrat Party, making him their second largest donor after hedge fund billionaire George Soros. Some commentators speculated that his post was also a veiled swipe at CZ's Chinese ethnicity, with others going on to posit that it was this tweet – made only a week before Binance's announcement that it would ditch its FTT holdings – that prompted CZ to initiate the selloff. The more conspiratorially minded members of the crypto scene suspected that it was CZ himself – or a close confidant acting on his instructions – who leaked the Alameda balance sheet to CoinDesk, in retaliation for Bankman-Fried's insult.

Whoever the culprit was – which, to this day, remains officially unknown – the leaked balance sheet was fatal for Alameda. Following its publication, a slew of revelations came to light around just how blurred the lines were between SBF's two companies. Among the most shocking of these was that Alameda had been collateralising loans with FTT; in other words, FTX's sister company had been taking the exchange's native token, pawning that out to lenders, and then using the borrowed funds to make bets on the market. The consequences of this were stark: the loans that Alameda used FTT to secure would be recalled if the price of FTT fell below a certain point. This in itself wouldn't be a problem, were it not for the fact that Alameda, contrary to the industry's perception of them as trading prodigies and stalwarts of the industry, were essentially insolvent.

The rumour at the time (which was substantiated in September 2023, when analysts went through Alameda's trading history, released in a government evidence exhibit) was that Alameda blew up during the Terra Luna collapse. They had huge leveraged long exposure to Luna and, when Luna fell, it brought Alameda down with it. The fund lost all its money, and then took out loans using FTT to try to trade their way back into the black. Were the loans to be recalled, Alameda would be finished. However, no one knew how tenuous the position of Alameda was. Until Caroline Ellison gave the game away.

'If you're looking to minimize the market impact on your FTT sales, Alameda will happily buy it all from you today at $22!' Thus wrote Ellison in a tweet confronting CZ on his announcement that Binance would be liquidating their FTT position. And, with this, she showed FTX's hand, and cemented the exchange's fate.

$22 was the price at which the Alameda loans would be recalled. CZ had his target. The firesale could get under way. CZ's team set to work and managed to breach the $22 price floor in under 24 hours. After this, it didn't take long for both FTX and Alameda to fold like a pair of cheap suits. Some assumed that, because it was Alameda that had received the dodgy loans, FTX would be sheltered from their collapse. But this couldn't have been further from the truth because, beyond handing over $5 billion worth of FTT to Alameda, FTX also operated a system of fractional reserves.

The fractional reserve process is commonplace within traditional banking. It involves banks only keeping a small amount of financial reserves on hand at any one time – not enough to cover all the assets they're holding on behalf of their customers. For example, if customers deposit a total of $10 billion into a bank, the bank may only keep $5 billion of this, and send the other $5 billion out into the financial markets. It gets put to work and generates revenue. It can be lent to other banks who may require it to cover a temporary shortfall, or to home buyers looking to secure a mortgage. Through this, interest is generated for the lender.

Of course, there is risk involved in this system: should customers all try to withdraw their funds at once, the bank won't have enough assets on hand to cover all withdrawals. Situations such as these are known as 'bank runs', and have calamitous consequences whenever they occur. However, the argument used by fractional reserve banks is that the chances of this happening are so minuscule that the rewards vastly outweigh the risks. And, in addition, ever since the Global Financial Crash in 2008, regulatory bodies around the world have put safeguarding measures in place to protect against the devastation of bank runs.

Banks in many jurisdictions are now required to segregate their clients' funds, with a ring fence around some or all of their retail deposits. In addition, following the global financial turmoil caused by the collapse of firms like Lehman Brothers, many governments started guaranteeing retail deposits themselves. In the UK, for example, the government set up the Financial Services Compensation Scheme, which reimburses up to £85,000 of customers' money should their bank collapse. And, lastly, to mitigate the risks inherent in the fractional reserves system, there are often strict rules governing what investments a bank can and can't make with their clients' funds; anything too risky is strictly forbidden.

It should not come as a surprise to hear that the fractional reserves process that FTX employed flouted every single one of these risk-management principles. And, being totally outside the scope of regulation, the exchange received no protections or guarantees from any governments. So, when they got hit with a bank run, the consequences for them were fatal.

In early November, users had already started taking their funds off the exchange in the wake of the CoinDesk article and the revelations it laid bare around Alameda's balance sheet relying heavily on the FTT token. Now, the news that those tokens were used to procure dodgy loans, Alameda's ensuing insolvency, and FTT's tanking price all coalesced, whipping up a tornado of fear that fanned the flames of panic. Amid this maelstrom of malpractice all coming to light at once, the inevitable happened: a bank run got under way.

Millions scrambled to reclaim their funds. The outflows were so severe that FTX simply couldn't handle it. By some estimates, on 5 November they should have had $8.4 billion in customer balances on the exchange. By 10 November, they had $1.1 billion – an 87 per cent drop. Had their customers' funds not been pilfered, then that drop shouldn't have been a problem. However, because Alameda had long been using FTX like a personal ATM, the limited assets actually held on their exchange – the ones that hadn't been handed over to Alameda – couldn't cover all the user funds fleeing the platform. When the taps ran dry, FTX halted withdrawals. And it was at that moment people realised that the balances displayed in their trading accounts were simply numbers on a screen. There was no money there. FTX had spent it all and had none left to honour withdrawals with.

SBF resigned as CEO of FTX on 11 November. The same day his exchange filed for bankruptcy. At this point, his formerly adoring fans stopped referring to him by the sobriquet of 'the crypto king', conferring on him the far less flattering (though much more accurate) moniker of Sam Bankrun-Fraud.

And it's easy to see why. Following the events of that fateful day, the market was sent into a tailspin. Bitcoin dumped to below $17,000. It was a level the flagship cryptocurrency hadn't seen in over two years, since the bull run began. The crypto winter had officially arrived.

And, that very same evening, even as fear and panic gripped the industry, and the charts flowed red with blood, I made my way across town, to a party we were hosting in Canary Wharf ...

23

Bahamas or Bust

The story doesn't end here. Far from it. Because even after FTX entered liquidation, things somehow managed to get worse.

As millions of frantic and furious investors tried to salvage their fortunes, they got desperate. For the vast majority, this despair had no outlet of relief or avenue of recourse. Distraught investors who had lost their life savings had nothing to do but scroll through social media for hours on end, searching for information on what was going to happen next. However, a small minority of victims decided to take matters into their own hands. They figured that, since they had been so unscrupulously screwed over, the gloves were off. There were no rules any more, and anything they could do to recoup their losses was fair game. Through the crimes and corruption of others, they had been made into victims. And now they were going to turn the tables and become the criminals themselves.

After FTX halted withdrawals and filed for bankruptcy, the internal mechanisms of the platform remained in operation. This came as quite the shock, as most expected the platform to shut down, be turned off or simply stop working after the bankruptcy filing. However, users were still able to log on, see their balances, and even make transactions. They were still able to trade. They just couldn't withdraw any funds from the exchange. After the initial surprise of the discovery, light bulbs started going off in users' heads.

Former FTX whales, with large balances on the exchange, began selling these off to individuals and organisations not caught up in the saga. For cents on the dollar. The buyers reasoned that, once the dust had settled, and the liquidators had been brought in and users were beginning to get reimbursed, withdrawals would reopen and they would be able to access the large balances they had just procured. Of course, there was a monumental amount of risk involved with this, and it was speculative at best whether it would even come to pass. Hence the significant discounts; reports circulated of some accounts being sold with a 95 per cent haircut.

This, in itself, wasn't illegal. But what followed undoubtedly was. On 11 November, while the world's media was focused on FTX's bankruptcy filing, a far more surreptitious story started spreading among industry insiders. Supposedly, FTX customers who had accounts registered in the Bahamas were having their withdrawals processed. Initially no one was quite sure why this was the case, or even if it was true. But then confirmations started coming to light, as well as explanations.

In December, roughly a month after his resignation from the exchange he had founded and bankrupted, SBF was arrested in the Bahamas – the jurisdiction in which FTX International was registered and headquartered – and extradited to the US. However, prior to his extradition he had remained on the island with his core team, in the same luxury resort community in which they had been living for the past several years.

Supposedly fearing for his safety, SBF decreed that the paltry resources still under the control of FTX – those that hadn't been given to Alameda or withdrawn in the bank run – should be diverted towards processing Bahamian withdrawals. He was still physically on the island, and the theory went that he was terrified about having hordes of local, irate customers baying for his blood, on an island rife with gang-related activity. This revelation sparked the imaginations of the more conniving former users of FTX.

'If anyone helps me KYC on FTX im giving 100k. I already submitted everything I need someone from FTX to process it.' This tweet was posted by the prominent crypto influencer AlgodTrading, the very same anonymous account who made the infamous bet with Do Kwon about the price of Luna. AlgodTrading's thought process was simple: FTX employees had more cause for being angry with FTX than pretty much anyone else. Not only had they all lost their jobs on account of the greed and corruption of the firm's inner circle, but they were also victims of the exchange's collapse. FTX employees received a large amount of their pay cheques in the FTT token, paid directly to their FTX trading accounts. So, for anyone who hadn't converted this into normal currency and off-ramped it into a bank account yet, not only had the value of their compensation been eviscerated, but it was entirely inaccessible to them.

As a result, not only were FTX employees looking for ways to get back at their old employer, but they themselves were also desperate to recoup their losses. And AlgodTrading, along with many others like him, saw in this an opportunity. If he could forge a Bahamian ID, or procure someone else's (or, for that matter, just submit any old piece of paper), he could then persuade a former member of the relevant team at FTX to process his KYC application. At which point he would be in possession of a Bahamian-registered account, and would then be able to withdraw his funds without a hitch.

His plan was devious and effective; it didn't take him long to find a willing accomplice at FTX. The six-figure payday, to someone who had nothing left to show for countless hours of toil, was simply too much to resist. Mere hours after posting his initial tweet, he was bragging about the success of his scheme, and how he had managed to withdraw millions from the bust exchange.

On seeing him boast about his own ingenuity, dozens of unimpressed onlookers were quick to highlight the high probability of his getting caught for it. The authorities, no doubt, would be conducting a meticulous post-mortem into the events currently transpiring, and coming down hard on everyone found to have acted illicitly. Many were also quick to denounce the sheer inequity of the situation. Because AlgodTrading was rich, and had a public platform, he was able to withdraw his funds. Whereas millions of ordinary customers had no such option, and no avenue of recourse whatsoever.

While AlgodTrading was a particularly egregious example of the rich and influential using their status and wealth to secure their own financial safety, he was far from the only culprit of this. Many others were setting up their own Bahamian KYC'd accounts. However, there was a problem: not everyone who wanted to withdraw their funds through this method knew a former FTX employee. This meant there was no way for their applications to get processed. While unfortunate for them, it presented a big opportunity to the people who already had KYC'd accounts set up. And this being crypto, where there is opportunity and urgency, the scams aren't far behind.

Reports started coming to light of FTX users with Bahamian accounts profiteering from the exchange's liquidity crisis. They would receive the internal balances of others with funds stuck on the exchange, charge a fee for withdrawing the funds, and then simply not send the money back to the person who paid them. So they got their fee and also stole the entirety of the balance they had been hired to save. For people with no moral compass whatsoever, the disaster engulfing FTX afforded them the ideal conditions for making a quick buck. They were looting during the blitz, and walking away from the disaster in a far better position than they had been in before.

And they weren't the only ones to look at the chaos and confusion taking place and see an opportunity for self-advancement in it all. Justin Sun – the founder of a major player in the industry, Layer 1 network Tron – was quick to capitalise. Sun is very much a main character in the drama that is the crypto industry; his token, TRX, once boasted a market cap of nearly $14 billion at its peak, and in November 2022 Bloomberg reported that Sun purchased a major stake in cryptocurrency Huobi (which Sun subsequently denied). He's also well known for his eccentricities, often referring to himself with the honorific 'His Excellency' – a title bestowed upon him by the government of Granada after they appointed him their Ambassador to the World Trade Organisation. In March 2023, Sun revealed his post was revoked; however, that hasn't prevented him from keeping the initials 'H.E.' in his Twitter profile.

Never one to let a good crisis get in the way of marketing his shitcoin, he made a public announcement saying that he had initiated talks with FTX in a bid to safeguard the Tron community. This 'safeguarding' took the form of guaranteeing the withdrawals of the TRX token from the bankrupt exchange. He would work with FTX to identify how much TRX was being held on the exchange, and then he would send the same amount to the platform – either in TRX itself or in stablecoins – so that they would have enough assets to process withdrawals.

This was a truly noble, altruistic idea. However, in a turn of events that surprised absolutely no one, Sun never managed to get any TRX out of FTX. He simply didn't need to; TRX surged in price after the announcement, so Sun had already reaped his rewards.

Because, while no one seriously expected anything to come of Sun's announcement, the whole industry was looking for false hope. For so long, SBF had been paraded around as the poster boy for digital assets. Here was the acceptable face of cryptocurrencies, not to mention the saviour of the industry after the Terra Luna collapse. And yet, after all that, he turned out to be just another fraudster. Everyone wanted to believe that there were still some good actors in the space. They needed to believe that.

And so the crypto commentariat, across both traditional and social media, wasted no time in lavishing praise on Sun. They didn't wait to see if his offer would come to fruition. They put their trust in his announcement alone and based their declarations of him as a hero of the industry solely on that. Which was exactly the outcome Sun was looking for. He had secured extraordinarily good PR, for both himself and his project – all of which was engineered at the expense of the FTX victims, who were fed false hope of salvaging their funds. When this never happened, the victims were left in a state of even greater despair.

And, egregious as Sun's disingenuity was, there were those who attributed even more sinister motives to his actions. Sun's plans not only netted him the best PR it was possible to obtain: they also presented a prime opportunity for any trading firms that still had access to FTX's platform to make a lot of money, fast.

Commentators noted that the consequences of Sun's announcement were an arbitrageur's dream. In the immediate wake of his announcement, the price of TRX surged by as much as 4,000 per cent on FTX, as users scrambled to buy the token in the hope they would be able to withdraw it from the platform. Traders who were able to deposit and withdraw from FTX freely had a prime opportunity to buy TRX on exchanges that were functionally normal and on which the asset hadn't been artificially pumped, transfer their tokens to FTX, and sell them at a 4,000 per cent profit.

Of course, there were no traders, firms or market makers that were able to withdraw from FTX. Apart from one: Alameda.

There was no proof that Sun had entered into such a deal with Alameda. However, for the victims of FTX, who had just witnessed SBF – a figure they considered to be one of the most trustworthy people in finance – commit some of the worst financial crimes in history, such an arrangement didn't seem far-fetched.

For Sun, these rumours were drowned out by the deluge of positive press that came his way off the back of his announcement. And he wasn't alone in being able to leverage the unprecedented crisis for his own gain. The architect of the FTX collapse – CZ himself – also had his PR machine firing on all cylinders. After the liquidity crisis that his FTT selloff triggered, but before FTX had filed for bankruptcy, CZ announced that he was preparing a rescue deal, to bail out the floundering exchange, protect its millions of customers, save the industry, etc.

Of course, this garnered him the highest plaudits from the four corners of the cryptosphere. The praise he received was reminiscent of that lavished on SBF during his spending spree in the aftermath of Terra Luna's collapse. The epithet of 'industry saviour' even made a reappearance (because things went so well for the last one of those ...). However, after receiving his applause – and innumerable news headlines – CZ abruptly pulled out of the deal. He cited disconcerting findings that arose during the due diligence process of the bailout. Whether CZ contrived the bogus rescue deal to get a detailed look under the FTX bonnet (which the due diligence process would have enabled him to do), or for the PR, or to put another nail in his competitor's coffin (industry alarm at CZ's backtracking from the deal exacerbated the bank run FTX was experiencing), or some combination of all these factors, remains open to debate.

But CZ's Machiavellian manoeuvres didn't stop there. The day after FTX filed for bankruptcy, Binance announced the launch of an 'industry recovery fund', to rebuild the industry and prevent contagion from FTX's collapse spiralling out of control. Binance pledged a billion dollars into the fund – promising to later ramp this up to $2 billion – to be used for 'a new co-investment opportunity for organisations eager to support the future of Web3'.

Essentially, they wouldn't be giving out grants or issuing free money to flagging firms; they would be making investments into crypto companies. And the companies on the receiving end of these investments would be expected either to pay the funds back later down the line, or hand over equity or tokens. An onlooker of a cynical disposition might interpret all this as Binance buying up crypto companies, likely at significant discounts owing to the liquidity crisis, thereby expanding its monopoly over the industry. And, as for the 'co-investment' aspect of the fund's structure, it should come as no surprise that one of the first co-investors to back Binance's initiative was none other than Justin Sun himself.

Meanwhile, as CZ and Sun postured, plotted, and revelled in unmerited praise, things at FTX were, somehow, getting even worse. In an inconceivably bad exacerbation to their already catastrophic problems, on 12 November, just hours after filing for bankruptcy, FTX was hacked.

The exploit took the form of an 'authorisation hack'. Hackers were able to alter FTX's code, override the withdrawal suspension, and turn the exchange's app and website into malware. If someone with the FTX app on their phone logged into the platform, their balance would be drained. If they went onto the website, Trojan horses were downloaded, which again drained the user's wallets. The scarce funds remaining on the exchange following the bank run were being plundered.

Hours after the funds started flowing out of the exchange, FTX general counsel Ryne Miller tweeted that the exchange was moving its remaining funds into cold storage. This stopped the outflows, but not before the hackers were able to make off with over $600 million. Twitter was immediately rife with speculation, with many people pointing the finger either at SBF himself or a member of his inner circle. They speculated that the intricate knowledge of the exchange, its mechanics and operating processes, along with the coordination required for a hack of that scale, made it highly likely that it was an inside job.

These theories were, ultimately, unproven. But the same can't be said of the other crimes SBF was accused of. In December, roughly a month after his resignation from FTX, SBF was arrested in the Bahamas. He was charged with wire fraud, securities fraud and money laundering, among a litany of other heinous acts. He was extradited to the US and subsequently released on a $250 million bail – the largest bail bond ever issued in the history of the US criminal justice system. Despite his parents coughing up the funds to bail him out – a truly sad state of affairs – he was recalled to jail, shortly before his trial commenced, for witness tampering.

It seems, therefore, that he had no inclination to leave his crooked ways at FTX. And, just as his turpitude continued unabated long after the collapse of FTX, the effects of the exchange's downfall were to be felt for a long, long time after its bankruptcy filing.

24

Exit

Just like with Terra Luna, the collapse of FTX spelt the sudden and irrevocable demise of a great number of firms across the industry. Contagion spread far and wide and seemed to infect even the healthiest of hosts.

One of the more notable, and surprising, casualties from the FTX collapse was none other than Galois Capital, the hedge fund that called out the tenuous technology underpinning Terra Luna. They had made a fortune shorting Luna during its collapse, and didn't hesitate to blow their own trumpets about their correct call.

'I said Luna & UST must be destroyed and it was so ... What else do you want? What more can I do?' This outburst of braggadocio was broadcast by Galois Capital's founder, Kevin Zhou, on the fund's official Twitter account. Zhou then followed it up with a slew of tweets lamenting Do Kwon's error in not asking for his help fixing the Luna / UST mechanism:

'You know what's funny. Not once did they reach out to me to ask for my help. I mean I'm among a handful of people in the world that understand their mechanism better than most of their own investors.'

'I even reached out. But he was too prideful to even respond. Pride goeth before the fall. And if you think about it, we were somewhat aligned before ...'

'Too late now. Supply lines are cut. His people are starving. Lunatic army and TFL employee mutiny soon. Pillage and loot what remains of the spoils of war.'

Ever since their call on that ill-fated project, Zhou and Galois revelled in their image as industry oracles, publicly patting themselves on the back at every opportunity. And yet even the hubristic hedge fund did not foresee the fate that befell FTX. Their flagship fund had half their money, some $100 million, on the exchange. When withdrawals were suspended, and the realisation dawned on the industry that the funds held on the platform would be stuck there forever, Galois wound down its operations. The self-proclaimed smartest guy in the room, Kevin Zhou, had the wool pulled over his eyes by SBF's contrived quirks and engineered eccentricities. And, ultimately, he had to bow out of the room. He would have done well to heed his own admonition: pride goeth before the fall.

Fatalities were also to be found in the most unusual and unexpected of places. Among these were Tom Brady, the NFL star and longtime brand ambassador for the failed exchange. FTX signed a sponsorship deal with Brady in 2021, paying the quarterback $30 million to promote them in television adverts, and to make an appearance at a conference FTX hosted in the Bahamas in April 2022. However, there was a catch to Brady's bung: it was to be paid in FTX stock. This seemed like a great deal at the time, when FTX was valued at upwards of $32 billion. But following the events of November 2022, Brady's stake in the firm was now worth exactly the same as the firm itself. Zero.

And the NFL star wasn't the only member of the Brady household to be affected by the exchange's collapse. His wife, the supermodel Gisele Bündchen, was also a brand ambassador for FTX, and her $18 million stake in the company underwent the same fate as her husband's. Things then went from bad to worse for the football player, as a group of FTX investors filed a class action lawsuit against him and other celebrities – including basketballer Shaquille O'Neal and *Seinfeld*'s Larry David – for promoting the exchange to their fans without due diligence.

It was difficult to feel too sorry for hedge fund managers and celebrities, however, when millions of ordinary people had lost their savings on FTX. When Terra Luna collapsed, it was estimated that $400 million got wiped off the markets as a result. FTX's implosion eviscerated a further $200 million from that, adding to the woes of everyone still clinging on to crypto in the hope of recouping their losses. And, of course, that's not to mention the direct damage that was caused to the exchange's users; the assessment from investigators was that over $8.9 billion, from more than 1 million customer accounts, was pilfered and handed to Alameda to fuel its staff's gambling addiction.

As for knock-on effects, not only were asset prices slashed across the board, but countless projects also shut up shop in the wake of FTX, leaving yet more users reeling from even further losses. This also occurred after the fall of Terra. However, there was a notable difference this time around. Whereas in the previous catastrophe contagion spread dramatically and projects folded very publicly, after FTX many projects wound up their operations quietly. Many were already insolvent – casualties of the Terra Luna collapse – or had long since run out of funds, having frittered them away licentiously during the bull run. Their departures from the world of decentralised finance had been in the pipeline for a long time before FTX's spectacular fall. The international news of the exchange's bankruptcy, and the relentless background noise around it, actually served as an expediency; it provided them with the ideal opportunity to slip stealthily away into the night.

And among the projects in this sorry state of affairs were our own ventures, Portent Protocol and Aquarius Drops.

Portent had been at death's door even before the demise of Terra Luna. Its token price had flatlined, and its relatively insignificant fundraise had all been depleted by bonuses and inflated salaries. As for Aquarius, it wasn't even able to complete its raise. New capital entering and being deployed in the space had already dried up following Terra Luna, and the fundraising landscape was now completely arid. Not even the most profligate and trigger-happy VCs, who punted money into anything with a pulse during the bull run, were writing new cheques.

For a while after Terra, some projects were still announcing fundraises. Bizarrely, these included a venture launched by Adam Neumann, the founder of office rental firm WeWork. Neumann was forced out of WeWork in September 2019, on account of eccentric behaviour, admitted drug use, and the company's poor performance. He entered the crypto space and, in August 2022, announced that his new project – a tokenised carbon credits play, similar to Paris Pact – had just received $350 million in funding. This was the biggest raise ever conducted by a project up to that point, led by the biggest VC in the industry (and one of the biggest in the world): a16z.

However, Neumann's announcement, and those like it, were misleading. Raises often take place months, sometimes even over a year, before they're publicised. The lag in closing a raise and announcing it to the public can give a false impression of the health of the industry. And, following FTX, even these delayed announcements came to a halt. Crypto companies weren't receiving any new investment and hadn't been for some time. Interest in the space, from both retail and institutional investors, was dead. Some were preserving capital and hibernating in order to survive the crypto winter. But many others simply left the space altogether – which, after all, makes sense; you can only get the rug pulled out from you so many times before you stop getting back on it.

Aquarius had only raised around 40 per cent of its hard cap target. All hope of completing the raise had gone out the window, so we simply had to return the funds left in the treasury. Which, by this point, didn't amount to very much: around 90 per cent of what we had managed to extract from VCs before the market tanked was gone. It had been spent, frittered away on salaries, bonuses and parties.

Most of our VCs understood this and simply wrote off the loss. For many of them, this wasn't their first market meltdown. They had weathered the collapse of the industry after the ICO era in 2017, so they were well versed in their investments going bust. Some even offered consolation, patting us on the backs for trying and telling us to keep our heads up. The influencers, on the other hand, were a different story. We had convinced a large number of promoters to buy allocations in our project, and these guys were far less sympathetic than the VCs. When we told them there was no money left to pay back their investments, several even threatened to sue to recoup their losses. A curt 'good luck with that' from Archie was all they needed to remind them that they had built their houses on a bed of legal sand.

Throughout the lifespan of our projects, we'd spent a fortune on legal fees, with large practices in exotic jurisdictions, to ensure that any litigation that came our way wouldn't even touch the sides. In a twist of irony then, the influencers who bought our allocations had actually helped fund the removal of their own legal recourse. It was the only instance I had ever come across of promoters experiencing what it felt like to be on the receiving end of a bad investment – a situation they put hundreds of thousands of their followers in on countless occasions during the bull run.

Closing Aquarius Drops, therefore, was a relatively straight-forward affair. We didn't have a publicly tradable token yet, so there were no token holders to worry about and no potential backlash from retail investors who had lost money. We just returned our remaining capital to our investors and silently slipped away. We maintained our social media profiles for a while, but gradually reduced the posting frequency, until we stopped altogether. There was no fuss and minimal mess. Which is more than can be said for Portent Protocol.

The token for our first project had been on the market for over a year. And it had been slowly but surely declining to zero. The token holders who hadn't dumped their bags, and who were holding out for a comeback, were not greatly enamoured with us, to say the least. On the increasingly rare occasions they did send messages into the project's official Telegram group, they were usually berating the team for incompetence or complaining about the ever-declining price. And it was the same story when they posted on Twitter, with the added kick of occasionally tagging either Miles, Archie, or both in one of their posts. They had long ago removed any reference to Portent Protocol from their bios, but grudges are long-lasting in crypto, and most of the retail who bought the token remembered them as the public-facing members of the founding team.

The news that the project was being closed could go terribly, and the whole team could find itself on the receiving end of a torrent of hate. This would be far from ideal, as Moonshot Advisors was still operational, and bad publicity was the last thing it needed. While the agency still had clients – mainly exchanges and large projects, who had raised enough to weather a multi-year bear market – belts had been tightened across the board, and the agency's revenues were feeling the strain. Add into the mix a swarm of scathing investors, venting their wholly justified fury about the failed Portent project, and that could be enough to tip the remaining clients over the edge, and incite them to fire Moonshot as their marketing agency.

The most difficult aspect of the closure was the situation with the liquidity pools. The token was still trading on Uniswap, and one other centralised exchange. This meant that there was still liquidity on both of those platforms, amounting to around $20,000 on each. Withdrawing the liquidity wouldn't just look like a rug pull, it would *be* a rug pull – in the purest, least equivocal, sense of the term. This would need to be dealt with, and no one was quite sure how.

Everyone on the team was panicking. Everyone was fraught with anxiety. Everyone except for me. By the time plans were being made to close out the two projects, I had resigned. I had been disheartened with the industry, and our role within it, for some time – from working with maniacs like Cillian, to being berated by clients like the baby-faced Jack, to the haunting message in the Terra Luna community forum. I had had enough. My tolerance for crypto, and the people at its helm, had been wearing thin for months. And now it was completely gone.

I can say now, with the confessional candour that hindsight lends, that it was sheer greed keeping me in the industry. I had never seen that much money before, and I was blinded by it. But gradually, after journeying deeper and deeper down the rabbit hole, I began to wake up to the reality of just how unpleasant it all really was. And when I heard about what FTX had been doing with their customers' deposits, my mind was made up. I would leave crypto, and never look back. I only wish I had made this decision sooner.

However, there was one final obstacle to overcome before I could put that cesspit behind me: my notice period. I was still tied to my positions until the end of the year. And, as chief communications officer, it meant I was tasked with disseminating the statement announcing the closure of the projects.

Miles gave me the statement to send out, which he had spent a whole week working on: Portent Protocol had fallen victim to the FTX fraud. The treasury funds were stored on the exchange. SBF and the Alameda team stole them. The only option was to close the project and withdraw the remaining token liquidity from the exchanges. Investors would have a deadline of 72 hours to sell any tokens they might still be holding. After this, the liquidity would be pulled.

I sent the announcement out. Three days later – which also happened to be my very last day at all of our companies – the liquidity pools for Portent were drained and the social media platforms were shut down. Our project, which we had once had such high hopes for, was finished.

There was no backlash. No one cared in the slightest. So many projects had shut down in the wake of FTX that little Portent Protocol didn't stand out at all. If anything, people expected it to happen.

One person – who was once our most passionate, committed community member, having been with us since before we launched – actually congratulated us. He was surprised we had lasted so long. Many of the other projects he invested in had kicked the bucket months ago. He was impressed and wished us all the best for our future plans. He said he was sure we all had bright futures ahead of us.

This depressed me infinitely more than the closure of our projects, and the profound sense of futility and wasted effort I felt, ever could.

Afterword

Grifters' Groundhog Day

Sending out that announcement was a fitting end to a chapter in my professional life that would be better left forgotten. If I could go back and never get in bed with the crypto bros, I would. After so long in the industry, I was left with one fundamental and inalienable truth: the whole space is rotten, to its very core. It's a cesspit, in which every financial crime under the sun takes place every single day – things that, were they to happen in any other industry, would result in long stretches behind bars for all those involved.

And yet, as much as I may want to forget, to stay silent and move on, I wholeheartedly believe that doing so would be inexcusably selfish. So many others I've encountered over the years have forgotten, or pretend they have. They've forgotten about the project they set up that failed, and that they then abandoned, leaving their investors holding the bag. They've forgotten that the founder they just invested in ran an ICO pump and dump in the last market cycle. They've forgotten that their favourite anonymous influencer promoted a project that pulled the rug – and made millions off of it.

Sometimes, events necessitate being remembered. And, sometimes, whistles demand to be blown. Because, while the world is rightly wary of the industry at this present moment, memories can be alarmingly fickle when a lot of money is in view.

I don't know what's going to happen to the crypto industry. There's every possibility that it will rise from the ashes. The halving is due to take place in April 2024. It's an event that occurs every four years, which halves the amount of bitcoin paid out to miners for verifying transactions, and which has historically caused the asset's dramatic price increases. There's a chance that, as you're reading this, the industry is in the midst of another bull run. And the crimes and corruption of the 2020–22 cycle have been forgotten. Along with the victims left behind.

I can only hope that, if that is the case, this record serves as a reminder of what the cabal of insiders who run the industry did with the unfettered licence they were given. With the blank cheques they were written. The blank slates on which regulations should have been carved. And the blank stares of journalists and media figures, who took their thirty pieces of silver and spoke the words they were told to.

I can only hope that, after the actions of SBF, Do Kwon, and the countless other characters in the rogues' gallery of crypto we haven't heard of – who will all hopefully get their day in court sooner rather than later – people will be dissuaded from having a punt in the murky and malevolent markets of crypto.

I can only hope that this story is not regarded as an object of mere interest or fascination, in the same way the memoir of a disgraced politician might interest or fascinate, but that it offers some insight into how the crypto industry really operates. That it provides a glimpse of what's really on the other side of the crypto coin. The side that the insiders didn't want you to see.